'Speelman and McGann's critique of the assumptions that underlie much contemporary research in psychology reveals the flaws that have impeded its development as a science. This book is a major work that should reform research practice in the field.'

Geoff Hammond, *Emeritus Professor, University of Western Australia*

'The book by Speelman and McGann has many nuggets of wisdom of which my favorite is their aggregation delusion, and additional delusions follow. I recommend the book for those who wish to become better researchers or better research consumers.'

David Trafimow, *Professor, New Mexico State University*

'Given its subject matter, I wasn't expecting to feel so invigorated, inspired, and hopeful about psychology once I'd finished reading. Speelman and McGann offer an incisive dissection of psychology's current ills, and a thoughtful discussion, with workable solutions, for how we can remedy them. I cannot recommend this book highly enough — everyone even remotely interested in psychology should read it.'

Louise Barrett, FRSC, *Professor, University of Lethbridge, Canada*

THE GREAT PSYCHOLOGY DELUSION

The Great Psychology Delusion takes an unflinching look at some of the foundational assumptions of psychological science. Exploring long-standing unanswered critiques of psychological research in a way that is detailed but accessible, the book brings together a wealth of material that challenges our understanding of what the science of psychology really is, and how the subject matter of that science should be conceived.

Identifying a Great Delusion (that there is a coherent discipline of psychology with sound foundations), the authors explore a number of more specific delusions regarding scientific practice in psychology. These include the problematic assumptions of core statistical analyses, questionable aspects of frequently used experimental designs, and continued frictions regarding the much-aspired-to scientist-practitioner model. The delusions produce the uncomfortable state in which we find much of modern psychological science – theoretically challenged, poorly replicated, and with questionable real-world value.

This unsentimental examination of the state of things nevertheless allows the authors to identify concrete steps that the scientific community can take to re-ground psychological research and move forward to a successful science studying the richest and most complex phenomena we know of: us.

This book will interest all people interested in psychological science, from undergraduate students to researchers.

Craig P. Speelman is Professor of Cognitive Psychology in the School of Arts and Humanities of Edith Cowan University, Australia.

Marek McGann is Lecturer in the Department of Psychology of Mary Immaculate College, Ireland.

THE GREAT PSYCHOLOGY DELUSION

Missteps, Pitfalls and How to Make a More Successful Psychological Science

Craig P. Speelman and Marek McGann

Routledge
Taylor & Francis Group
LONDON AND NEW YORK

Designed cover image: Marek McGann

First published 2026
by Routledge
4 Park Square, Milton Park, Abingdon, Oxon OX14 4RN

and by Routledge
605 Third Avenue, New York, NY 10158

Routledge is an imprint of the Taylor & Francis Group, an informa business

British Library Cataloguing-in-Publication Data
A catalogue record for this book is available from the British Library

ISBN: 978-1-032-82290-7 (hbk)
ISBN: 978-1-032-81540-4 (pbk)
ISBN: 978-1-003-50387-3 (ebk)

DOI: 10.4324/9781003503873

Typeset in Times New Roman
by Newgen Publishing UK

Craig:
For Mum, who advised me to have an open mind, and for Dad, who taught me to be sceptical.

Marek:
For Mum, who always sees the person, never lost in the people, and for Dad, who still inspires.

CONTENTS

PREFACE

Marek and I began the journey that has culminated in this book in 2010 when he invited me to a workshop he was organising on enactive psychology. Even though I knew nothing about the topic, Marek was keen for me to present to the enactive community some of the skill acquisition material from a book I had published a few years previously with Kim Kirsner. The workshop was held in Tipperary in the Republic of Ireland. In my talk I included a section on my attempts to develop a simulation model of the theory that Kim and I had presented in our book. I had tried to simulate the data that I thought was typical when people perform the lexical decision task for multiple trials with repeated words. Essentially, my presentation was focussed on how the simulation attempt failed because it predicted perfectly smooth learning curves for individual performance. I discovered, once I thought to look closely, that individual data was far from smooth. Although the enactive audience were polite in their reception of my talk, it was only Marek who wanted to discuss this particular finding in more detail. This sparked many conversations about how psychology's predilection to focus on data averaged across many individuals meant that important detail about individual behaviour was being overlooked.

Our initial focus on the problems associated with averaging led us to consider the reasons that psychology researchers aggregated data across people. The more we delved into the issue, the more we were astounded to learn that many others had considered this issue before and written stark warnings of the pitfalls of relying on aggregated data to generate conclusions about how *people* behave. We were even more astounded to note how little effect such entreaties had had on the research practices of mainstream psychology. Largely, the earlier warnings had been ignored. These warnings did not feature in my own education, but I do recall, when commencing my first lecturing position at a university on the other side of the country, a colleague asked me my thoughts on the nomothetic/idiographic issue. I did not have a clue what he was talking about. I read a couple of the papers he passed on to me on the subject, but given that the issue did not seem to feature in any of the skill acquisition papers I was eagerly consuming at the time, I soon forgot all about it. That is, until I started looking at the performance of individual participants in my own research. It was like a whole new world had opened up to me, but one that was scary in its apparently chaotic nature. Certainly, there were few obvious patterns to be discerned.

Marek and I spent many conversations wondering why the issues of aggregation were so readily ignored by mainstream psychology. It was obvious to us that focussing on individual performance meant explaining behaviour was a lot more complicated than papers in mainstream psychology journals implied. Maybe it was this complexity that attracted researchers to the simplicity offered by aggregation. But as we considered the aggregation issues in more depth we realised that continued use of aggregation resulted in a number of other problems with the way research is undertaken in psychology. Ultimately, we concluded that psychology research involved many questionable assumptions and practices, which means that not only is the knowledge base of the field questionable but so are the interventions in applied areas that are based on this knowledge base. Furthermore, researchers and practitioners are either unaware of these problems, or they are not concerned by them. Neither of these states is desirable for a field that professes to be a science.

And so we were determined to add our voice to those that came before, but we were keen for the message to not be easily ignored. Some have questioned our use of the word "delusion" to describe some of the unjustified assumptions inherent in mainstream psychology research, suggesting it might come across as too confrontational. We are unapologetic here – when we are conveying a message that has such importance for the status of psychology as a science, we want people to feel confronted by the dire state of the current situation. Psychology researchers need to take notice of the problems we identify in this book. There are some hard lessons to digest in the first part of the book. We know because we have had to come to terms with them ourselves. They are lessons that do not sit well with the psychology education we both experienced. And yet, most psychology researchers will be aware of the problems that have recently been identified with the field, such as the reproducibility crisis. Many of the solutions that have been proposed to remedy these problems are mostly attempts at doing what we have always done but doing it better. In this book, our primary message is that the way we have been doing psychology research is wrong in many respects, and that we need to find different ways of doing it. And as clear as we are about this message, in the second part of the book we are also clear on the strategies that can forge a different path.

I would like to thank Marek for collaborating with me as we have made this journey. Our discussions on the various topics in this book have been the most enjoyable part of my research activities over the last 15 years. I have learned so much from Marek, particularly how academic writing does not have to be as dry as I was taught to produce. I would also like to thank my academic home, the School of Arts and Humanities of Edith Cowan University, for allowing me the space to undertake such a large project as this book. The time and space to consider such a long-form project is a scarce luxury these days. Finally, I would also like to thank my wife, Nichole, and our kids, Maggie, Stella, Lauren, and Bob, for inspiring me to do well.

CS
March 2025
Perth, Western Australia

I undertook my doctoral studies part-time at the University of Sussex while working in my first full-time teaching position for the small independent college, DBS School of Arts. These two facets of my working life both involved taking a critical perspective on how mainstream psychological research and work in the broader, inter-disciplinary field of cognitive science were conducted.

Part of my teaching involved addressing the perennial issue of what a science is and whether psychology is one, along with a number of other controversial issues regarding biases, philosophical tangles around ethics and free will, and an exploration of non-mainstream perspectives.

My doctoral research, meanwhile, followed my increasing interest in the important role of embodiment and brought with it a greater appreciation for understanding context, ecology, and concrete activity in our understanding of psychological phenomena. These sensitivities would be sharpened as I adopted what is considered an "enactive approach" to cognitive science, one which is centred on living beings making sense of and being intimately engaged with their environments.

Perhaps due to the powerful influence of context I did not fully grasp how much these two aspects of my work related to one another until much later. But the enactive approach places a significant emphasis on the development and dynamic deployment of skills, and so when browsing a publisher's stall at a conference, I picked up a book entitled *Beyond the Learning Curve*, which promised a new way of thinking about skill, I was intrigued. Reading it, I was struck deeply by how, in paying attention not to generalities but to specific individual cases, Craig Speelman and Kim Kirsner used the tools of traditional cognitive psychology to ultimately undermine that mainstream approach, challenging some of its most fundamental preconceptions.

My reading of the book coincided with my organising, along with friend and colleague Fred Cummins, a summer school on the enactive approach to cognitive science. I was tickled by the idea of having someone present who worked entirely within an approach to research that was heavily criticised by enactive thinkers, but whose attention to data had led to a surprising overlap in some key conclusions. I suspect Craig felt a bit like a Beatles fan at a Grateful Dead concert, but I maintain there was real value in having different voices present at the event, and more importantly, he was still speaking to me afterwards.

What followed has been the most productive collaboration of my career, and a lot of fun to boot. What is more, there has been a gradual dawning on me, as we explored more deeply into the history and development of practices in psychological science, that the two aspects of my work are more tightly bound up than I had first realised. This book provides no attempt to persuade the reader of a single specific approach to psychological science – that would be self-defeating as an ambition. Indeed, perhaps the biggest take-home message we hope to get across is that psychological science too quickly foreclosed on a valuable diversity of methods and theoretical viewpoints and will benefit greatly from an opening of minds to a deliberately pluralistic investigation of behaviour and experience. Nevertheless, I find myself much better able to articulate with my students what is valuable, and what is necessarily limited, in the research work that psychologists undertake, and how to tell the difference. While there has been a continual running to keep a syllabus up-to-date with the roiling crisis of crises in psychological science over the past decade and a half, through conversations with Craig, exploration of histories, and developments within enactive, ecological, and dynamical approaches to research, I have also increasingly developed a confidence that such efforts are not in vain. More to the point, this work has involved an ever greater appreciation for the humanity of scientific endeavour – that many factors other than "data" play a role, and that these need not undermine but are essential to science. This includes the importance of rhetoric, coalition building, professional incentives, and other pragmatic details. The ecology of science.

There is of course much more work to do, and I look forward to being able to teach it to my students as we as a community go about it. I'm very grateful to Craig for our collaborations, for his patience and good humour as I have lost track of time differences, and for his willingness to traverse the globe to keep things moving forward.

In the vein of work's ecology, I am grateful to my academic home for the past 20 years, Mary Immaculate College, and the culture and community of humane and human work that is crucial to the place and the people there. In particular, the Department of Psychology has provided support both directly and indirectly. The time and space to take for work is made, not found or met by accident, or chance. For me, support arrived from leadership, Department Head, and champion, Niamh Stack, who held workload at bay, so work was done. Among my colleagues, too, the person upon whom this project most imposed, and worked hardest to provide room to allow it, was Suzanne, to whom I feel a gratitude that words alone are inadequate to express. My love to all of my girls, Suzanne, Amara, and Calla, who are the reason for it all.

MMcG
March 2025
Limerick, Ireland

ACKNOWLEDGEMENTS

Roll credits! While two people will be credited as authors on the cover, this book benefitted from the efforts of a great many more.

A number of people provided very useful feedback on various sections, arguments, or whole chapters (in some cases where the material formed part of earlier works). These comments substantially improved the work as it progressed and played a significant role in improving the final text. In this light we are very grateful to Lou Barrett, Berna Devezer, Suzanne Egan, Kerry Greer, Harry Heft, Miranda Lucas, Cillian McHugh, Basil Vassilicos. Also valuable has been feedback on several talks about this material to the Edith Cowan University Experimental Psychology Unit.

Marek completed some of the early parts of the writing process while taking research leave and sabbatical from teaching at Mary Immaculate College. Marek is thankful for the opportunity for that leave, and for the space it provided to undertake this work. What is more, on returning from leave certain accommodations were also made to support the continued writing process, with the help and support of Niamh Stack in particular, without whose intervention the whole project would have faced significant delays. Niamh maintains a very positive *esprit de corps* in the Department of Psychology at MIC, one which has ensured that while there may be differences of opinion on some of the topics presented in this book, there is space and encouragement to explore them. I am thankful to work with the likes of Lorcan Cronin, Suzanne Egan, Michelle Glasheen, Niamh Higgins, Paul Mulcahy, Elaine Murnane, and Marc Scully.

The work of the Midwest Psychological Field Station is explored in a number of chapters of this book. Our own understanding of this work has been supported by a vibrant community of researchers, particularly those involved in an international symposium held in Roskilde, Denmark, in April 2022. Marek is grateful to Sofie Pedersen, Jytte Bang, and Cillian McHugh for their role in organising that meeting, and to all of the participants of the symposium for fruitful and highly productive conversations.

Two people in particular read and provided feedback on the entire text of the book, and we are deeply grateful to Geoff Hammond and Trish Purnell-Webb for their positive comments, questions, and critical observations, all of which supported improvement of the final text.

We would also like to offer our thanks to the editorial team at Routledge, who provided a welcome and clear-minded support throughout the process. Adam Woods initially championed the project, and Georgia Thompson, Shraddha Saikia, and Shruthi Maniyodath shepherded it expertly through to production.

Finally, our families have put up with a lot of distraction, absence, odd pronouncements, and the occasional very strange text message, over quite a long period of time.

PART I

Missteps and Pitfalls

1

THE GREAT DELUSION

Delusion: an idiosyncratic belief or impression maintained despite being contradicted by reality or rational argument.

(Oxford Dictionary)

Psychology is one of the most popular subjects to study at universities across the globe. As professionals, there is no area of human life in which psychologists are not embedded – from marketing to clinical psychotherapy, organisational management to education, sports and performance to community development, and neuroscience to the criminal justice system. As a professional group, we have persuaded generations of people that psychology offers insights worth spending years studying, and almost everyone that they would be better off if they had access to the advice of a psychologist.

The value of those insights, and that advice, is underwritten by knowledge produced through scientific endeavour. The scientific literature of psychology is now a massive, sprawling edifice, incorporating many different perspectives and methodological approaches, analytical techniques, and reporting standards.

It is becoming increasingly clear, however, that all is not well with this enormous monument to scientific effort. Indeed, some of the core foundations of contemporary psychology are so unsteady that what appears at first glance to be a sturdy construction is little more than a Potemkin facade. This is not a matter of fine-tuning otherwise sound principles – there are fundamental concepts and methodological assumptions which cannot bear the load that is asked of them.

The result is a *perception* of knowledge and understanding that is, simply, mistaken. It is a Great Delusion, and it is time to face up to it.

Psychology is diverse, and no error will be universal. But nor is it the case that we can recognise we have been getting something badly wrong, determine to change how we do things going forward, and yet still continue building on the same foundations. Facing up to our delusions means taking stock of what kinds of things we can have confidence in, and what we need to

DOI: 10.4324/9781003503873-2

question. It means questioning what kinds of advice we can honestly give to our clients and being ready to change how we approach even longstanding practice. Which of our interventions are sound? Do our tests measure what we think they do, and what we claim they do? What should we teach, and what long-held, widely known "certainties" should we remove from the curriculum?

Our aim in this book is to frankly (and to be honest, *uncomfortably*) dig into the foundations of psychological science. We are not the first to do so. Part of our discomfort will be reporting just how long-standing some of these crucial, fundamental criticisms of scientific practice have been. We're not even the first to suggest that there might be something delusional about the current status quo in the discipline (Hughes, 2018, p. 148). But through insistent repetition, with an aim not to speak to a technical, methodological audience, but to a broader, more diverse one, we hope that we can play a part in raising awareness of these vintage issues, as well as articulating some lesser recognised ones.

We do this not to be destructive, but to help open up and expand scientific practice, to ground it more firmly, supporting future growth. We are ambitious for psychological science, but not prescriptive, or exclusionary as to what that future should look like. The point is not to offer some vision of a One True Psychology. Instead, through a clear-eyed account of how things currently stand, we seek to recognise and promote a wide range of positive steps to take, paths that are varied but valid, and in keeping with the principles of rigour and systematicity that are definitive of effective science.

Interesting Times for Psychology

It certainly is interesting times for psychological research. For more than a decade now we have been embroiled in a particularly heated period of reflection, critical self-appraisal, and even a certain amount of soul-searching. The research literature is replete with discussions of existential crises (Ferguson, 2015; Hughes, 2018), around practices of research design and conduct (John et al., 2012; Nosek et al., 2022; Pashler & Harris, 2012), analysis of data (Nuijten et al., 2015; Scheel et al., 2020), and construction of theories (Eronen & Bringmann, 2021; van Rooij & Baggio, 2020). Research practices that have been used widely for decades have been scrutinised, incisively dissected, and found wanting.

It would seem, at present, that there is an unusually broad recognition that things must change. The long but effective process of self-correction that is defining of scientific enterprise has kicked into high gear, and the old structures and practices sedimented into typical psychological research are being shaken loose, to re-settle at some point into new, more reliable, more valid, and more satisfying organisations.

These are simultaneously new and long-standing circumstances for psychological science. On the one hand, many, if not all, of the problems that have led to this disciplinary reflection have been around for decades. Indeed, as we will see, the essence and character of psychological science have been contested from its very beginnings.

On the other hand, the level of commitment to changes in research practices, analytical techniques, construction of theories, elimination of fraud, and other reforms represents something new. Not only have there been immense efforts put into developing the evidence base to support such reforms (e.g., Ebersole et al., 2016; Ebersole et al., 2020; Klein et al., 2018; Klein et al., 2022; Open Science Collaboration, 2012), whole frameworks for scientific practice (UNESCO, 2018) and specialised graduate programmes (Bishop, 2023) have been proposed to address them. Journals have changed their criteria for submission, review, and acceptance. Indeed, the toxic impact of some traditional publication and dissemination practices has prompted significant changes in that area too. The long history of critical analysis and arguments for the need to revise or refine core theoretical and methodological assumptions has prospects now for an unusual level of impact. They can find a rich medium for growth in the freshly ploughed ground of psychological practice.

Our intention for this book is to offer our voice in chorus to those who have gone before, but also to provide for the reader a combination of both historical context and accessible presentation of some technical, often abstruse, methodological points and their theoretical implications. Within the psychological literature, the present combination of novel critical enthusiasm and long-standing critique is striking to us for two principal reasons. The first is the excitement and optimism that we feel given the fervent recognition of the need for reform, and the possibility for improvements to psychological science that arises from this widespread awareness of the issues. The second is that, given such critical self-reflection is inherent in the very notion of scientific practice, why has it taken so long, and how can we avoid this current opportunity falling to the same inaction? Given that most of the criticisms now in debate are decades old (if not more) it behoves us to understand what constraints have prevented such upheaval before now, and what needs to happen to ensure the most positive and productive outcomes in the coming years.

There are, therefore, a number of aspects to this story. Some of them are scientific, relating to theoretical and empirical practice, some of them sociological and historical, relating to the ways that scientists organise themselves and their disciplines. But it all starts with a first, basic, misapprehension, a Great Delusion, if you will.

In the rest of this chapter, we will briefly review historical arguments that psychologists have always been a fractious and diverse bunch, but also have benefited significantly from a pragmatic coalition of empirical researchers, theorists, and practitioners presenting a united front. The Great Psychology Delusion is that, despite there not really being a single coherent field of study, practice, or disciplinary project, we have mostly convinced ourselves and key players in society more generally that there is such a thing as a science of psychology. More formally:

> ***The Great Psychology Delusion:*** The belief that psychology is a valid science despite the fact it rests on a number of untested and/or invalid assumptions.

Now, this definition includes a very triggering phrase for many psychologists, so we should quickly note that our disagreement with the claim that there is a science of psychology is not with the term "science", but with the small and deceptively powerful obfuscation achieved by the singular article "a".

Historian of psychology Christopher Green (2015) has strongly made the point that not only is psychology not a unified discipline, but that it will never be. There is no small set of general principles, no core set of basic phenomena, from which a coherent scientific enterprise can be derived. As Green puts it, psychology is a "congeries of idiosyncratic interests bundled together more through administrative and diplomatic efforts than by underlying intellectual coherence" (Green, 2015, p. 210).

This seems a rather petty point with which to take issue. Psychologists are very aware of the breadth and complexity of our subject matter. Surely, one might think, that a fine-grained coherence hasn't yet been achieved doesn't mean that we need to be too critical. The establishment of the institutions of a discipline, and the web of apparent mutual support between scientific development and real-world practice provides justification and legitimacy for both. The rest will follow in time. Such is the very nature of scientific progress. Over the past century and more, the broad appeal of the many facets of experience, behaviour, and people generally, as topics of personal interest and motivation, has ensured not just viability, but vibrancy, to programmes of study. Simultaneously, the very real concerns of personal, social, and public good ensure a field of practical value and public investment. On first blush, it might appear that the Great Psychology Delusion is a rather harmless one – there has been much to recommend it, and the costs seem slight.

But this is, we argue, a misapprehension. It may be that there are historically defensible reasons for allowing the delusion to skew our perceptions of ourselves and our actions as professionals. It has been the case for quite some time, however, and is increasingly apparent, that the costs to the advancement of both science and professional practice are great indeed. The delusion is not benign. That there is no coherent endeavour that properly encompasses the disparate ways in which psychologists' work is related to a tendency to conceptual slippage – referring to quite distinct things using similar vocabularies. Examples of this abound in psychology. We will spend some time, for example, examining how phenomena that occur at different scales, or even different domains, are described with the same words. Think of every time the press of a response button, the performance of a computational evaluation, or a neural process in a brain localisation study are all pointed to with the same term, such as "decision" or "inference". The result of such slippage is a failure to make important distinctions.

As we will see, the Great Delusion is a product of a number of more specific (we hesitate to say "lesser") delusions. These specific delusions are conceptual errors that produce misperceptions. We see coherence where things are at odds, consistency when things are diverse, and implications where there are none.

Early struggles over the identity of the discipline have given way to an archipelago of really quite distinct scientific endeavours. Diversity of course is a strength, so long as it is recognised and embraced as such. Where it is overlooked, dismissed, or differences elided, then problems arise. We argue that this failure to systematically, deliberately, and accountably address the complexity and variety of scientific practices gathered under the broad umbrella of the term "psychology" plays a significant role in the recurrent, and long-standing critiques that are ever-present in the research literature. We will argue that the more specific delusions, what seem like a number of different problems, are in fact more related than they seem, symptomatic of the conceptual slippage which is partially hidden by the inappropriate perception of psychology as more unified than it really is. The Great Delusion thus prevents us from properly perceiving the evidence of its own falsity.

A misperception that different scientists are actually studying distinct facets of the same thing means that what appears to be productive cross-pollination between domains may in fact be contamination that invalidates work rather than supporting it. What seem to be sound guidelines from one field can become misleading when confidently followed in another, and all without us realising what is happening.

The welter of concerns that have been raised about psychology can be disorienting (to the point that some have suggested that we have a "crisis crisis" Medaglia & Fernandez, 2022). In what follows we wish to demonstrate the value of becoming aware of the Great Psychology Delusion, showing how awareness of the error can reveal the ways in which these different criticisms are related. They are not quite the same but grounded in the same conceptual confusions that give rise to the Delusion in the first place. In particular, we discuss three broad recurring criticisms that are often discussed as though entirely distinct, but which we believe are in fact related.

The first criticism is the confusion of the individual and the collective, an implicit assumption underlying a large portion of psychological research that people are ultimately interchangeable. In the recent literature this issue has been addressed in terms of the validity of different forms of statistics, and seen particular discussion regarding the topic of "ergodicity" (Hunter et al., 2024; Molenaar, 2004, 2008a; Speelman & McGann, 2020). We will further argue, however, that this issue is partly a problem of a certain blindness to the differences between different scales of phenomena.

The second criticism relates to the poor state of theoretical work in psychology – both the weakness of extant theories and the lack of much that could be described as scientific progress (McGann & Speelman, 2020; Szollosi & Donkin, 2021; van Rooij & Baggio, 2021). The effective development of a theory requires that scientists both have a reasonable grasp of the question they are interested in – what it is they want to know – and a very strong understanding of how evidence relates to that question. Different ambitions prompt different kinds of theories, which in turn are informed, tested, and either supported or falsified, by different kinds of evidence. For theory to progress, rather than flounder, the relationships between question, theory, and evidence, must be clear. Several factors, not least of which is the confusion of the individual and the collective, mean that these relationships are not at all clear in much of contemporary psychological work.

The third criticism is that of the "research-practice gap", and regards the seemingly distinct ways in which psychological researchers and applied psychological professionals approach their work. This is in some ways a specific example of the confusion of theory, question, and evidence we have just noted. The mismatch between the intentions, values, and standards of evidence of researchers and practitioners means that on the one hand, there is much scientific work that has not been put to good use in applied settings, while also many serious questions from applied settings that need addressing but on which science has had very little of value to say.

None of these criticisms is new. Despite their vintage, however, none of them has been adequately addressed by psychologists to the point that we could be confident of them being overcome, or even effectively engaged with, in the foreseeable future. How is it that this can be the case? Part of the problem, we will argue, is the Great Psychology Delusion is an error that ensures we will repeatedly take ideas from one domain of psychology and misapply them in another. An error that suggests that what is being studied by one group of psychologists is not a different phenomenon to that studied by others, but is just an alternative perspective on the same one. Overcoming this delusion will mean recognising those distinctions, and shifting our perspective, our methods, and the evidence and analyses, more deliberately and effectively to fit our aims and ambitions. It will not mean entirely divorcing one domain of observations and research from others, but it will mean that we will be better able to orient ourselves and direct our research in light of those distinctions.

We call this problematically messy conceptualisation and practice a Delusion in order to highlight, indeed to be polemical about, its erroneous character, but also to acknowledge that this is not the product of deliberate conspiracy or malice. It is, though, a historical legacy we must learn to overcome. The first step to getting over a delusion is to recognise it as such. There is no such thing as a coherent science of psychology, and there never has been.

The Diverse Origins of the Psychological Sciences

The breadth of challenges faced by psychology seems striking, though in reality is nothing new. William James famously quipped to the publisher, on delivery of the manuscript for his magisterial *Principles of Psychology*, that it was "a loathsome, distended, tumefied, bloated, dropsical mass, testifying to nothing but two facts: 1st, that there is no such thing as a *science* of psychology, and 2nd, that W. J. is an incapable". He would have a similarly critical view in his later *Psychology: A Briefer Course*, on the final page of which he would opine:

> A string of raw facts; a little gossip and wrangle about opinions; a little classification and generalization on the mere descriptive level; a strong prejudice that we have states of mind, and that our brain conditions them: but not a single law in the sense in which physics shows us laws, not a single proposition from which any consequence can causally be deduced. We don't even know the terms between which the elementary laws would obtain if we had them. This is no science, it is only the hope of a science.
>
> *(James, 1892, p. 468)*

From a figure considered one of the fathers of psychology, these seem rather pessimistic views.

The foundation of psychology as an independent discipline in Europe is typically attributed to the work of Wilhelm Wundt, who set up the first laboratory in Leipzig around the same time James was doing so in Harvard, as well as writing the first textbook in Europe, and founding a journal dedicated to psychological science. Wundt's ambitions for psychology were quite specific, aimed primarily at providing disciplined and systematic information to address philosophical debates regarding perception, the mind, and to a certain extent metaphysical issues. Initially intending psychologists to become influential within departments of philosophy, Wundt and more particularly his students faced a backlash from that community, and so became increasingly dependent on the prospect of institutional existence quite independent of philosophy and any endeavours associated with it (Danziger, 1994). The result was a swift historical move away from Wundt's conception of what psychology was to be.

Danziger (1994) describes the early decades of the twentieth century as a "repudiation of Wundt". This involved a rejection of the narrow, cautious focus on particular aspects of perception and experience in the laboratory, shaped by philosophical considerations, but also the grander project of his *Völkerpsychologie*, on which he would publish over the latter half of his career. The term *Völkerpsychologie* famously has no direct English translation, but is typically framed as "folk psychology" or sometimes "cultural psychology". It involved a recognition by Wundt that human behaviour and experience was not simply an individual phenomenon but rather is shaped and influenced continuously by the cultural practices, mythic narratives, and customs of a person's society. *Völkerpsychologie* is perhaps most famous for its lack of impact on the discipline of psychology more broadly, but demonstrates again for us the complexity and non-unitary character of psychological science from its inception, even for those doing the incepting.

A few years after James and Wundt founded the first laboratories for psychological research, and while James was struggling with the manuscript for *Principles*, in the United Kingdom Francis Galton had begun work on the physical and physiological measurement and evaluation of people, differentiating and ranking them according to a variety of dimensions, in the service of his intentions for a eugenics movement (Cowan, 1972). Galton's work developed during a time when increasing urbanisation (increasingly dense, complex populations) along with the burgeoning of modern state organisations and management of society, fed an enthusiasm for scientific principles to underpin (or rationalise) public policies and interventions. It was a period of significant innovation in the production and use of population statistics due to Adolphe Quetelet (who we will meet again later), along with a sweep of theories from phrenology, to physiognomy, to particular interpretations of the work of Darwin. These numerous sources of concepts and data provided the bases of a variety of new social endeavours in the domains of public health, education, mental health, criminality, and more. What are now often described as applied fields of psychology initially arose quite independently of psychological science, often even a little before the founding of those first laboratories in Leipzig and Harvard (Richards, 2010).

Galton's "anthropometric" work involved a plethora of simple measures including height, weight, grip strength, head size, lung capacity, and sensitivity to various auditory and visual distinctions. It would provide a catalyst for the expansion of quantified evaluation and planning in the practical domains that would form the bedrock of psychology's claim to real-world relevance. James McKeen Cattell, who had been a student of both Wundt and James, attributed to Galton the inspiration for "mental tests and measurements" (Cattell, 1890), and played a crucial role in the argument for a socially engaged and practical psychology. The psychometrics, and even more so the statistics that evolved from Galton's work (MacKenzie, 1981) would be fundamental for the development of intelligence, educational, and capability testing underlying many applied fields.

These tests were not integrated with or derived from physiological measures or laboratory work on perception, reaction time, and other aspects of experience that formed the bedrock of experimental psychology following Wundt and James and had even less to do with philosophical concerns that remained powerful motivations for many.

If psychology was so variegated in its origins and organisation, then, how did it come to be that universities organised departments of psychology that brought these disparate professionals together under one roof?

Putting Up a United Front

What constituted psychology in its first decades of existence as an independent discipline was something of a mish-mash of new social endeavours and new research approaches in search of a home. During this time a disparate body of academics and professionals formed various alliances, some principled and some pragmatic, as they sought to create a solid foundation on which to build.

Flowing from the academic, experimental, and laboratory research were the students of Wundt, James, and others, who set up departments across a number of colleges. To solidify their positions they sought a place within the existing structures, which for many included moving into positions of secularising the moral formation of the university student body (Richards, 2010). Many universities in the US in particular required all of their students to complete classes in morality and civic-mindedness (often taught by the university presidents in their role as religious pastors). As society and education modernised, there came pressure to provide a principled, scientific basis for such education, and it was here that many psychologists found reliable, consistent roles from which to grow within the academic structures of the time.

The goals of academic psychology around the turn of the twentieth century were, therefore, unclear and controversial (O'Donnell, 1985). At this time university psychology tended to have three different facets to it, and different leaders in the field had different ideas about how they should be prioritised. Those three facets were psychology's role in addressing philosophical problems regarding experience, experimental laboratory work, particularly in physiology, and addressing practical social problems.

On both sides of the Atlantic, but in the United States in particular, there also existed a strong pressure for psychological science to have a practical usefulness, to justify investment and inclusion in universities strongly shaped by powerful business owners providing private endowments. Men and women working in the fields of organisational, educational, and criminal psychology all stepped up and found increasing influence within both academic and applied settings (Danziger, 1994). Practical applicability was a currency that appealed to patrons and colleges, though it challenged the fledgling science, which had barely begun to find its feet, let alone provided sufficiently advanced scientific work which could be applied with rigour to real-world circumstances. On the one hand, pioneers were still disagreeing on what the very principles of psychology would be; on the other, they were making promises such as "we can do as much for education and mental life in general as physics does for railroads, bridges, and electrical engineering" (Scriptures, cited in O'Donnell, 1985, p. 139). O'Donnell (1985, p. 139) argues that many of these early psychologists got ahead of themselves. Not waiting for the underlying scientific understanding to catch up, many psychologists "who were talking like physicists, were working like engineers".

In the early years of the American Psychological Association, then, that organisation provided an appearance of unity by which psychologists of different stripes could demonstrate the maturing of their discipline, and worthiness for the time, space, and resources of universities. In fact, though, this apparent cohesion camouflaged a rather fragmented understanding of what psychology was and what it should be. That is, even the founding members of APA didn't agree on what a science of psychology actually was (O'Donnell, 1985).

The association nevertheless performed its institutional duty well, in *representing* the existence of a single discipline, even as departments in different universities waxed and waned depending on the commitments of their heads and graduate students to different forms of investigation (O'Donnell, 1985). The broad umbrella gathered but did not integrate disparate communities; willing, but not achieving, the development of a unified discipline. It seems that the only coherence actually managed by these early psychologists was administrative, though this was still a significant achievement hard won.

As the departments bedded in and generations turned over, students appeared who were products of these administrative successes. They might come to specialise in some particular aspect of psychological work but were introduced during their studies under the general rubric of psychology sampled from across these disparate fields. For students of later generations, the various projects and endeavours of these different scientific communities were all part of the same piebald profession.

No Such Thing as Applied Psychology

Several historians agree that the most significant pressure on the development of psychology as a discipline at the turn of the twentieth century and into its early decades was the push to develop practical applicability (e.g., Danziger, 1994; O'Donnell, 1985; Richards, 2010). The domain which saw the most significant effort was that of education, though as we have noted already, there were also developments in areas such as organisational, criminal and forensic, and clinical work. It was likely not a coincidence that this occurred at the same time that the United States was making new, significant financial investments in public education. In his presidential address to the APA, James McKeen Cattell (1896, p. 144) raised the prospect of psychology offering significant value to the education system of the United States where "more than one hundred and fifty million dollars, collected by enforced taxation, is spent on public schools". O'Donnell (1985, p. 152) reports that of 27 doctoral students of G. Stanley Hall in the 1890s, nearly three-quarters ended up in teachers' colleges, training schools, or child-study departments. The creation of the infrastructure for public management of education involved the professionalisation of teachers (new requirements for formal qualifications), as well as, crucially, the recording and tabulating of standard data from schools for the purposes of administration (Danziger, 1994). This created an entirely new scale of educational phenomenon, and a new market for methods of measurement and analysis to fulfil the needs of that new scale.

The application of a psychologist's mindset to practical social problems tended to involve the creation and use of domain-specific anthropometric tools – that is, this applied work owed more to the work of Francis Galton than it did to that of James, Wundt, or any of their intellectual antecedents. In this sense, as Richards (2010) notes, it is potentially misleading to refer to it as "applied psychology", given that that suggests an underlying "pure" science which has been adapted and implemented in real-world settings. Indeed, in these early years, the influence was more likely to go in the other direction – in the early 1900s, experimental work would start to take on the methods and analytic techniques used by the applied psychologists.

Danziger (1994) notes what he describes as the "triumph of the aggregate" during this period, in which experimentalists moved away from research on individual observers in introspective or perceptual experiments, in favour of samples of multiple participants. Initially, this shift towards groups rather than individual rapporteurs of experience or perception appears to have been a result of a change from using trained observers (typically, the psychologists themselves) to untrained participants. As the subjects were increasingly naive, so multiple measures allowed for estimates of error, and the aggregate was considered a better representation of the underlying principle being investigated than any one observation alone. Over time, the use of statistics that were first developed and deployed in the practical fields would come to be incorporated, and indeed to dominate, analysis of laboratory results (Danziger, 1994).

The relationship between the fields of applied practice and laboratory research is therefore quite different in psychology to a number of other sciences. We will explore this issue in more depth in Chapter 6, but for the moment we might note that the typical structure of qualification and professional practice is quite different for psychologists than for most other professionals. For instance, though biology and medicine are essentially intertwined, they are studied separately, and a person can be a qualified medical professional without first having a base degree in biology. This is true for engineering and physics, pharmacy and chemistry, and indeed pretty much every other profession you care to name.

But not psychologists. Application and research are so oddly related to one another in psychology due to a history of fraught, unclear and often contested practice through the short lifetime of the discipline. This is compounded by the converse cases of professions with long histories that developed entirely independently of any scientific practice, but are now clearly recognisable as an applied domain of, well, *some* kind of science of psychology (consider teaching, for instance).

Critically Reflecting on Our Disciplinary Diversity

The various strands of historical development that were pressured together by the interaction of ambitions and incentives around the institutionalisation of psychology in its early growth never really integrated. In a famous APA presidential address, Cronbach (1957) lamented the lack of unity within psychology, identifying "two disciplines of scientific psychology". It is worth noting that when deciding on labels for these two groups he alluded not to a subject matter or set of phenomena that united each, but to their methods: the experimentalists and the correlationists. The experimentalists worked with small numbers of participants in laboratories, attempting to discern the general (shared) principles of psychological functioning. Their attention was directed to the universals of human mental operation, and how that consistent apparatus worked differently under differing, controlled, conditions. The correlationists worked further afield with larger groups of participants generally in their natural settings, as it were – schools, organisations, and other institutions. They used questionnaires and various measurements or indicators of amount and sought general patterns or associations within those arrays of numbers. Their complementary interest was in the many ways that people vary, behaving differently in apparently similar circumstances.

Though there could always be found examples of correlationists who had dabbled in experiments, or experimentalists who engaged with individual differences, the perception was of groups that were not just distinct, but motivated by differing values. Cronbach (citing Pastore, 1949, before him) describes correlationists as having an applied bent with a relatively conservative character. Using methods originally designed to estimate the heritability of life outcomes (in the service of eugenics), correlationists essentially seek a finely grained perception of the ways in which our systems of education or work select people for success and failure, inclusion or exclusion. Their work essentially helps improve the efficiency of these selection and filtering systems.

For Cronbach, experimentalists, on the other hand, address more rarefied questions, with less direct relevance to the operation of society, but with the aim of providing means of changing outcomes for any given person, or indeed, everyone.

Cronbach's commentary codified a broad observation regarding scientific efforts relevant to the understanding of behaviour and experience and has become a landmark citation since.

Flis and van Eck (2018) have provided some evidence for Cronbach's observations through digital bibliometric analysis of the APA's PsycINFO database of journal articles. Examining the co-occurrence of 3000 key terms across publications in indexed articles from 1950 to 1999, they mapped a landscape of the research literature. What they found was two reasonably distinct lobes or hemispheres of work. The collections of key terms that ran together in each case appeared at first glance to be a reasonable fit for Cronbach's two disciplines. On the one hand, terms such as "experiment", "magnitude", "mechanism", and "stimulation", tended to show up together more often, rarely seen in the company of the likes of "attitude", "intervention", "occupation", or "policy" which hung out in the other lobe of the keyword map.

The analysis offered a somewhat telling finer-grain perception of the state of things, however. While the experimental hemisphere seemed reasonably tightly, or at least consistently connected, the opposite hemisphere was somewhat more diverse, with various distinguishable regions of tightly connected keywords. Flis and van Eck (2018) suggest that what Cronbach (1957) gathered together under the single title of "correlationists" might in fact be more disparate. Indeed, this area of the map appears to include the quintessential example of the correlationists in individual differences work, but also distinct applied fields such as psychotherapy, education, and clinical intervention.

Not only did the keyword maps seem to uphold the general existence of Cronbach's two distinct domains of work, this division remained consistent, with very little change, across each of the five decades of publication examined. In 1957 Cronbach had commented on what he saw as the first signs of integration of the two major groups, based on their shared commitment to a scientific psychology. As would be confirmed decades later by Flis and van Eck, reflecting on progress in 1975, Cronbach was less optimistic. The means of integration promised to be more systematic inclusion of individual differences being taken account of in experimental work. By the 1970s such work was widespread, and some have taken Cronbach's (1975) recognition of that as evidence of the desired integration. However, to Cronbach, it was clear that the complexities such experimental work introduced were not likely to offer the foundation for a unified, reliable science of psychology that he (and so many others) had hoped for. Cronbach would refer to the myriad "interaction effects" made apparent by factorial and more complex research designs as leading psychology into a "hall of mirrors that extends to infinity" (p. 119). Illusions within delusions within illusions it would seem. Cronbach (1975) recommended caution and humility to psychologists of all stripes, and a critical awareness of the limits to the kind of knowledge that typical research methods can provide us.

While humbling, we need not be overly dissuaded from psychological research by Cronbach's reflections (indeed, he himself did not counsel despair). Once we recognise that psychology is not unified, and pause for the moment in any attempt to force some kind of unwarranted integration, we can use the diversity of approaches to help us identify some of the ways in which various kinds of psychological science differ from one another. Making these differences explicit, and disciplining our consideration of them, will help us make clear to ourselves as a group of like-minded professionals how our different efforts relate to one another. This is very valuable in our current circumstances, as we critically reflect on the strengths and weaknesses of scientific practice across psychological research. When are our different methods compatible with one another, and when are they not? Where should we expect resonance and productive insights, and where should we carefully keep concepts separate to avoid confusion? When does cross-pollination become contamination?

Reflecting on our Differences

Discussion of psychology's "two disciplines" tends to describe the different camps in complementary ways. Generalisations are always contested of course, and we have already noted that there are probably more than just the two that Cronbach named for us. We will explore these issues with more nuance in a moment, but the coarse outline looks something like this: experimentalists are interested in within-participants differences (often between conditions), and correlationists are interested in between-participants differences (often within conditions or settings). Experimentalists have a focus on mechanism and the development of causal theories, correlationists with distributions, patterns of occurrence, and largely descriptive accounts. Experimentalists are interested in figuring out general underlying principles or even laws of behaviour and experience, correlationists pay more attention to actual, specific, real-world implications and relationships.

These are clearly distinctions that matter to psychologists. Just as it is telling that Cronbach decided to identify sub-disciplines with their preferred methodology, so it is that when we examine the three characteristic distinctions we find differences that matter for psychologists. For our present purposes, then, whether these are accurate summaries of different forms of scientific psychology is immaterial (variations are inevitably more complicated than a list of simple binaries like this). It is the description of psychology's disunity *along these dimensions* that tells us what dimensions are considered worth distinguishing for the psychologists doing the describing.

We do not think it coincidence that these three key dimensions resonate with the three recurring criticisms of psychological science that we have identified above. The within-between distinction struggles with the relationship between the individual and the collective aspects of human behaviour. The differences in priorities of mechanism and description between experimentalists and correlationists have been repeatedly used to criticise the lack of sound theoretical development (most explicitly aimed at the correlationists, but the problem exists across the board). And the differences of interest between abstract generalities and real-world specifics are a core wedge maintaining the research–practice gap. These aspects of psychological sciences represent not just nuances, but importantly, critical differences that militate against any easy unification of different psychological sciences. Unpacking this issue in detail will take several chapters, but it is worth pausing now to briefly touch on each in turn.

The Individual, the Collective, and Matters of Scale in Psychological Science

The shift from observations of individuals to the observation of groups may not seem at first to be something that needs critical reflection. This is simply *more*, after all. We are still interested in the same phenomenon, the same behaviour, experience, or personality trait. The move to making multiple measurements spread across a number of different people rather than focusing on an individual was a step taken to strengthen scientific validity. It was researchers taking steps both to facilitate awareness of our own errors – not being led astray by individual coincidence or outlier – and also to enable generalisability of our measurements – the wider variety of measures we make, the more likely we are to encompass the full range of natural probabilities.

The shift in scale of work from one, to some, to many, is not, however, entirely innocuous. There is a difference, obviously, between measuring a tree and measuring a forest. Just what those differences are can be hard to elucidate clearly. Scale matters, but it is only in the past few years that we have started coming to terms with just how and why it matters. Horton (2021) and Di Caglio (2021) have both recently advanced theories of scale, addressing the question of what it is that changes between scales, and how we should understand those changes. We will explore this issue in much more depth in Chapter 7. For the moment, we can help to inform our intuitions, looking for now at just the broad outline of the concepts that matter.

That trees and forests are different things is readily apparent, not least from that distinction being enshrined in a warning proverb or cliché about how paying attention to one can blind you entirely to the other. Certainly, there is a relationship between them – a forest involves a bunch of trees. Indeed, this relationship is much more subtle and thorough-going than our simple intuitions would have us believe. Wohlleben's (2016) delightful popular introduction to the ecosystems of forests describes a myriad of subtle ways in which the population of trees interact with each other, with the earth, the landscape, and the complex web of systems (mycelial networks, water and mineral cycles, birds, insects, and other wildlife) that make up that ecosystem.

A forest is not just a collective noun for tree. It is not just "more" tree. As we shift from the scale of the individual tree to the ecosystem of the forest, we encounter a distinct category of phenomenon rather than just a multiplication of the basic one.

As Di Caglio (2021) notes, this is the case across all aspects of the natural world – from physics, and chemistry, to medicine, meteorology, and sociology. When we shift in scale we orient ourselves differently to the world and what phenomena there are to encounter. When we change scale, say, zooming in from seeing the forest at a distance to picking out and focusing on a particular tree, we don't just magnify our initial perspective, we change the resolution at which we are observing. Things too small to be seen when looking at a forest become apparent when looking at an individual tree.

The resolution of our observations and measurements can have a very significant influence on the outcomes of those measurements. This is called a *scaling relation* (for a useful outline see van Orden et al., 2003). The most famous illustration of a scaling relation is Benoit Mandelbrot's (1967) discussion of the length of a coastline. If you measure, say, the circumference of the island of Ireland with a metre stick (with great patience and care), you will come to one answer about how long that coastline is. If you were to use (with even more patience and care) a ruler just a centimetre long you will end up with a measurement that is quite a bit longer.

Scaling relations mean that the scale at which we observe our phenomena of interest will have a direct impact on what phenomena we observe. They also mean that we must be very careful at all times to be *conscious of the scale at which we are making observations*. The scale at which we are making our observations will play a role in what measurements and records are possible, what specific phenomena we are observing, and also what kinds of methods and analytic techniques are valid for those observations.

That different scales tend to have different methods or apparatus associated with them (Di Caglio, 2021; Horton, 2021) means that it is difficult to keep more than one scale in view at a time. We will explore this in more depth in later chapters. For the present, we can recognise that for psychology (in nearly all cases) phenomena proper to individual human beings are at a different scale than phenomena proper to groups or populations of people. Scale imposes itself on psychological research in the form of a demand to keep straight what the relationship is between the individual and the collective, between a person and people. We will argue in the coming chapters that a lack of explicit recognition of this fact is one of the things that undermines psychological research and one of the roots of many ills in replication, reproducibility, and analytic validity that have beset the field, and led us to the polycrisis in which we find ourselves. This elision of the distinction between individual and collective, which occurs through the aggregation of data, is one of the core specific delusions that sets us on course for the Great Delusion.

It will take some time to unpack the problems that arise from this scalar misapprehension. Chapters 2–4 are all focused on different aspects of conceptual slippage attributable to this confusion, most clearly illustrated, and most explicitly discussed in the recent literature, on the topic of *ergodicity*. Ergodicity is a strict definition of the conditions under which collapsing across scales of description can be legitimately done. A key characteristic of an ergodic system is that the behaviour of a sample as a whole can be used to predict the behaviour of a single individual in that sample. There are two conditions for this: that each member of the sample is essentially interchangeable, and that the behaviour of each of the members does not change over time. It is likely obvious to the reader, and we will note in more detail in the next chapter, that this condition is rarely, if ever, the case for groups of human beings. Let's face it, we're probably among the least ergodic things in the known universe. This is a fact that has significant implications for a wide range of typical practices in psychological research of various kinds.

The complex relationship between the individual and the collective is not just a factor in the first of the three distinctions between Cronbach's experimentalists and the correlationists that we have outlined. This issue also provides a useful lens on our understanding of the different ways in which theory is developed and deployed in psychology, as well as the differing focus on the laboratory vs. the field. Indeed, as we turn our view to these distinctions with this sensitivity in mind we will notice interesting ways in which Cronbach's simple dichotomy breaks down. While it was useful as a first-pass coarse distinction to help us see some of the complexity in the population of psychologists and their orientations, the ways in which it does not apply allow us a finer-grained perception of some crucial issues in the organisation and priorities of psychological professionals.

Conceptual and Theoretical Clarity

Cronbach (1957, p. 675) noted that correlationists tend towards descriptions of patterns, distributions of traits or tendencies within a target population, but offered little, at the time, by way of theories that explain those patterns and afford accurate or confident predictions. In 1975 he would note both his own and others' lamentations about the failure of theoretical progress (p. 116).

Unfortunately, matters have progressed surprisingly little in the intervening half-century. Indeed, theoretical progress in psychology across the board has been notably weak and one of the recurring concerns for critics. Clinician and individual differences researcher Paul Meehl (1978) famously upbraided psychological researchers for their conceptual sloppiness and failure to develop theoretical frameworks that could support some kind of incremental or systematic progress in improvement of our understanding of behaviour and experience. We will explore some of the limitations of theoretical development in the psychological sciences throughout the book, particularly in Chapter 5. For the moment, we can note that our contemporary literature remains negative in its judgements of the state of the art (e.g., Ferguson & Heene, 2012; Gray, 2017; Guest & Martin, 2021; van Rooij & Baggio, 2020). The recent uptick in papers addressing a range of different facets of theoretical development, however, provides both a liveliness to the recognition and discussion of the issue, and a wealth of new resources, that offer hope for imminent positive changes in this domain.

There are a number of different factors that underpin weaknesses in psychological theorising. The conceptual slippage that results in psychologists sliding between scales of phenomena, losing track of the differences between persons and people, is only one aspect of this. It does, however, present a useful means of ingress into this question, and while it does not account for all of the problems, it usefully illustrates how the varied facets of criticism levelled against scientific practice in psychology are not entirely distinct.

In Chapter 5 we will illustrate this problem with the recognition that there are different kinds of theory, which play different roles in the development and progression of scientific understanding. Different theories have different relationships with evidence, which in turn implies different priorities and weightings for methods appropriate to those data. Where the confusions explored in Chapters 2–4 result in unreliable contact with our phenomena, our confusions about theories result in unreliable connection between different goals and objectives of research. This prevents scientists working on different aspects of psychological phenomena from being able to orient and relate their work to each other. Problems with our grasp of the individual and collective, and scientific theory, make the Great Delusion almost inevitable.

Sliding carelessly between levels of description of phenomena and explanation, undisciplined in the handling of relations between the individual and the collective is at play here just as it is in the breakage in logic between within-person and between-person empirical work. The conceptual slippage remains in play too, in the third of the major critiques we will address – what is sometimes called the "research-practice gap", the too-frequent mismatch in explanations, focus, and understanding between empirical research and applied professional practice.

The Gulf Between Research and Practice

Cronbach suggested that correlationists focus more on applied settings, but by turning our sensitivity to scale on this stated difference in priorities we can see that any simple description of experimentalists as individual-focused, and correlationists as collective-focused, starts to break down. Indeed, in professional practice settings, we find another set of psychologists, dedicated both to real-world, applied psychological phenomena and a tight focus on individuals. Many, or most, of these psychologists do not fit easily into Cronbach's dichotomy. Indeed, Flis and van Eck (2018, p. 354) suggest that the supposed "correlationists" are a rather heterogeneous group, determined more by what they are not (experimentalists) than what they are. One thing that thus becomes apparent is the disjunction between how scientific knowledge of psychological phenomena is advanced and how it comes to have an impact on regular people's lives.

Professionals in clinical, educational, health, and other settings, are focused directly on helping specific individual people, with their innumerable particularities and idiosyncrasies. One of the challenges that such professionals must face is how to translate knowledge about distributions and populations, or supposedly general and generic principles of psychology, to the individual person with whom they are working at a given time. Making effective use of the knowledge that we have is not a straightforward task, and inevitably demands judicious sensitivity on the part of the practitioner more than technically accurate implementation of a fixed and dependable set of principles (Carter, 2002).

Looking Ahead

It is important for us not to underestimate this lack of overall coherence in the psychological research literature. The temptation is to downplay (or even laud!) this as simply a matter of specialisation – a division of labour, the careful focusing of efforts that is characteristic of maturing, advancing science. Molecular biologists and zoologists don't cite one another with great frequency, and use often distinct technical vocabularies, but no one fears the incoherence of biology as a science. It seems an odd inferiority complex that would lead us to draw such a conclusion for psychology.

But things do not quite look that positive for us psychologists. The history of the biological sciences is a disparate web of efforts that are sometimes more, sometimes less related to one another. Over time various theoretical edifices have emerged and consolidated – ecology and ecosystems, evolution, and others – that provide a superstructure across which different specialisms can align and calibrate their efforts when necessary.

From the time that it began to coalesce as an independent, named professional endeavour, psychology has not yet managed to produce anything similar. The threads of specialism did not diverge from a common root, nor are they connected by a theoretical scaffold. Historians have a tendency to recognise the coherence of psychological research as arising not from a shared subject matter, a collection of phenomena that form a reasonably natural, easily sensible category that can be approached from different perspectives. Rather than organised around *phenomena*, psychologists seem to be organised (where they are organised at all) by the *methods* they have adopted as techniques of investigation (Danziger, 1994; Stam, 2000; see also Gigerenzer, 1991).

Despite this cross-pollination of methodologies, however, the various continuing historical strands of professional development remained quite separate. Most psychologists adopted the same relatively small number of statistical tools, but little was done to properly characterise the conceptual relationships to which these tools were being applied. The result is a misapplication of tools and inferences from one domain to others.

Reflecting on our past and present, then, we are faced with the uneasy conclusion that as a scientific endeavour psychology is rather a mess. Reviewing the evidence for the validity, reliability, and coherence of psychological scientific practice (or rather, the regrettable lack of same) a person might be driven to hopelessness. The delusion of a coherent psychology is starkly at odds with its unkempt, indeed chaotic, reality. Is there a way to clean ourselves up? It is tempting to throw up our hands and walk away, but your authors, dear reader, are an optimistic pair. Now, we certainly do not promise to fix things – that is beyond the scope of a single text, and our aim is not to propose some hegemonic vision of the One True Psychology. The subject matter and values of psychological scientists are too diverse for that. A useful first step in getting over our delusions, however, is to orient ourselves so that we can better perceive how things are. The landscape may be complex, but we can still orient ourselves within it, and learn to find our way carefully. Our aim in setting out the material in the following chapters is to make ourselves and you, our readers, sensitive to some of the key points at issue so that we can address them openly, honestly, and indeed, scientifically. It is science's great strength that once the problem is better understood, solutions become almost inexorable.

The development of psychology does not require everyone to study the same thing, use the same methods, or even agree on the best ways in which to link the science that is done in the laboratory to the real world. It does, however, require us to be able to orient ourselves with respect to one another and to be able to communicate and negotiate clearly around these issues in particular cases, when necessary. To do this, we need to think more clearly and specifically about how different subject matters, methods, conclusions, and applications relate to one another. In Part I of this book, we set out the challenges we face so that we can address them clearly. In Part II, we provide some tools that we believe can help us in this endeavour to discipline our understanding of phenomena, theories, and methods.

Through the rest of this first part of the book, we explore different facets of psychological science that need to be taken apart and understood. We explore a number of facets that comprise the Great Psychology Delusion. In most cases the point is not to uncover novel or startling realisations. Indeed, as our brief foray into history has already made clear, these are largely issues that have been explicitly acknowledged in one form or another since the inception of the position of "psychologist" as paid employment. Our aim, rather, will be to bring such disparate discussions together, as well as to elucidate how sometimes different points relate to one another and can be used to give us a sense of how different aspects of psychological endeavours are oriented with respect to one another. Part I is therefore an attempt to take a step back, through careful and critical examination identifying important landmarks and features of the landscape of psychological science.

We will find a number of interrelated themes recurring. Winding through several of these problematic aspects of psychology is our failure to properly get to grips with the relationship between the individual and collective. The first-person perspective of our subjectivity, as well as fundamental tenets of legal and civil society (especially in the Western countries that have dominated the conduct and publication of psychological research), gives individuality, and the individual human being a crucial role in our understanding of behaviour and experience. This individuality occurs within, and as part of collective phenomena, described in universal or encompassing terms, generalising across some, much, or all of behaviour and experience as they are observed and measured. Psychological phenomena occur at multiple different scales, therefore, and we will find it increasingly important that we be able to keep track of and make sense of the scale at which research is being conducted and analysed.

Part of what makes keeping track of this relationship between the individual and the collective so tricky is the diverse roles for theory in psychological research, and the diverse attitudes to theory building that exist among researchers. In getting to grips with certain methodological delusions, we will find theoretical uncertainties having an important role to play.

Finally, the break between applied and basic research in the psychological sciences represents a diversity of values that makes for an uncomfortable frisson of tension between psychological researchers with different priorities. We finish Part I with an examination of the research–practice gap, and what respectfully and effectively addressing it may look like.

The chapters of Part II provide a more positive outlook. The examination of methods, theory, and values in Part I allows us to review the wealth of resources available on these matters. In Chapter 7 we address the issue of scale in depth – the different frames of reference used within psychological research and how to orient ourselves deliberately and systematically with regard to them. Taking scale into account will involve widening the range of methods both in the production and analysis of data beyond those that are currently dominant.

Rather than re-inventing the wheel, however, we will find that there already exist a plethora of valid and effective methods in the extant literature. Chapters 8 and 9 explore this variety, and there we argue that what is needed is not a starting from scratch in methods or theory, but a more effective deployment of this wider range of methods. There is no way to know which methods or theoretical frameworks will be most productive, but a reinvigoration of that diversity will play a role in finding out.

In the final two chapters, we reflect on the huge body of existing work, and what value can still be derived from it given the critical conceptual and methodological questions that must be borne in mind when engaged with it. The critical perspective we adopt throughout is not a dismissive one, but a means of discerning. We close, then, with a looking forward to the possibilities of a successful science of psychology, and the promise of a polycrisis put to good use.

We turn first, though, to examine the fraught relationship between a person and people in psychological science, and one of the most pervasive and resilient misconceptions extant in research practice: the Aggregation Delusion.

2

THE AGGREGATION DELUSION

A Science of People, or Persons?

It is possible to characterise many conclusions that psychologists report about their research with one simple phrase: "People do…". That is, researchers attempt to highlight something about human behaviour that is typical of "people". But it is important to consider carefully what is meant by such a phrase. For instance, by "people" do researchers mean "all people", "a majority", or maybe "a sizeable minority"? In reports of psychology research, this is rarely specified. However, the strong implication is that the researchers have uncovered something they believe to be *general* to humans. That is, psychologists are concerned with discovering universal truths about psychological functioning (Hamaker, 2012; Van Geert & de Ruiter, 2022, p. 94).

Why might psychologists be interested in this? If we can know something that applies to all humans, we can then know something about specific humans. That is, if we know something about what *people* do, we can know something about what a specific person is likely to do. For instance, imagine that when studying, people learn material better by attempting to recall the material on several occasions rather than re-reading the material on several occasions. Such knowledge can provide advice to a struggling student preparing for an exam. Similarly, if people suffering with depression are known to better respond to Cognitive Behavioural Therapy (CBT) than to conversation with a hairdresser, then this is useful information for a therapist dealing with a new patient with depression.

All of this makes sense. It follows the same sort of logic we see applied throughout other sciences. Having deduced the general principles of motion from countless observations of physical objects, from balls to planets, physicists can predict how particular objects will behave when moving in a particular context. Armed with this knowledge, physicists can determine the trajectory a rocket travelling from Earth requires in order to meet an asteroid travelling through space at a particular velocity and with its own trajectory.

Chemistry is another science where precise predictions of future events are not only possible but routine. For example, the oxidation of propane results in heat and light, and several by-products, as described by the following equation:

$$C_3H_8 + 5O_2 \rightarrow 3CO_2 + 4H_2O$$

DOI: 10.4324/9781003503873-3

Our knowledge of the mechanism underlying this chemical reaction is so precise that, on the basis of this equation, and information about the surrounding conditions and the initial mass of propane and oxygen present, we can predict how much energy is released and the mass of the by-products. The predictions will vary depending on the surrounding conditions, and the extent to which materials are contaminated with other elements. Nonetheless, if we have knowledge of these factors, it is possible to modify the predictions and/or estimate the degree of error associated with the prediction. The precision of such predictions is so high that production processes can be planned and the costs associated with each stage estimated. In a commercial process involving such chemical reactions, very little is unknown or left to chance.

How well does psychology do in this type of endeavour? How well can psychology predict the behaviour of individuals on the basis of general principles derived from data collected from groups of people? Not well at all, it turns out. Nothing like the precise prediction in the chemistry example is currently possible in psychology. We cannot, with certainty, predict what a particular person will do in a certain situation let alone attempt to predict the magnitude of some aspect of their behaviour. Why might this be the case? Why might a discipline that claims science-status, as does psychology, fail to match the predictive abilities of chemistry? The simple answer reflects possibly the only firm, uncontested psychological fact; that a person's behaviour is determined by many more factors than exist in the sorts of chemical reactions about which we can make precise predictions. There are so many factors that influence human behaviour that we do not know them all, nor how they interact to affect behaviour. To make matters worse, we cannot even be sure that there are universal principles underlying human behaviour that are currently obscured by the plethora of factors that impinge on the nature of that behaviour. And yet psychology, in its efforts to live up to its mantle as a science, undertakes research with a similar approach to that of other more established sciences. That is, it assumes there are universal principles underlying behaviour, applies methods designed to sift through the morass of unimportant influences on behaviour to find the major factors that can explain behaviour, and uses this knowledge to predict individual behaviour.

Since around 1939 the dominant paradigm in Psychology has become one where many individuals are tested under similar conditions, measurements of their behaviour are aggregated, and average behaviour is used to characterise how people in general behave (Danziger, 1994; Lamiell, 2019). In this chapter we argue that this paradigm is flawed as it does not deliver on its promise to produce information about universal principles of behaviour. We also argue that adhering to this paradigm in the face of its shortcomings is delusional.

The Aggregation Delusion: The assumption that the psychological mechanisms that underlie the behaviour of people are similar to the extent that they can be uncovered and examined by aggregating measurements of behaviour from groups of people.

The Aggregation Delusion is an assumption of universality of human experience and behaviour organisation that is increasingly exposed as an assumption that has survived only because it has not been tested. When the complexity and the richness of human behaviour both within and between people are acknowledged and explored, then a host of related delusions in psychological research practice become illuminated (the topic of subsequent chapters).

There are many ways in which psychology generates aggregate measures of behaviour, but calculating the mean is probably the most obvious and the most commonplace. In the following section we consider some implications of relying on the mean to characterise behaviour. Focussing on the mean is a convenient way of highlighting many of the issues aggregation creates for psychology. Several other issues are considered after this section.

How Mean is the Mean?

A common introductory lesson in psychology involves measuring a group of humans on some variable and calculating the mean of the values. This mean value is then discussed as representing the average performance of the group, as if this value provides a representative substitute for the group's data. It is our view that rationalising a set of data into one value is a theoretically loaded practice that can be misleading and possibly erroneous. While the mathematical tool itself is theory neutral, its use within the community of scientific practice within psychology is not. We argue here that the mean, used without care, can cause illusions of stability and reliability in behavioural data, which in turn leads to inappropriate conclusions regarding the underlying nature of the psychological system. Our principal intent in what follows is to make the assumptions inherent in typical scientific practices more explicit, to expose them for critique. Our examination of the mean is therefore less a statistical one than a theoretical one.

The most common form of the mean that is used in psychology is the arithmetic mean. This represents the sum of all the values in a set divided by the number of values in the set. Although other forms of the mean are used in psychology (e.g., geometric, harmonic), our arguments are mainly confined here to the arithmetic mean. Our concerns, though, are mainly with the use of measures of central tendency, so our arguments apply in the general sense to all forms of the mean.

Textbooks used in introductory psychology courses on statistics and research methods typically refer to the mean as a measure of central tendency and often contrast it to other measures of central tendency such as the mode and the median. All such measures are used in situations where data sets contain some variation (i.e., not every score has the same value). The aim in calculating one of these measures, then, is to generate a value that sits somewhere in the middle of the distribution of scores. On the relatively rare occasions that the particular importance of measures of central tendency is mentioned, it is as an indicator of the typical or most likely scores within the distribution (e.g., Dancey & Reidy, 2008, p. 44; Haslam & McGarty, 2003, p. 135; Howitt & Cramer, 2011, p. 25). These "typical" scores are "summary" or "descriptive" statistics, providing at least some insight into the basic characteristics of the distribution in question.

However, while all of the data in a distribution are involved in calculation of the arithmetic mean, it remains a matter of judicious use as to how well the mean represents those data. Summaries are vital to good communication but used too frequently and uncritically they provide an impression of reliability or consistency that distorts the normal state of affairs. It is this sometimes careless overuse of the mean and its too frequent use without other statistics as a summary of distributions with which we are concerned here. In particular, the over-reliance on the mean (even though we all, of course, know better) expresses a way of thinking about distributions and variability that we believe poses potentially grave problems for our science. Introductory textbooks typically indicate that most measures of anything related to humans, and indeed any biological system, produce a distribution of scores. These distributions are commonly normal in shape (although see Micceri, 1989). That is, they have a shape that corresponds to the Gaussian distribution, which has a symmetrical shape, with most scores clustered around the middle of the distribution, fewer scores at the tails, and a smooth transition from the middle to the tails (see Figure 2.1). The mean, therefore, sits perfectly in the middle of the normal distribution (as do the median and the mode).

The Gaussian distribution is also referred to as the "normal law of error" (Boring, 1920), suggesting that scores on either side of the mean represent some error of measurement. Adolphe Quetelet, the first to apply this law to social and biological data, suggested that the mean of a distribution of human measurements, such as of a set of heights, represented nature's ideal value and that values on either side of the mean were deviations from nature's ideal (Howell, 2002).

Relying on the mean of a set of scores to represent the set appears to carry with it the assumption that the variation in values observed around the mean is somehow erroneous. Whether it be that our methods of measurement are faulty, or that individual humans represent "deviations around nature's ideal", or both, values around a mean are often considered noise, and the only way to eliminate this noise is to average it away. What we are left with, then, is an approximation to the "true" value for that human dimension. It is this assumption regarding the interpretation of noise, and the truth value of the mean, that we think requires questioning. This assumption has several subsidiary assumptions that we tackle below and conclude that they are difficult to justify. So too are some of the implications of using the mean to infer features of the mechanisms that give rise to human behaviour.

The uncritical or unreflective use of the mean in much psychological research makes us problematically blind to variation and distribution amongst the data we collect. In focusing narrowly on the mean, we make ourselves blind to potential variation and complexity in our data and in the cognition and behaviour those data represent. The assumptions we identify as underlying the uncritical use of the mean are, effectively, assumptions about certain characteristics of the psychological system, characteristics that tell us more about the theoretical goggles we are wearing than about the behaviour we are observing.

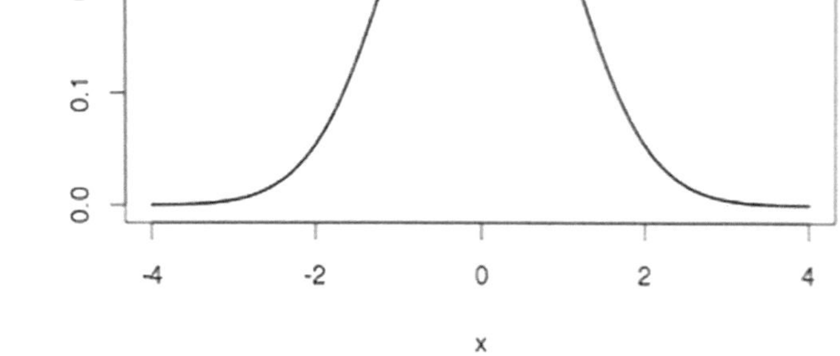

FIGURE 2.1 The Gaussian, or "normal", distribution. X represents the measured variable, and Y represents the probability of occurrence of particular values of X.

Assumption 1: There is a true value that we are trying to approximate when we measure humans on some dimension.

What is it about human behaviour we are trying to eliminate by averaging? In our own field of cognitive psychology, it would seem we assume that in each head there is a mechanism that is common to all/most people, but which is obscured by our noisy measures and/or our noisy heads. That is, in our experiments, we expose a group of people to the same conditions. Everyone is assumed to respond similarly to these conditions because their cognitive mechanisms are similar. Unfortunately, the data we collect from these people are not identical, and we assume this is because our measurements are not perfect and that there are a myriad of tiny and random effects that conspire to create noise in the data. Still, if we test a sufficiently large sample size, averaging should enable us to observe the characteristics of each cognitive mechanism unobscured by the noise.

The main question that occurs to us when we consider this scenario is why do we assume that everyone has the same cognitive mechanism? Just as we would not readily accept that each person's height is some deviation from an ideal height, it is odd that we would accept that each person's brain works in exactly the same manner. Certainly, this is the assumption that our research methods in cognitive psychology rest upon, and yet there does not appear to be any attempt to justify it. This is the strong version of the assumption. The weak version is that we assume that people have pretty much the same cognitive mechanism. This, however, is not a version that helps. If we accept that people have slightly varying cognitive mechanisms, using the mean to draw inferences about these mechanisms – that is, to get a picture of some average mechanism – we end up with a mechanism that may not exist in anyone's head. More on this later.

One means of justifying this assumption could be to point to other systems in the human body and note that they all tend to work in similar ways in each individual. For example, the heart operates in the same manner in each person and although some viable deviations from the standard exist (e.g., atrial septal defect, dextrocardia), the vast majority of people have similar cardio-vascular systems. Most of the other major systems in the body also have the same uniformity across the human species, from the cellular to musculo-skeletal levels. In response to this justification, however, we would point to the fact that the brain has one major difference to the other systems in the body – it changes its mode of operation as a function of experience. (Other systems in the body do this also (e.g., the cardio-vascular system responds to regular exercise by becoming more efficient), but this is usually in a quantitative manner, whereas the brain alters its functioning (at least its role in the organisation of behaviour) in not only a quantitative, but also a qualitative manner (Patel et al., 2013).) We consider this response further below, but for now we suggest that the assumption of common cognitive mechanisms is one that can be challenged and probably should not be the starting point in explaining human behaviour.

Assumption 2: Averaging helps us to eliminate the noise in our measures to see the true value.

We have no issue with the common statistical notion of sampling error. This is the notion that, when sampling from a population of scores, each sample will have a mean that is likely to vary from the mean of the population with a fairly predictable probability. That is, there are likely to be many samples with means that fall fairly close to the population mean, and a much smaller number that have means further away from the population mean. The chances of obtaining a sample mean close to the population mean are increased by taking a larger sample.

The problem we have with sampling is more in the interpretation of sampling error. Just as we have a difficulty with the concept of the mean reflecting a true value on some variable, we also find it challenging to accept that sample values on either side of the mean reflect noise in the data. This interpretation suggests that these variations in values are not psychologically meaningful. Instead they are a nuisance factor that requires elimination. Indeed, if this noise did not exist, if we could measure "true" values directly, we would have no need for inferential statistics such as the analysis of variance (ANOVA).

Despite there being something of a tradition within psychology pointing out the difficulty in this assumption (e.g., Doherty et al., 2013; Meehl, 1978), standard practice would appear to hold tight to it. Just as there are no obvious justifications for the argument that the mean reflects some true value, we have discovered no explicit attempts to justify the elimination of variance as a "cleaning-up" activity. It just appears to be the done thing.

A crucial mathematical (as opposed to psychological/theoretical) assumption regarding the use of the average to eliminate noise is the shape of the distribution in question. For the assumed Gaussian curve, averaging provides us with a clear representation of the centre of the distribution, the "noise" to either side being averaged away. In a sobering and landmark paper, Micceri (1989) noted that normal curves are very rare in real psychological data. To calculate the mean in the hope of eliminating noise or getting some glimpse of a "true" or even a typical value hidden in the variation is simply to overlook reality in favour of a comfortingly elegant mathematical ideal (Freedman, 1985).

One problem with this assumption is apparent when one considers possible reasons for sample values varying from the sample mean. One obvious reason is measurement error. All forms of measurement are associated with some degree of error. Typically this is related to physical features of the measurement process. For example, imagine three contractors preparing quotes for paving a driveway. They each measure the proposed driveway in order to estimate the number of pavers and time required to complete the job. It would be no surprise if the three contractors arrive at slightly different measurements for the length of the driveway. One may have placed the end of the tape measure a little further from the road than the other two. Another may not have removed every kink in the tape measure before noting the length. And the third could have viewed the tape measure from a slightly indirect angle when reading the length. This variation thus occurs for a range of reasons, none of which are systematic and so constitute random effects related to the measurement process. It is this sort of variation that is most likely to be normally distributed (Mlodinow, 2009, pp. 135–136).

The problem for psychology is there are likely to be other reasons behind variation in sample values in psychological contexts. There are at least two prominent reasons. One is there may be differences between individuals in terms of the processes underlying the behaviour being measured (more on this below). The other is that within each individual, these processes, even if the same, may not be stable, such that repeated measures of the same individual will vary, but also measuring different individuals at the same time may be capturing the same process but at different times (more on this also below). These two reasons for sample variability are not likely to be random but in fact reflect something germane to the psychological processes in focus, and so should not be discarded as unimportant noise. Being non-random means they are unlikely to be normally distributed, and so cannot be treated like random noise in any statistical analysis (e.g., removing through averaging, or assumed equivalent to other sources of random variation such as occurs in ANOVAs). Therefore, averaging across many measurements may not be providing an estimate of a "true" value.

Assumption 3: Any inability to use the mean as a reliable measure of a stable characteristic is a product of weaknesses in methodology or calculation (i.e., it does not represent a failure in the initial assumption that a true value exists).

Assumption 2 implies that averaging is necessary because our methodologies are inherently faulty in that they cannot be expected to provide perfect measures of the variables of interest. To some extent, this assumption is indisputable, considering that even measurements of physical properties (e.g., length, temperature) carry with them conventional measurement error values. In psychology, however, we take this assumption further than in the physical sciences. Although we accept that there are features of the physical environment that will affect the accuracy of any measurements we take, we are also concerned with the validity and the reliability of the measures. Validity reflects whether we are measuring what we think we are measuring. Most often psychological variables are not directly observable so we need to construct measures that are directly observable and argue that these reflect the operation of the unobservable mechanisms we are interested in. Even if we assume that our measures are valid in this sense, the reliability of these measures concerns psychology greatly. Indeed, Psychological Test Theory makes explicit this notion by indicating that each score on a particular test reflects the true value for that person on the test, plus error (Novick, 1966). The concern with reliability extends even further in the case of measuring the behaviour of one person. In cognitive psychology, we do not seem to believe that our measures are capable of producing an accurate reflection of the state of a person's cognitive system at some point in time. Indeed, if we exposed a person to the same stimuli, under the same conditions, on several occasions, and recorded their reaction times (RTs) in responding to those stimuli, we would likely average the individual RTs, on the assumption that each RT could not reflect the "true" RT for that person in that condition.

There is little doubt that there would be variance amongst the RT values recorded in this situation but what is the justification for assuming that each RT is a deviant of the true value? Instead of assuming that each RT is the true value plus some error created by seemingly random processes, could it not be possible that each RT reflects the state of the cognitive system *as it is at that point in time*? By this we mean, behaviour in response to the experimental conditions reflects not only the external conditions, but also the state of the cognitive system as the behaviour is occurring. The system will be in a different state to the one it was in on the previous occasion when an RT was recorded, and to the state when the next RT is recorded, if for no other reason than the fact that the system has experienced a repetition of the experimental conditions and made the same responses. The assumption then that taking the average of measures from repeated trials will provide a reflection of some stable element of the cognitive system seems fanciful given that the system could not be stable if we keep giving it experiences. This is a psychological reflection of the Heisenberg Uncertainty Principle – by measuring a system, we are influencing the system and hence affecting the very thing we are trying to measure. Unfortunately, averaging several scores will not result in a value that reflects some stable feature of the cognitive system. Instead, this stable feature may not even exist (Van Orden & Stephen, 2012).

Assumption 4: The noise in our measurements represents the effects of variables unrelated to the one being measured.

Part of the justification for averaging scores appears to be the assumption that scores on either side of the mean reflect error. This error can be error of measurement, as considered above, but it can also reflect the operation of many factors that influence behaviour. There is recognition in psychology that humans are sensitive to a vast range of variables, and any measurement of one variable is going to show the effects of many of these other variables too (hence the widespread usage in psychology of statistical methods such as Factor Analysis and Structural Equation Modelling). However, we assume that these effects have several characteristics. One is that they are random, and the other is that they operate independently of the variable we are interested in (i.e., the one we are currently measuring). Essentially, then, this error is assumed to be analogous to white noise in a radio signal. As such, calculating the mean is assumed to be just like fine-tuning a radio signal – in both situations, noise is eliminated to enable a clearer perception of the signal. Again, though, we wonder what justification there is for such an assumption. Below we consider whether it is appropriate to assume that the variance in a set of scores is a reflection of variables that are random and independent of the variable we have measured.

Interpretative consequences of using the mean.
The mean is often used as if it is a good representation of a group of scores. Clearly, it is only used when there is variation amongst scores – if there is no variation, then the scores can be characterised easily as so many scores of the same value. When there is variation amongst the scores, some measure that reflects the middle of the distribution of scores is considered to be a good reflection of the type of score that is observed in that set. As this variation in the set increases, however, the confidence one has in the mean being a good reflection of the group decreases.

This raises an issue with respect to the testing of differences between groups in an experimental design. Standard inferential statistics compare the variation between groups with the variation within groups in order to determine whether the scores in one group are significantly different to those in the other group. In spite of its name, then, ANOVA is rarely used to determine whether differences exist between the variances of two or more samples. Although there is explicit recognition that it is variance we are considering, ultimately the conclusions that are drawn in such situations concern whether the mean of one group is different to the mean of the other group. So, even though the statistical test explicitly considers the degree of overlap between the distributions of scores in the groups, the final conclusion is phrased in terms of whether one mean is significantly larger than the other.

The extent to which such a conclusion is a fair reflection of the state of the distributions is of course affected by the size of the difference between the means but it is also influenced by the amount of variation in the distributions, and the number of scores in each distribution. Thus, it is not uncommon to see significant differences between means reported where the differences are very small. This will happen when the variation within groups of scores is small, and/or the number of scores is large (Cumming, 2012, chapter 12).

In the end, though, a conclusion that the mean of one group is different to the mean of another group can end up being translated as one condition improved performance more than another condition, or similar. But is this an accurate summation of the outcome of the statistical test, and for what purposes are such conclusions used? When one concludes that one condition led to better performance than another condition, at best the implicit conclusion is that, on average, or generally, this condition improves performance. But, as is clear from the above characterisation of inferential statistics, there may well be significant overlap in the scores between the two conditions. For instance, if Condition A led to better overall performance than Condition B, there could well be scores in Condition B that were better than scores in Condition A. In other words, the final conclusion may represent an accurate description of the state of affairs for a subset of scores, but not necessarily for the whole set. Many undergraduate statistical courses and textbooks include such caveats in the discussion of the outcome of statistical tests, but the practices of scientists and standards of review and publication in journals involve few checks or balances against this kind of concern (see Marmolejo-Ramos & Matsunaga, 2009 for examples and explorations of good practice in this regard).

Inferential statistical tests generally do not provide information regarding the number of cases that do or do not match the pattern of results represented by the difference in means. It is, of course, a trivial matter to generate such information. Doing so can provide illuminating results. For example, we (Speelman & McGann, 2013) reported the results of a classroom exercise exploring the word superiority effect, where detection of a letter is found to be more accurate when the letter is presented in the context of a word than when presented in isolation (Reicher, 1969; Wheeler, 1970). Although the standard word superiority result was found with these data and supported by a statistically significant superiority in the word condition, when individual scores are considered, almost half of the over 500 people in the experiment provided results that either showed no difference between the conditions (i.e., identical accuracy scores in each condition) or showed results that were the opposite of the effect. This observation raises a serious question over the validity of using inferential statistics to assess differences between means. If we just examine the differences between means and focus only on whether or not this difference is statistically significant, we can end up with a conclusion that describes the effect of the manipulation as if it has had the effect on all or most of the individual scores in the data set. In other words, the mean difference can ultimately represent all of the differences, whereas in many situations this may well be inaccurate. Without investigating the data beyond the means, one's confidence that the means reflect the overall results should be low (e.g., Balota & Yap, 2011).

One heavy-handed solution to this problem would be to confine our theorising to situations where the differences between conditions are so clear that there is no need for inferential statistics to determine whether or not differences are significant. An example of such a clear difference between conditions would be where 80% of participants in one condition show results that are higher/larger/better/faster than 80% of participants in another group. This would be a difference in performance that would be obvious, has a good chance of being replicated, and everyone would believe. Confining ourselves to effects that are this obvious would limit the number of phenomena that require explanation and may reduce the current preponderance of seemingly unrelated phenomena and theories. Other solutions have been proposed before. One is to report effect sizes along with the results of significance testing (Cohen, 1994). This does not, however, address the issues we have identified because effect sizes are mostly used in comparisons of means. In this context the effect size is just a way of characterising how large the difference is between the means, in relation to the variance observed. Another solution is to report confidence intervals with means (Cumming & Finch, 2005). Again this does not entirely solve the problem because a confidence interval is just a measure of average variance, and so glosses over details of a distribution of scores.

An illustration of how problematic averaged data can be comes from Heathcote et al. (2000). The target of their investigation was the Power Law of Learning. This refers to the observation that improvement in the speed of performing a task with practice has a characteristic pattern: performance improves by large amounts early in practice but these increments in performance get smaller as practice proceeds. The smooth trend in these learning curves can more often than not be described well by a power function (see Figure 2.2). Such curves have been observed in fields as disparate as cigar rolling (Crossman, 1959), reading mirror-reversed text

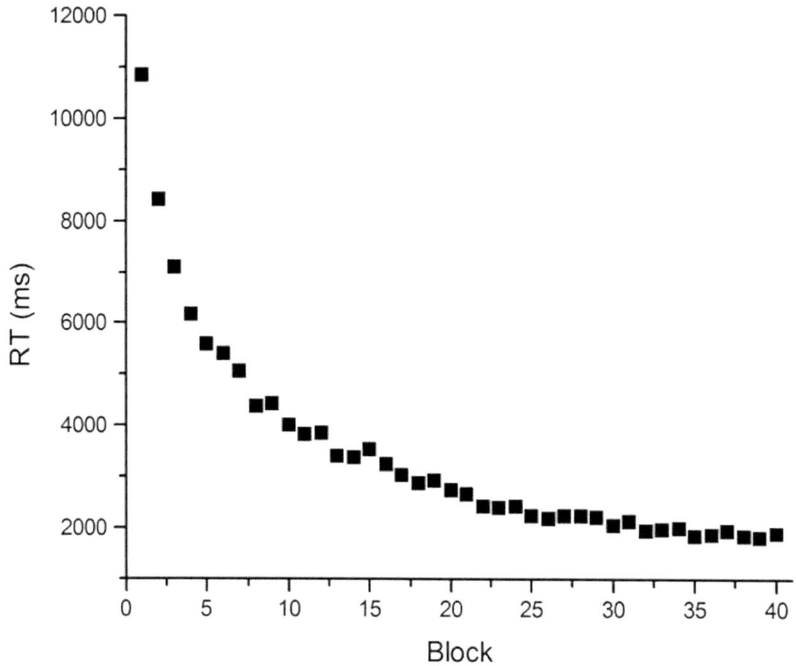

FIGURE 2.2 Mean RT data from practice on an arithmetic task. Participants (N = 40) solved an equation $[(x^2-y)/2 = A)]$ with eight repeating (x,y) pairs, determining whether A was "odd" or "even" for each pair, for 40 blocks of eight trials.

(Kolers, 1976), and implicit memory (Kirsner & Speelman, 1996), and are similar to retention and forgetting curves in memory (Ebbinghaus, 1885). So ubiquitous is this observation that it has been said to comprise one of the few laws in psychology (Newell & Rosenbloom, 1981), and the one fact that requires explanation by any credible theory of skill acquisition (Anderson, 1982; Logan, 1988). Heathcote et al. (2000), however, called into question the lawfulness of this relationship between performance speed and practice. They demonstrated that power functions result from averaging any group data with a downward trend. The important point here is that power functions can appear in averaged data, even when they do not occur in individual data. Certainly, if individual data is inspected, smooth learning curves are rarely observed. Although performance usually gets faster with practice on a task, performance from trial to trial almost never follows a smooth downward trend (see Figure 2.3).

So, why should theories attempt to explain power function learning if it does not actually exist in individual performance? The assumption of many cognitive theorists appears to be that individual performance does not reflect the real behaviour they wish to explain, and that averaging is required over many trials and many people to remove the noise from the data that is obscuring the real pattern. In the case of the Power Law of Learning, it appears that skill acquisition theorists assume that learning is smooth and follows a power function, and therefore, their theories must posit a learning mechanism that produces power function learning curves. It is possible, though, that this assumption is misguided. Rather than assuming that learning must follow a smooth trajectory, and so average data must be used to observe this smoothness, why not accept that what appears to be noise in the data is actually an accurate reflection of the

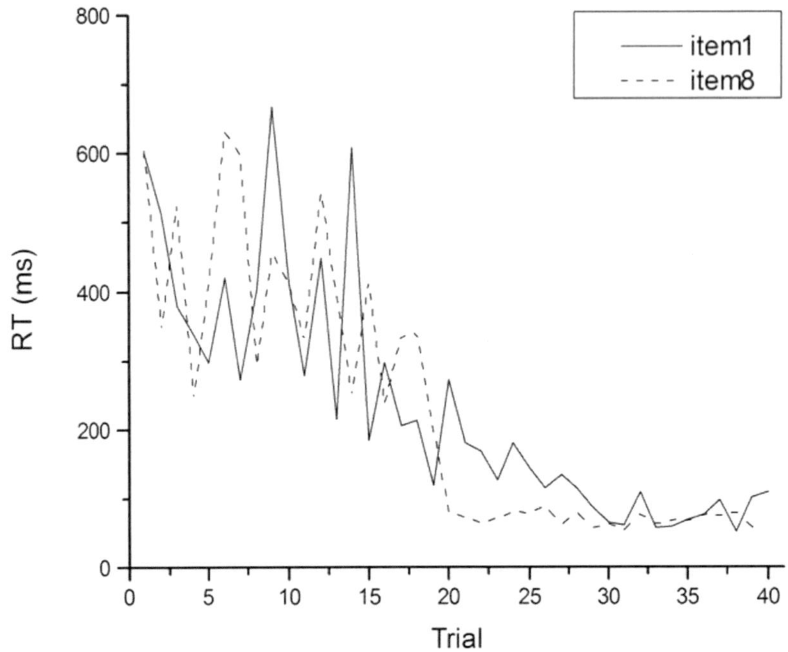

FIGURE 2.3 An individual's RT as a function of practice for specific items in the arithmetic task of Figure 2.2.

cognitive processes underlying performance? The lesson for all theories of cognitive processes, then, is that proposing mechanisms to explain mean performance may provide explanations of behaviour that does not exist. This lesson also applies to all areas within psychology where quantitative methods are used to aggregate data across individuals in attempts to discover universal principles underlying behaviour – this exercise may be misguided.

Aggregation to Principles to Prediction: How Well does this Work in Psychology?

Statisticians will tell us that the results of a statistical analysis of a sample of aggregated data can be generalised to another sample from the same population to the extent that the two samples are similar with respect to a number of properties (e.g., number of elements in the samples, that members of the sample are homogenous on a number of relevant variables, and so on). That is, properties of the first sample, such as the mean, and the variance, could be generalised to predict the mean and variance of the other sample, if the samples are similar. This is fairly uninformative, however, as it boils down to predicting that one sample is like another sample if the two samples are alike.

What statisticians will say is more informative though is that information about a representative sample will enable us to say something about the population from which the sample was drawn. Specifically, some of the characteristics of the sample, such as its central tendency (e.g., mean) and its distribution (e.g., variance), can be seen to be good estimates of similar characteristics of the population. A statistician will probably be happy to stop there, but in psychology we rarely do.

To summarise what we have covered above, psychology researchers have adopted a slightly different approach. On the basis of aggregated data, some value will be calculated to represent the "typical" behaviour. Commonly this will be something like the average of the measurements taken from each person in the sample. This average will then be used to characterise the group's performance, and then all discussion will be centred on this value. For instance, it will be used to compare groups tested under different conditions. Thus, the average, or mean, is a shorthand for "what the group did".

Psychology researchers also go a further step by characterising their results as if a mean applies to all people in the sample, as if the mean reflects what "people do" (DeJesus et al., 2019; McManus et al., 2023; Speelman & McGann, 2020; Speelman et al., 2024). In other words, the average result is generalised to the individuals that make up the group.

An important question, then, is how well can the general principles of behaviour derived from aggregated data be used to predict behaviour in individuals? Our first response to this question is there is not as much evidence on this point as one might expect. Since the early days of psychology, a massive amount of data has been published on average group behaviour under a range of conditions, but in most cases it is only assumed that the reported average behaviour is a good prediction of the behaviour of individuals. Rarely is pertinent data on this question ever considered or reported. There are, however, some relevant reports that, at the least, should make one wonder about the validity of this assumption.

Studies where effects observed in aggregated group data do not predict individual behaviour can be divided into two types. One set involve data patterns observed in group data that are not observed in individual data (e.g., individuals show no pattern (i.e., no effect), or different patterns). One example comes from research examining eye scanning patterns on pictures of faces. Mehoudar et al. (2014) replicated the often-reported group-level behaviour which is a triangular pattern between the eyes and along the nose. When individual level behaviour was examined by Mehoudar et al., the triangular pattern was rarely observed, with the only common feature being that individuals showed idiosyncratic patterns. Another example is provided by McManus et al. (2023) who found that, in a review of ten studies on moral cognition, none of the studies reported more than 50% of individuals in their samples exhibited results that matched the group data pattern. And, of course, the word superiority effect replication study we described above (Speelman & McGann, 2013) found that almost 50% of the sample did not show the word superiority effect evident in the aggregated group data.

The other type of study where aggregated group data does not predict individual behaviour is where the behaviour of individuals, or sub-groups, are opposite to the effect observed in the group. Such a possibility was famously identified by Simpson (1951), who demonstrated that trends in sub-groups could differ from (or are even inverse to) the aggregate trend when the groups are combined, an observation that has come to be referred to as Simpson's paradox. Kievit et al. (2013) discuss several examples of this from a range of fields in psychology and conclude that the paradox "is most likely to be observed when inferences are drawn across different levels of explanation (e.g., from populations to subgroups, or subgroups to individuals)" (p. 1). For example, Hamaker (2012) reported different relationships between typing speed and the frequency of typographic errors in groups and individuals. At the group level the correlation is negative. That is, experienced typists are both faster and more proficient. At the individual level the correlation is positive, such that the faster a given individual types, the greater the number of mistakes she or he will make relative to their own performance at slower speeds.

It is difficult to determine whether these examples reveal a general shortcoming with psychological research because it is not commonplace for researchers to consider how well effects observed in group data predict individual level behaviour. When researchers have considered this question, there have been mixed outcomes (e.g., Moore et al., 2023). That is, in some studies, group effects are demonstrated by the majority of the individuals in the group, which might indicate the effects are universal. But in other studies, this is not the case. Which raises the question of why might group data not predict individual behaviour? To answer this requires consideration of why psychology researchers aggregate data across people in the first place. Why can't we derive general principles of human psychological functioning by observing the behaviour of one person, or perhaps a handful of people? The most likely response would be that people vary in so many ways. For any behaviour one cares to measure, peoples' responses are likely to be diverse. Some people are fast responders, while others are more considered. Some find logic problems easy, whereas others struggle. For this reason, measuring a small number of people is unlikely to provide a reliable or representative estimate of what is general to all humanity. In other words, data collected from individuals is "noisy" in that it reflects not only the variable of interest, but also idiosyncratic factors associated with the nature of individuals, plus measurement error inherent in any measure of human behaviour (Speelman & McGann, 2013). Thus, as any statistician will tell you, if your estimates of some value entail some error of estimation, it is best to take many measurements and calculate a value that reflects the centre of the scores. The average or mean is the most typical. Further, the more estimates used in this calculation, the more "accurate" an estimate of the value will be.

Now couldn't researchers improve their estimates by focussing on one person, but taking multiple measurements from that same person, and then calculating an average? As we indicated above, one potential problem with this approach is that a person performing the same behaviour repeatedly changes rapidly – what we call learning or practice effects on one hand, and fatigue and habituation effects on the other. The process of studying the phenomenon in which we are interested therefore changes that phenomenon, creating difficulties in understanding and interpreting the observations made at any given time.

The preference for large group studies is often provided with some historical context in research methodology books. For example, according to Robinson (1981, pp. 47–52), Fisher (1925) was the first to advocate comparisons between treatment and control conditions, with more than one "subject" in each group. He also advocated a statistical approach to these comparisons, which demands large numbers of subjects (N) to provide the best chance of detecting differences between the groups. Following Fisher's recommendations to incorporate random allocation to groups, and ANOVA techniques, psychology researchers developed the ability to identify cause and effect relationships between variables. According to Robinson (1981, p. 310), psychologists were so excited by this capability they "began to equate good experimental research with large-N designs". Another research methodology text adds, "The view even arose that to study an individual participant was somehow unscientific and that real science was performed only with groups of individuals" (Ray, 2000, p. 274).

So psychology settled on a solution of observing groups of people under the same conditions, and aggregating their data into some measure of average performance. It is important to understand the basic assumption underlying this approach. *The only situation in which aggregating scores of any kind makes sense is when it is assumed the scores all reflect something similar.* The values, of course, do not need to be identical. If they were, there would be no need for aggregation and averaging. Indeed, the scores are expected to vary, but the variation is assumed to reflect the operation of a similar mechanism. For instance, if recall scores are recorded for a group of people performing a memory test, each individual's score is assumed to reflect the same basic memory operations involved in processing information, storing that information in memory, and then recalling that information at some later time. These operations are all assumed to be similar in all the people observed. *If the researchers did not assume this, there would be no reason to aggregate the scores across people.*

Consider a scenario where a researcher believed that some peoples' memory systems functioned such that forgetting was due to information stored in memory decaying in strength with the passage of time, whereas forgetting in others' memory systems was caused by interference such that new information blocked the recall of old information. If the researcher held this belief, there could be no reason for aggregating scores across people who the researcher believed varied in these basic memory mechanisms. The average of those scores would reflect some Frankensteinian mishmash of two quite different memory mechanisms. Simply, the average would have no meaning. It would be akin to the average of apples and bananas.

Because psychology researchers often attempt to discover universal principles of behaviour (Hamaker, 2012; McManus et al., 2023; Van Geert & de Ruiter, 2022, pp. 125–135), they do not start by assuming there are several different principles operating in the one group of people. The starting assumption is that the behaviour of a group of people will reflect the same underlying psychological mechanism (Richters, 2021). Measurements of this behaviour are aggregated together because the researcher assumes that each person's score reflects the operation of this same mechanism and so provides a window on the general principle underlying everyone's behaviour. Calculating the average score then provides a measure of this principle as it operates in the human population. This approach is most obvious in experimental designs where interest is on the effect of manipulating an independent variable (e.g., experimental treatment vs. control) on a dependent variable (e.g., scores on an anxiety scale). It is important to note, however, that the same approach is inherent in any research that involves a correlational design. Analysing the scores from a group of people with some form of correlation analysis involves the aggregation of scores from two or more variables in order to arrive at conclusions that reflect some general principle underlying some human characteristic (e.g., neuroticism is positively correlated with anxiety).

Thus, psychology researchers assume that the same mechanisms underlie behaviour in similar contexts for all people, make numerous measurements, and aggregate them, taking averages of a group to be a better measurement of a given phenomenon than a single measurement of an individual person. It is worth unpacking this assumption a little further. Essentially researchers assume that each individual in a group possesses a similar set of psychological mechanisms in their heads which underlie the behaviours observed by the researchers. By aggregating data derived from these behaviours, the researchers believe they can arrive at generalisations about those mechanisms that are possessed by each individual.

This underlying assumption that all people are essentially the same and the mechanisms giving rise to their observed behaviours are identical and interchangeable in this way is therefore a significant load-bearing tenet of a very large proportion of psychological research. This assumption is almost entirely implicit (Kroupin et al., 2024). Despite having been raised in some detail in recent years (e.g., Beck & Jackson, 2022; Lamiell, 2019; Molenaar, 2004, 2008b; Rose, 2016), it has seen surprisingly little discussion in the methodological reform literature, especially since so many questions have been raised regarding the validity of this assumption.

What evidence is there to support this assumption? Very little, as it is an assumption that is rarely stated let alone tested. The aggregation process is set forth in core and advanced methodological training and textbooks, and so seldom raised for reflection that many researchers rarely consider the implications for our understanding of individual people. Indeed, it is easier to find evidence contrary to this assumption. Such evidence comes from across the range of sub-fields of psychology. Perhaps most explicit are findings from longitudinal work in developmental psychology that identifies multiple development paths to similar outcomes. That is, children learn and mature to perform the same thing but do so in different ways, meaning that the underlying mechanisms are not general. This has been shown in areas such as posture control and locomotion (Adolph et al., 2010) and reaching and hand–eye coordination (Thelen & Smith, 1994). Such patterns are not confined to motor control, however. Knight and Fischer's (1992) work on reading development indicate multiple routes to effective reading performance (though the routes are not as reliable as one another), while Karmiloff-Smith (2000) describes evidence indicating that something such as face recognition can be done in more than one way, and the manner in which individuals perceive and respond to emotional faces is done in a variety of ways (Carlisi et al., 2021). Bucciarelli and Johnson-Laird (1999) describe multiple ways of drawing inferences that differ between people, and Speelman and Kirsner (2005) explore a wide range of impacts of individual differences not just on performance on various cognitive tasks but on the way in which the performance is accomplished. Conversely, classic work by Shoda et al. (1994) illustrated that two children with the same score on observed aggression measures might nevertheless have notably different patterns of aggressive behaviour. This wide diversity of developmental pathways and underlying cognitive mechanisms undermines the simple assumption of similarity in such mechanisms when participants engage in a given experimental task. The recognition of just how fundamental this issue is for psychology has seen some recent work (see Yarkoni, 2022 and commentaries).

As mentioned above, part of the rationale for aggregation is the awareness that people do differ from each other. However, this acknowledgement of individual differences within the majority of psychological research allows for variation, but only insofar as people are taken to possess the same cognitive mechanisms that vary within limits along a small number of dimensions. These can only be quantitative, not qualitative distinctions in the mechanisms that give rise to observed behaviours (Anastasi, 1937, p. 29). But what if human beings are capable of finding quite different ways to achieve similar end results? What if there is more than one way for a person to develop to adulthood capable of key skills required in their society?

Evidence for the possibility of such differences exist, particularly in domains such as disability studies, where we see people with bodily differences often achieving indistinguishable performance in a specified array of tasks, but doing so in a manner quite distinct from what is commonly expected (Devlieger et al., 2003). Similar findings have also been evidenced where developmental disorders affect brain development, but some perceptual or motor skills remain "normal" despite the neural means by which those skills are enacted necessarily being very different to what would be considered typical (Karmiloff-Smith, 2000). Indeed, research (e.g., Ayoub & Fischer, 2006; Cantor et al., 2019) suggests that even "normal" development is much more varied than we would have believed, and apparent consistency in localisation of brain function is largely a product of statistical aggregation of measurements across people. The area of brain imaging, too, is grounded in the assumptions of aggregation, which has been discussed as under-recognising individual differences in the organisation of brain function which in turn is responsible for very low reliability of localisation conclusions (Bennett & Miller, 2010, 2013; Hunter et al., 2024). Zilles and Amunts (2013) examined a range of ways in which group-based analyses of neuronal structure can lead us to overlook information about individual differences in neuronal structure and change in structure over time that offers crucial clues to the processes underlying brain development.

Ergodicity

To understand the limits on aggregation revealing universal principles of behaviour, it is important to be aware of the conditions that must be satisfied for such a thing to occur. That is, under what circumstances can the average of aggregated data be useful in understanding the behaviour of the elements of a sample? Or, when can the average of a sample be used to predict the performance of the elements?

We already highlighted above how, even when dealing with large samples, sample-level statistics still come with costs and assumptions. These issues have been discussed to varying extents within psychology for at least the last 60 years (e.g., Cronbach, 1957), and there has been a recent resurgence in interest (Fisher et al., 2018; Rose, 2016). Molenaar (2004, 2008a; see also Molenaar & Campbell, 2009) and others (e.g., Hamaker, 2012; Rose, 2016) have fought to raise awareness that, in counterbalance to the apparent benefits, the cost of using samples and averages in order to estimate psychological variables is that almost all comparison and theorising of those variables must occur at that sample level. Psychological theories in this case must be actuarial descriptions of the behaviours of populations, not specific descriptions or explanations of the behaviour of individual people. In other words, mean-based statistics only allow generalisations to the means of other samples, not to individuals. We can draw conclusions about the individual members of those samples only in very specific circumstances, where we can show that the sample in question (as a system of variables) can be considered "ergodic".

The ergodic theorem, proven by the mathematician Birkhoff (1931), shows that the behaviour of a sample as a whole can be used to predict the behaviour of its individual components only in those cases where two criteria apply: (1) all of the members of the sample are essentially interchangeable with one another; and (2) the members of the sample, and the sample's average behaviour, do not change over time. (More technically, the average of the sample's behaviour over time is the same as the average of all of its potential behaviours at any given moment. For other versions of these two criteria, see Molenaar (2008a) and Schmiedek et al. (2020).) Gas molecules (e.g., hydrogen (H_2)) in a sealed vessel would be considered an ergodic system because all elements (molecules) are identical in all respects.

On the basis of these criteria, it is clear that human beings, and groups of them, are quintessential examples of non-ergodic systems (Hunter et al., 2024). No two human beings (even monozygotic twins) are so identical as to be interchangeable on most variables. In addition, people's tendency to change over time not only over long developmental timescales, but also the shorter timescales of practice and learning, is a perennial thorn in the side of within-subjects designs (Molenaar, 2008a). And yet, any method of analysis that involves measuring a sample of people on some dimension and using the average value as a predictor of individual behaviour or, crucially, as a description of individual psychological function will be assuming that the system observed is ergodic. In such circumstances, psychologists are committing what Molenaar (as described to Rose, 2016, p. 64) refers to as the "ergodic switch" – studying something that is not ergodic and acting as if it were. In a non-ergodic system there is no reliable connection between the results of the sample-level statistics and those of the individuals that comprise those samples. We can generate means from raw data, but we cannot generate those raw data from their means. This fact matters a great deal when we are trying to develop theories that describe, explain, and predict the behaviour of individual people from the calculated measurements of many of those people (Hamaker, 2012).

Fisher et al. (2018) have recently provided a clear and substantial illustration of the falsity of ergodic assumptions in six data sets from what would typically be considered high quality research projects in psychology. Re-examining these data sets, they were able to investigate the differences between statistics calculated over samples as a whole, and over the measurements of the individual members of those samples. They found that individual participants were much more variable than the samples they belonged to, with intra-individual variance ranging from two to four times that of samples constituted by those individuals. Similar observations have been made in a correlational context. Hamaker et al. (2007) demonstrated that while the factor structures of personality scale scores were stable across a sample of 60 participants over time, within participants factor structures varied (and were almost never the same as the group). (For further examples of the non-ergodicity of psychological processes, see Gernigon et al. (2023).)

Clearly, the conditions of ergodicity never apply to humans. Therefore, the average of group data can never be used to develop general principles by which we can understand the individuals in a group. And yet, most psychology researchers behave as if this is not the case. Psychology acts as if groups of humans are ergodic. We have suggested that conducting research on the basis of such an assumption with no basis is fallacious, and so we have used the term "ergodic fallacy" (Speelman & McGann, 2020). Our term for describing this behaviour is deliberately more strident than the gentler "ergodic switch" term used by Molenaar. The latter carries the connotation that there is something quaint about the way psychology researchers go about their work. In our view, there is nothing quaint about making a major mistake. Our aim in this book is to call out such behaviour for the delusion that it is so that future generations of psychology researchers can avoid the mistakes that litter the discipline's history. And these mistakes are not only in the way we interpret our data and analyses, but possibly more importantly, those errors impact the types of predictions and decisions we make about individuals. We demonstrate these issues in later chapters.

The problem is not a new one and has been raised repeatedly by others to little apparent effect on mainstream research practices or standard interpretation of findings (Danziger, 1994; Estes, 1960; Grice et al., 2006; Grice et al., 2017; Lykken, 1991; Smedslund, 2016). It is possible that the message has been lost partly in the method of presentation, which has for the main part been couched in fairly dry (if thorough and comprehensive) statistical arguments and formulae (e.g., Haaf & Rouder, 2019; Williams et al., 2020). At the least, the solutions provided by others to the ergodic fallacy have clearly lacked the "cut through" to shift mainstream methods of analysis. But this is not something that we can afford to ignore, confident that our methods and analyses are robust to the violation of this assumption. It speaks to some of the most common forms of psychological research, and as such, the ergodic fallacy is substantially responsible for the breaking of the vital feedback loop between the phenomena proper to the discipline, and the theories purported to explain them.

The Problem of Measurement in Psychology

While the ergodicity issue places hard limits on what aggregation can deliver in terms of discovering universal principles of behaviour, there is another problem that must be considered to justify aggregating measures of behaviour across people. This problem relates to the rationale for aggregation mentioned above. That is, the main reason for aggregating measurement across people is those measurements are assumed to reflect something similar about each person. One side of the "something similar" issue is related to ergodicity. Another side of the issue is whether the scores one ends up with through the data collection process actually represent comparable properties about the people that were measured. This may not be too difficult an assumption to justify when the measurements are objective features of behaviour, such as reaction time, number of items recalled, and heart rate variability. Justifying the assumption, however, faces significant challenge when the measurements come from self-report responses on psychological rating scales, such as those used to measure depression, anxiety, attitudes, personality, and happiness.

In a series of articles that present a devastating case against the way measurement is construed and operationalised in psychology, Uher (2022a, 2022b, 2023) highlights several problems associated with the use of rating scales to answer questions about psychological processes. Of relevance to the issue of aggregation is the common practice in psychology of asking people to provide ratings of their experience or feelings. For instance, in the Depression and Anxiety Stress Scale (DASS; Lovibond & Lovibond, 1995), an instrument commonly used to indicate signs of depression and/or anxiety, a person will be asked to respond to the following item: *I couldn't seem to experience any positive feeling at all.* The person is asked to reflect on their experiences over the previous week, and to give a rating of 0 to 3, where the numbers are supposed to indicate the degree of experience (e.g., to some degree), or the frequency with which something was experienced (e.g., most of the time).

Amongst several problems with such rating scales, Uher (2022a, 2022b, 2023) suggested the vagueness of the response categories provided in these scales means they may be interpreted differently by respondents. This assertion was supported by Simpson (1944) who asked students to indicate how they interpreted frequency terms such as "usually", "occasionally", and "rare". A large range of responses were observed for each frequency category. For example, 25% of the sample indicated they would select "usually" to describe something that occurred 90% or more of the time, whereas another 25% of the sample would use this term for something with a frequency of 70% or less. Uher (2022a, p. 2537) also notes that the interpretation of such terms may vary depending on the experiences being rated (e.g., "often" may mean different frequencies for talking compared to sneezing). Furthermore, the same ratings may not reflect the same quantitative information. For example, the numerical value that is assigned to a rating of "small" for a bicycle will not have the same quantitative meaning as the value assigned to a rating of "small" for a train. Moreover, the common assignment of numerical scores to an agreement scale (i.e., Strongly Agree = 5, Agree = 4, Neither Agree nor Disagree = 3, Disagree = 2, Strongly Disagree = 1) is problematic for the quantitative operations that are typically performed on such scores (Uher, 2022b, p.25). For instance, although Strongly Agree (5) surely indicates more agreement than Agree (4), can Agree (4) really be considered more agreement than Neither Agree nor Disagree (3), when many might consider the latter as indicating "Not Applicable"? Also, it is possible that people may consider agreeing and disagreeing as different ideas rather than as opposite ends of the one dimension, negating the appropriateness of one scale to measure both ideas.

The problems identified by Uher cast doubt on the assumption that people interpret response options on rating scales in the same way. As a result, we cannot be confident that the scores assigned to the options selected by respondents are comparable values. Each respondent could be providing scores for the items on a scale using psychological dimensions and processes that are different for each person. Certainly, there is little justification for assuming these dimensions and processes are the same for all respondents on a scale. Thus, there is little justification for aggregating such scores across people as is commonly undertaken in the many forms of statistical analyses used to assess the reliability, validity, and factor structures of such instruments. This then calls into question the validity of any attempt to measure psychological phenomena using rating scales.

The Aggregation Delusion

So, psychology is aggregating for reasons that are not valid. And aggregation does not deliver on its promises. For this reason we invoke the notion of the Aggregation Delusion. The Aggregation Delusion is an implicit assumption that, for the purposes of psychological research, people are fundamentally interchangeable. Despite the fact that outside of the psychological laboratory there is nothing in the world *less* fungible than a human being, the methods of a great deal of psychological research require people to be essentially the same in all key respects save those regarding the independent variable (or its equivalent).

Some implications of the Aggregation Delusion that will be considered in subsequent chapters include the following:

- Common methods in psychological science are not viable for their intended purpose. If the aim is to uncover general principles of behaviour, aggregating people will not reveal such principles. To make claims of universality, or at least generality, these claims must be based on some measure of the proportion of people to which the principle applies.
- There may be no general principles. It may be the case that people are not sufficiently similar that such principles can be derived or are useful. If this is the case, the nature of psychological science will need to be revisited.
- There may be some general principles, and so people are pretty much alike, in which case aggregation makes sense. However, we will not know this unless we check on whether people are similar in some respect. So, it is not justifiable to start a research endeavour by assuming this to be the case, as is currently common practice.

It is important to note that when psychology does try to uncover general principles of behaviour or function, it determines this not by aggregation alone. Some form of experimentation is also used to uncover cause–effect relationships. Unfortunately, problems associated with the Aggregation Delusion also creep into the logic associated with the experimental designs utilised in psychology. This issue is considered in the following chapter.

3

THE DELUSIONS OF EXPERIMENTAL CONTROL, GROUP COMPARISON, AND CORRELATION

The Delusion of Experimental Control

One fundamental feature of the design of psychology experiments is the notion of control. The concept of experimental control requires people to be tested under the same conditions (e.g., the circumstances of the laboratory or testing situation, the sequence of experiences, events, or presentations being manipulated by the researcher, the stimuli presented to participants for responses, participants' mode of responding, the researchers themselves), assuming they will behave in essentially similar ways. Responding in a "similar" way here acknowledges that people's responses will vary quantitatively along some measurement scale (manifest as variance in data), but not qualitatively. Indeed, testing situations are usually so constrained that people are not able or allowed to respond in qualitatively different ways. Doing so invalidates their behaviours and ensures that their data do not form any part of the researchers' interpretation of what has happened. For instance, if participants are performing a Stroop task, and are required to speak into a microphone to provide their colour-naming response, singing into the microphone will disqualify their responses from the analysis.

The concept of control is a general one in psychology, beyond just experiments. Questionnaires that are used to measure attitudes, personality, and mental well-being are typically standardised to control for a plethora of variables that may affect responding and thus affect interpretations of the responses. So, for instance, the same form will be completed by every person being tested, the same duration will be allowed for completion, and participants' mode of response will be kept uniform. If, for example, an item on the questionnaire requires a response along a 5-point Likert scale (e.g., ranging from Strongly Agree to Strongly Disagree), providing a response beyond the extremes of the scale would be disallowed. So too would providing a written clarification of the response provided.

The importance of control in an experimental situation is revealed by a brief survey of research methodology textbooks on our bookshelves. Invariably these books (e.g., Haslam & McGarty, 2003, p. 46; Robinson, 1981, p. 72) state that the ability to draw causal inferences from controlled experiments relies on being able to equate groups on all things other than the independent variable. These other things are often referred to as confounding, secondary, or error factors. Ray (2000,

DOI: 10.4324/9781003503873-4

p. 165) implies that controlling for a variable virtually eliminates its effects, and further "…stressed the logical necessity of beginning our experiments with groups that can be assumed to be equal" (p. 202). Our survey indicated universal agreement on this point, and the texts describe various means by which groups can be organised to ensure this equivalence (e.g., matching, randomisation, discussed below), but rarely was there any consideration for whether such methods are sufficiently successful to justify the assumption that experimental groups are indeed equivalent.

On the basis of the Aggregation Delusion, we argue that this assumption regarding control is not valid, and indeed constitutes another delusion.

> ***The Delusion of Experimental Control:*** The assumption that if people are treated in the same way, and tested under the same conditions, their responses will be homogeneous enough that they can be treated as a well-constituted sample from a pre-specified population of behaviours.

Any study that involves testing groups of people under similar conditions has the aim of generalising the results of the group to some population from which the group was sampled. To be precise, the population is in fact the behaviours under study, not the people. This population reflects all responses collected under the particular conditions of the experiment. The individual participants are considered instances of an ideal, or average, individual, and so their responses constitute independent estimates of the average population response. The assumption of control, then, is once again that people are interchangeable, that their behaviour is "ergodic" such that we can predict the behaviour of a person in a particular situation by studying the behaviour of many people in that same situation. Their average response will provide us with the best estimate of how another person would respond.

The Delusion of Experimental Control is not really a different delusion to the Aggregation Delusion. It is an expression of that delusion as applied to a particular scenario. That is, where the Aggregation Delusion assumes that people are similar enough that measurements taken from them can be aggregated, the Delusion of Experimental Control assumes that people are fundamentally similar enough that they will respond to a particular experimental situation in a similar manner, and so their responses can be considered instances from the one distribution of responses (Diener et al., 2022). Both beliefs are delusional because they mistakenly assume that people are ergodic.

The Delusion of Experimental Control is essentially an assumption of cognitive generality – that there is a single, canonical set of cognitive and psychological mechanisms that give rise to behaviour (Richters, 2021). Similar behaviour is assumed to necessarily be the product of similar psychological mechanisms. Furthermore, the Delusion of Experimental Control holds that a controlled situation has the same meaning for each person exposed to it, and so, because of their similar psychological makeup, they should respond similarly to that situation. This assumption is similar to one that underlies the use of self-report items in psychology questionnaires which is similarly problematic (see Chapter 2). An implication is that for the purposes of psychological experiments, people are interchangeable and the average of individual measurements over many people will provide the same information as an average of many measurements of an individual person: the "ergodic assumption". This assumption is rarely considered nor tested, and when properly examined is often found to be violated (see Chapter 2). Psychological diversity and the lack of ergodicity impose severe constraints on the concept of experimental control and demand a greater degree of explicit justification of methodological and analytic practices than are currently extant within psychological research.

Furthermore, the invalidity of the ergodic assumption underlying the Delusion of Experimental Control contributes to another delusion, the Delusion of Group Comparison.

The Delusion of Group Comparison

Grounded in the same quicksand as the Delusion of Experimental Control is the Delusion of Group Comparison. A great deal of psychological research involves the comparison of two or more groups of people. Each group is treated or presented differently according to a variable under the control of the experimenter (whether directly, in experiments, or through assignment to groups according to the inherent characteristics of the participants, in the case of quasi-experiments). Indeed, in many areas of psychology, and indeed in many other human sciences, a version of this kind of experiment – the randomised controlled trial (RCT) – is considered the gold standard of research. Any measured differences in the pattern of observations between the groups in question are explained with reference to the difference in presentation or involvement of this experimenter-controlled variable – the independent variable.

The issue of the control assumption identified above as the Delusion of Experimental Control also applies to this situation where multiple groups are compared. In this case, the control is extended to the multiple groups, and exerted by ensuring that the groups are treated in as identical a manner as possible, except for the experimental treatment condition. For example, two groups could be treated in exactly the same manner, except one group receives some additional treatment (the experimental group) that the other group does not (the control group). Importantly, such a design assumes that the people within the experimental and control groups are essentially equivalent with respect to the variables under examination, insofar as they would all respond similarly to the treatment condition if they experienced it, or to not having the treatment condition if that was their experience. As before, the problem with this assumption is that it is rarely tested, and data exist which cast doubt upon it (see Chapter 2). Thus, any difference in behaviour between the two groups may be a result of the different experimental treatments they received, but it could also be due to pre-existing differences between the individuals that lead to different ways of responding to the experimental conditions.

There is often some recognition of this control problem, but it does not extend to the possibility that experimental participants differ in the psychological mechanisms relevant to the behaviour in focus. What is acknowledged is the possibility of variation along one or more shared dimensions of potential change that will impact their responses on the dependent variable being measured in the experiment. These other dimensions are typically not under the direct control of the researcher, in that they cannot be manipulated. They are often referred to as confounding, extraneous, secondary, error, and even nuisance variables.

If confounding variables are left to vary naturally, it is possible that people will be allocated to conditions in such a way that one condition contains many people who would score high on some measure of a confounding variable, and the other condition contains low scorers on that variable. For example, if participants differ in terms of academic ability, this could affect their performance on a problem-solving task they are required to complete as part of an experiment. One group could be dominated by people of higher ability, and the other might have a majority of people of lower ability. This would create a situation where a difference in performance between the conditions would be difficult to interpret. The difference in performance may be associated with the manipulation of the variable of interest (the independent variable). Alternatively, the difference could simply be due to the pre-existing differences between the groups in terms of the confounding variable. For instance, if the condition with the high ability majority solves more problems than the condition with the low ability majority, one would be tempted to interpret the problem-solving difference as just due to the pre-existing differences in academic ability.

There are several means by which researchers attempt to control for such differences between participants and so ensure group equivalence. The first two methods to be discussed all require that the researcher know something about the possible confounding variables prior to observing the behaviour of interest. This information essentially provides an index of the degree to which the participants vary from each other on the confounding variable. The final method does not have this requirement; however, it does make assumptions about how the process of allocating participants to conditions affects the distribution of differences in the confounding variable in the various conditions. These methods are some of the ways that researchers have addressed issues of potential non-equivalence of groups, which must be overcome to apply the logic of group comparison. It is important to note, however, that in presenting these methods here, we are not endorsing them as viable options for dealing with the delusion issues we have identified. As we demonstrate below, they don't.

Matching

One method for dealing with potential confounding variables is to measure people on these variables and use this information to allocate people to conditions so that the conditions are roughly equivalent, on average, with respect to the confounding variable. There are various means by which this process is undertaken, but the principle they all share can be illustrated with an intelligence example. If we have a measure of each participant's intelligence (e.g., their score on the Raven's Progressive Matrices test) at the commencement of the experiment, we can rank order the participants on the basis of this information. If the experiment has only two conditions we could allocate the person with the highest intelligence score to one condition, and then the second person on the intelligence list to the other condition. We could then proceed in this manner, allocating people in the 1, 3, 5, 7, … positions on the list to one condition, and those in the 2, 4, 6, 8, … positions to the other condition. This process would result in conditions with roughly equivalent average intelligence scores. Some researchers might be concerned that the process just described would result in a slightly biased allocation because, for every pair of participants, the highest scorer would always be allocated to the same condition. So, an alternative method would be to allocate those in the 1, 4, 5, 8, … positions to one condition, and those in the 2, 3, 6, 7, … positions to the other condition. Other variations on this theme are available to researchers (e.g., D'Amato, 1979, p. 37; Ray, 2000, p. 213), but one would have to be extraordinarily confident in the accuracy of measurement of the confounding variable to be so concerned about the possible bias inherent in various allocation strategies to then consider more complex methods.

Matching is not restricted to only one confounding variable per experiment. It is possible to control for multiple confounds through matching; however, the difficulty in organising equivalent groups increases multiplicatively with each new confound added. For instance, one might consider not only intelligence as a possible confound in the problem-solving experiment but socio-economic status (SES) also. Let's say we have information (low, medium, high) about the SES of each participant. Matching in this case would require both experimental conditions to have similar distributions of intelligence and SES such that these were roughly equivalent. This would mean, at a broad level, that there were participants in both groups who had high intelligence scores and were from low SES areas, other high-scoring participants who were from medium SES areas, and some high-scoring participants from high SES areas. There would be a similar requirement for all other levels of intelligence. It is not only more complex to develop a scheme for allocating people to conditions in the two-confound case, it can often be a challenge to have sufficient people in the sample in all the categories of the confounding variables to satisfy the matching requirements.

Pre-testing

If matching proves impractical with respect to ensuring group equivalence, researchers can still use the information about participants obtained prior to the intervention in a number of ways, all of which are designed to approximate an equivalence process. In some situations, this information involves a variable that is different to the main dependent variable but is correlated with the dependent variable. For instance, in the above example where the dependent variable was performance on the problem-solving task, and the other variable was intelligence as measured by performance on the Raven's test, the intelligence information can be treated as a covariate in a statistical test such as the analysis of covariance. This test can control for the correlation between the covariate and the dependent variable, and effectively remove it from the variance in the dependent variable. The remaining variance can then be analysed for any signs of variance that are associated with the intervention. The upshot of this technique is that pre-existing differences between groups on the covariate (intelligence in this case) are to some extent equated through a statistical process, and so mimics the ultimate aim of a matching process.

Sometimes an experimental design allows for participants to be measured on the dependent variable *prior* to the intervention, as well as afterwards. Thus, each participant is measured twice, and so the design is often referred to as *repeated measures*. For some participants, the two measurements will be before and after the intervention (i.e., the experimental group). For others (i.e., the control group), they will just be on two occasions, separated by a time period that is similar to that experienced by the experimental group. This type of experimental design, also often referred to as a "Pre-test Post-test" design, enables a researcher to check on the equivalence of the groups prior to an intervention (i.e., by comparing mean Pre-test scores on the dependent variable), but it also enables each participant to act as their own control. When we considered matching above, we focussed on the idea of creating a situation where participants were compared with people of similar abilities (e.g., intelligence) in terms of how well they performed on the problem-solving task. This was so that problem-solving performance only reflected the differences in treatment and not also pre-existing differences in intelligence. A repeated measures design achieves the same end by comparing a person's performance before an intervention with their performance after the intervention, thus eliminating any effect of pre-existing individual differences. In the problem-solving experiment, the assumption would be that there is no change in the intelligence level of each participant throughout the experiment. This constancy in an important confounding factor means that any change in performance can then be attributed to the intervention as that is the main thing that has changed during the experiment.

It is possible that something else has changed for participants in such an experiment besides the effect of the intervention. Just being tested multiple times can change a person, in a multitude of possible ways (e.g., Ray, 2000, pp.145–149). They might become sensitive to the issues being explored by the researcher, and so alter the way they respond, either to fit with the researcher's aims or to thwart their attempts to "control the way I think". It's also possible that having performed a task once, a participant can become better at the task, or they could become fatigued or bored. In essence, although a repeated measures design has enormous advantages associated with using participants as their own controls, it also comes with several disadvantages associated with such testing effects. A control group is therefore considered important in repeated measures designs, as these allow assessment of the degree to which testing effects occur when no intervention has been experienced. Thus, the performance of an experimental group might change in a particular direction, from the Pre-test to the Post-test. The performance of a control group could also change in the same direction. If the extent of change in both groups is similar, then the changes in performance could be more a result of testing effects than anything associated with the intervention. On the other hand, if the experimental group showed a larger change in performance than the control group, then the typical interpretation of such a result would be that, although there might have been some testing effects present, the intervention also had an effect over and above those of the testing effects.

Randomisation

We noted above some difficulties with creating equivalent groups through matching. A further difficulty is that it is not possible to match for everything. It may not even be possible to know what to match participants for. A different approach to designing an experiment with equivalent groups of participants is to randomly allocate people to groups or conditions. The assumption with this approach is that, if the sample is large enough, and the number of conditions is not large, any pre-existing differences between participants, on any variable, will be "averaged out". That is, the distribution of scores for a variable for the people within each condition should be the same for all conditions. As a result, the average score on that variable should be roughly the same for all conditions. And this applies to all potential confounding variables. It is important to note that random allocation to conditions is assumed in Null-Hypothesis Significance Tests (NHST) (as is a random selection from the population). An assumption that participants within experimental conditions are essentially equivalent on variables other than the independent variable is required for the probability of events in the experiment to be estimated. If this assumption is violated, the validity of an NHST is questionable.

As noted above, the RCT is considered the most effective means of managing the potential limitation of experiments with respect to pre-existing differences. The assumption of this approach is that random assignment to groups will ensure that pre-existing differences in abilities will be balanced across the conditions, and so result in approximately equal ability levels in each condition. From the survey of research methodology books in our collection one could be forgiven the impression that random allocation to groups guarantees group equivalence of pre-existing differences. For example, according to Elmes et al. (1995, p. 231, italics added), randomisation is "...a more common technique to *ensure* the formation of equivalent groups of subjects". Robinson (1981, p. 76, italics added) claimed that "with randomisation, the effects of the variable are *equated* between the groups, thereby removing the *possibility* that any difference noted between the groups was a function of the variable in question". Similar sentiments were expressed in books by Haslam and McGarty (2003, pp. 46–47), Maxwell and Delaney (1990, pp. 7–8), and Ray (2000, p. 163).

Random allocation to conditions does *not* guarantee equivalence of pre-existing differences (e.g., Elmes et al., 1995, p. 231), and occasionally wild discrepancies can result. But such discrepancies can be checked before, and even after, an experiment is conducted, although this is rarely done (Van Geert & de Ruiter, 2022, p. 152). Nonetheless, such an approach cannot remedy the likelihood that individuals within the groups, and across the groups too, differ in terms of the psychological mechanisms that underly the relevant behaviour. Thus, any difference between the groups' behaviour may not be safely attributed to just the differences in treatment conditions. The difference could merely have been a result of pre-existing differences in the way individuals respond to the treatment conditions they experienced. How this might affect the interpretation of an experiment's results is illustrated in the following two scenarios.

Let's first consider the possibility that there are qualitative differences in psychological mechanisms amongst the participants in an experiment. If these differences are given sufficient freedom to be demonstrated, they would be evident as different behaviours. That is, behaviours that are qualitatively different. As mentioned above, though, experiments are typically designed so as not to allow such degrees of freedom in participants' responses. Wildly different responses are generally discarded for reasons such as being "inappropriate", "revealing inattention", or "participants not following instructions". Another possibility is that similar behaviours may result from quite different underlying psychological mechanisms (see Chapter 2), and so observing the same behaviours in different participants does not automatically indicate the operation of similar psychological mechanisms. Both scenarios considered here complicate the interpretation of results from experimental designs. The assumption that eliminating such differences between participants through the various research design control measures is not safe without evidence that the measures have been successful. Nonetheless, there is a more serious concern with respect to the assumptions underlying group comparison in psychology experiments.

In addition to the problems just identified, the comparison of groups in controlled experimental designs suffers from an insurmountable problem of logic. Such designs rely on the controlled differences between groups, and the assumed equivalences within and between groups in terms of all other variables, in order to infer the existence of experimentally induced differences between the groups. Even if the problems identified with control and allocation to groups did not exist, there is one other fundamental problem that threatens the interpretation of results collected with such designs. This problem concerns the inference that an observed difference in the behaviour of an experimental group compared to a control group was caused by the experimental treatment. The inference assumes that the experimental treatment caused a change in behaviour in the experimental group that would not have occurred if they had not experienced the experimental treatment. In other words, if they had been treated like the control group, they would have behaved like the control group. The problem with this inference is that it is an ultimately unjustified assumption. In such between-group designs, the researcher never has the opportunity to observe the experimental group under control group conditions, and so cannot know how they would have responded under those conditions. The researcher assumes that the observed behaviour of the control group is an appropriate indicator of how the experimental group would have responded under those conditions. But, for the reasons already articulated with respect to control, this is not a safe assumption. Ultimately, then, the researcher never gets to directly observe the effect they assume to have occurred in the behaviour of any individual. That is, the change in behaviour that the experimental treatment is assumed to have caused is only ever *inferred* from comparisons of group behaviours (Eronen, 2020), and these comparisons are based on dubious assumptions. We must ask ourselves, then, if we cannot observe an effect directly in the behaviour of an individual, does such an effect exist in any real sense? If the effect is only apparent in the carefully controlled situation of an experiment, and relies on the dubious aggregation of results from groups of individuals, and the equally dubious comparison of such groups, does this effect actually explain anything like natural behaviour? We argue that the answer is "no" and that the belief that a difference in performance between two groups of individuals who are associated with the manipulation of a variable is evidence that the manipulation had an effect on behaviour is therefore delusional.

The Delusion of Group Comparison: The assumption that, if participants in one condition had been tested in another condition, they would have behaved similarly to participants who had originally been tested in that condition, and vice-versa.

Despite the excitement that early researchers felt about the possibility of investigating cause–effect relationships in psychology through group comparison experiments (Ray, 2000, p. 274; Robinson, 1981, p. 310), the Delusion of Group Comparison suggests that, at best, group comparison in experiments can only be suggestive of such causal relationships (Hunter et al., 2024). A great deal of information about these relationships is not provided by standard between-groups experiments. To illustrate this point further, we provide a concrete example of the Delusion of Group Comparison in operation.

A Worked Example

Bargh et al. (1996) reported an experiment that has become famous, not only because it has attracted a label (the Florida effect), but because it has been the target of several criticisms related to the various crises besetting psychology, such as the replication crisis (Doyen et al., 2012; Mac Giolla et al., 2022; Romero, 2018). We focus on this experiment here for other reasons. The previous criticisms of the Bargh et al. experiment may all be damning in the sense that confidence in the existence of the Florida effect has been diminished, but it provides a clear illustration of the arguments and both delusions presented above.

The experiment we consider here is Experiment 2 in Bargh et al. (1996), where a group of young people are exposed to several trials in which five words are presented, and instructed to form four-word sentences from these words. For half of the group, in half of their items, one word was a word associated with being old (e.g., worried, Florida, old, lonely, grey). For the other half of the group, these old-associated words were replaced by neutral words (e.g., thirsty, clean, private). At the completion of this scrambled sentence task, the group primed with the old-associated words were observed to walk down a hallway outside of the laboratory significantly more slowly than the group exposed to neutral words. Bargh et al. concluded that this result "suggest(s) that exposing individuals to a series of words linked to a particular stereotype influences behavior nonconsciously" (p. 237). That is, by presenting words to some participants that are associated with being elderly, it primed the elderly stereotype in the minds of these participants, which had a slowing effect on their walking speed.

This is a between-groups design, with no Pre- vs. Post-test measure of walking speed. So, an obvious concern with the result is that the primed group could just have been slower walkers.

Without some form of prior measure of walking speed, we can never know. Bargh et al. would probably defend the result by saying participants were randomly allocated to conditions, and this would reduce the chances of a walking speed bias resulting from allocation to condition. This would reduce the chances of a bias occurring, but it does not eliminate the possibility. Hence the need for a check of prior walking speed.

Bargh et al.'s observations regarding the effect of priming on walking speed were based on a statistical comparison of the aggregated walking speeds of one group with the aggregated walking speeds of another. As suggested above, without more information about the general walking behaviour of the experiment's participants, we cannot jump to the conclusion that the experimental manipulation changed the behaviour of some of the participants, specifically those in the "old" primed group. The only safe conclusion here is that one group is statistically different to the other in their walking speeds. Importantly, this means that the aggregated results of the groups differ. There is no information available about a *change* in behaviour. To draw the conclusion that the manipulation caused a change in behaviour is courageous.

Another feature of the Bargh et al. design means conclusions about the possible effect of a priming manipulation are difficult to reach. The behaviour of two groups of people were compared. Why did Bargh et al. compare groups of people to try to observe the effects of priming? Presumably, Bargh and colleagues felt that the primary observation they were going to make – walking down the hall from the laboratory – was such that they would not be able to observe them do it again without there being possible confounding factors that might affect that behaviour (e.g., increased familiarity of the route might speed walking; the tedium of an extended experiment might slow walking; being asked to walk the same route again might raise suspicions in the minds of the participants which could have an unknown effect on walking speed). To avoid such a minefield of alternate explanations for a change in walking speed, each participant could only be observed walking once. So, rather than compare the walking speeds of a person after being primed, and after not being primed, we suspect that Bargh et al. would have thought it better to compare the walking speeds of people who were primed with those who were not primed. But still, the question remains – why are *groups* of people compared? Comparing the walking speed of one person who had been primed with that of another person who had not been primed might raise suspicions that any priming-related slow walking could just have been a result of pre-existing differences in walking speed between the two people. To address such a concern, psychologists typically compare groups instead of individuals, on the belief that having large enough groups, and random allocation to groups, will reduce the possibility that prior differences will have an impact on observed results. As mentioned, though, this strategy does not eliminate the possibility that groups start off differently. Furthermore, it creates another problem that is apparently unknown to most psychology researchers. We say "unknown" because no one talks about it in their reports of their studies. There are less generous speculations which we will not consider here.

By comparing the performance of groups of people in the manner reported by Bargh et al., researchers are assuming that the people in each group are essentially the same in some respect that is important to the phenomena under examination. In the Bargh et al. experiment, the assumption is that, if the priming effect exists, the people in the priming group would all have a similar psychological mechanism operating in their brains that is affected by priming in the same way and so the behaviour of everyone in this group would be affected in the same way. It is probably safe to assume that researchers do not expect that people within a group would be affected by their manipulation *to the same extent*. A great deal of attention is paid to the amount of variance that occurs within the data of a group of people. Indeed this is central to the sorts of statistical tests that are typically performed to make comparisons between groups. Nonetheless, there is still the working assumption that people exposed to the same experimental condition will be affected in the same way. In the Bargh et al. study, this assumption would be that the Florida effect would be such that the people in the priming group would walk slower after the priming manipulation. They might all differ in the extent to which their walking has been slowed, but the assumption is that all people in the priming group would be affected in the same way. If Bargh and others do not start with this assumption, then it is worthwhile asking why have they put all those people into that group, and treated them the same. Comparing their results with the other group with some form of NHST is based on the assumption that each person is an element from one population of elements that are effectively the same thing: that is, they have the same form of psychological mechanism that is affected by priming in the way described. Their results are aggregated together to provide an approximation of the population behaviour. The problem with this assumption is that it is rarely tested, and when it is, it is often clear that the assumption is not warranted (e.g., Speelman & McGann, 2013).

Several scenarios are possible with the Bargh et al. design that would have all given rise to the reported significant difference between the two groups: (1) everyone in the priming group is slowed by the priming effect; (2) the majority of people in the priming group are slowed by the priming effect, but a minority are not affected at all and their walking speed remains the same; (3) a minority of people in the priming group are affected by the priming effect, and in a dramatic way such that their walking speed is significantly slowed, but the remainder of the group are either unaffected by priming or are affected in a different way (their walking speed is slightly increased). Bargh et al.'s design would not enable the discovery of which of these scenarios, or others, occurred in his experiment, at least not without closer inspection of individual results.

To summarise, Bargh et al.'s Florida Effect experiment demonstrates all three delusions we have considered to this point. The data from many people are aggregated together on the assumption that the people are similar enough in some respect that each person's behaviour reveals the operation of a similar mechanism (i.e., stereotype priming) and so each person's behaviour can be treated as instances of the same phenomenon (The Aggregation Delusion). No evidence was provided to support this assumption. Bargh et al. assumed that by treating participants within a particular condition (either the "old" priming condition or the control condition) in exactly the same manner, participants within a condition would interpret their task in the same way, would respond to the items in that task in the same way, and would be wired in such a way that a primed stereotype would influence their behaviour in the same way (The Delusion of Experimental Control). This assumption was not tested in the experiment. Finally, by interpreting the slower average walking speed of the "old" primed group as demonstrating the priming effect of the elderly stereotype, Bargh et al. have assumed that the average walking speed of the control group is a valid indication of the average speed of the "old" group if they had experienced the control conditions and so is a useful point from which to gauge a change in behaviour (The Delusion of Group Comparison). There was no observation of the "old" group under control conditions, and so no justification provided for this assumption. Indeed, no change in behaviour was observed.

We have not targeted the Bargh et al. experiment for any reason other than that it is an example of a simple experimental design often used in psychology, and that it illustrates the types of assumptions, analyses, and interpretations associated with such experiments. The points we have highlighted in this experiment that we consider to be invalid are endemic in much of today's experimental psychology. Although we do not claim that, as a result, the conclusions that follow from such research are wrong, we do argue that the assumptions underlying the methods by which those conclusions were reached are questionable. If they are re-considered, and found to be unjustified, then we recommend researchers revisit the original research questions and consider alternate methods for assessing them.

The randomised controlled trial holds a much-vaunted position as the pinnacle of powerful research designs, but one of the most basic implications of the issues outlined above is that there are more robust means available and in use within psychological science. The simple shift from a "between-group" to a "within-group" design provides us with a means to examine with a much higher degree of resolution many of the phenomena that psychologists are interested in observing. Though there are more constraints on the kinds of research questions that can be asked compared with between-group comparisons, within-group comparisons provide a means of recording individual instances of a given phenomenon – a particular change in behaviour from one condition or setting to another, for instance – that is quite impossible in a typical RCT. We consider further the value of such individual instances of a phenomenon in the next chapter.

The issue with group comparisons is not only that half the data is always missing (i.e., we don't observe participants in the "other" condition; Eronen, 2020). It also represents a situation that has no direct connection to any real-life situation. For instance, imagine the following conundrum: "would someone perform mental rotation better, such as in the classic experiments reported by Shepard and Metzler (1971), if they practised that task, or played a version of the game Tetris?" The typical approach to addressing this question in psychology research would be to perform an experiment. In this experiment participants would be randomly allocated to a mental rotation practice condition or a Tetris playing condition. Then everyone would be tested on the mental rotation task. Statistics on the data collected in this last phase might show an advantage for one group over the other, but as we have described in the Delusion of Group Comparison, since we do not observe people in both conditions, we cannot say that one condition resulted in a greater change in the participants in the superior condition.

A further problem with the group comparison logic is that the comparison can never occur in reality. Just as someone cannot be in two places at once, there are some forms of comparison that do not make sense for any individual. So, in the mental rotation vs. Tetris example, it is not possible for a person to answer the conundrum with respect to themselves. If they had practised mental rotation, and then performed the mental rotation test, this result could not be sensibly compared with a later test result that followed subsequent Tetris play. The latter result will obviously show some influence of the previous mental rotation practice, the effects of Tetris play, and the previous mental rotation test. Thus, for any one person, they can never know if their performance on the mental rotation test would be better following Tetris play or by practising mental rotation. This is just one of those conundrums we can never definitively resolve. It is similar to the many scenarios often referred to as "Sliding Door" moments (cf Stephen & Van Orden, 2012).

One serious implication of assuming that people tested in an experiment all share a similar psychological mechanism relevant to the phenomenon under investigation is that, if this assumption is not valid, then the chances of replicating any effects observed in the experiment are likely to be low. If people within experiments are not homogeneous in terms of their fundamental psychological mechanisms, and so respond to controlled conditions in different ways, then the observation of an average group effect will be a reflection of a combination of idiosyncratic psychological mechanisms that are unique to the particular sample of people tested in the experiment. Any attempt to replicate the effect with a different sample of people will inevitably result in another unique combination of idiosyncratic psychological mechanisms which is unlikely to match the specific combination examined in the original experiment. As a result, the average group effect for the new experiment is likely to be different to the one originally observed. It should not then be surprising that psychology is experiencing a replication crisis (Baumeister et al., 2022; Gernigon et al., 2023; Open Science Collaboration, 2015; Tang & Braver, 2020; Wallot & Kelty-Stephen, 2018).

The Correlation Delusion

One of the first things that we learn in statistics is to be careful and critical when it comes to correlations. Say it with us: *correlation does not imply causation*. Amen and inshallah.

The ubiquity of this mantra perhaps leads us to a certain complacency as to the depth of its implications. This simple phrase contains within it one of the deepest critiques of psychological science – longstanding in discussions of our scientific practice, and with a burgeoning recent literature. The reason is that this snappy, unanimously agreed-upon phrase carries the payload of a crucial demand for well-developed theory. Let us unpack it.

A correlation is a quantification of the relationship in the variation of two sets of numbers. When examined pair by matched pair, any similarity in their risings and fallings can be represented simply on a single dimension ranging from –1 (a perfectly anti-phase relation in which one set of numbers falls by precisely the same proportion as the other rises), to +1 (a perfectly in-phase relation in which both numbers rise together in proportionate lockstep).

A consistency in the way two things vary is *prima facie* evidence that they are related in some way. We are perennially tempted to consider the possibility that as one thing changes, it causes the other to change with it.

Famously, of course, demonstrating the existence of such a relationship, even a reasonably strong one, is not sufficient to infer a *causal* relationship. The frequency of eating ice cream and of wearing short trousers are correlated, but it is unlikely that slurping a scoop of rum 'n' raisin produces in the licker an irresistible urge to change into a pair of shorts. The simplest explanation here is that both variables are at least partially consequent on a third variable – hot weather, for example.

Our consideration of the mantra typically ends there. *Correlation does not imply causation.* All that we need to do is stop ourselves from succumbing to the temptation of assuming a direct causal connection, where other relationships might also be present. Rarely do we consider carefully what *is* required for a causal inference, and what kinds of ambitions we should have in seeking them.

If correlations don't imply causation, then what is it that we are looking for when we look for correlations? The answer, of course, is causation.

Scientific explanation involves the telling of stories that provide an accurate and preferably precise account of how things come to be the way that they are. While there are stages of scientific work which are not directly concerned with identifying causal relationships, these are early and intermediate stages. Approaching causal accounts is the ultimate aim.

In psychology, correlations are often used to implicitly evaluate conclusions about causal relationships. This may seem erroneous to many psychology researchers because of the training mentioned above. Nonetheless, interpretations invariably have causal connotations. Merely concluding that two variables are "associated" provides little explanation for any phenomenon. Such knowledge has no utility without some theory as to the mechanism by which the variables are somehow connected. Even if the two observed variables are not directly connected in some causal relationship, there will be some indirect causal connection implied, possibly through other variables. If this is not the case, does describing two variables as being correlated have any true value (Eronen, 2020)? And yet, concluding a causal relationship from a correlation is not justified for more than the usual reasons indicated in introductory research methods lessons. The main reason is that in most correlational research each data point in the correlation calculation represents two bits of information about an individual. Thus, the relationship between the two variables under examination by the correlation analysis is never observed in any individual. It is only inferred by extrapolating from the results of many independent individuals. Again we can ask, does this relationship exist? By using the data points from a large sample of people, we infer a relationship between the two variables. However, this extrapolation is based on the ergodic assumption that each person in the sample is the same in some respect (i.e., with respect to the relationship between the two variables of interest), and so are independent estimates of this relationship. But this assumption is rarely commented upon and never tested.

Students are often instructed to display data collected on a categorical variable (e.g., nations) as a histogram rather than as a line graph. The reasoning is that there is no justification for connecting information across the levels of a categorical variable. If the variable is continuous (e.g., amount of practice), the data can be represented as a line connecting the various data points because there is clear justification for connecting them, particularly when the data points come from the same person or people. In a scatter plot of data that someone analyses with a correlation, the correlation implies a connection between the dots (i.e., does a linear function describe the data well?), and yet it is debatable as to whether either of the variables in the scatter plot should be considered continuous when scores on each of them come from different people. As such, the relationship between the variables indicated by the correlation is possibly a fiction. In the context of psychological research, extrapolating from a correlation between two variables to a claim that there is some connection, possibly causal, between those variables is not justified, and in our view, delusional.

> ***The Correlation Delusion:*** The assumption that an association between two variables, suggested by paired measurements on these variables taken from a group of individuals, indicates something about a relationship between these variables that is shared by each of those individuals.

The Correlation Delusion shares underlying assumptions with the Aggregation Delusion and its offspring: the idea that human beings are ultimately interchangeable and the measurement or recording of one can be substituted for the measurement or recording of another. We can illustrate the implication of such an assumption with respect to a fairly common example in psychology. Imagine that someone has reported a positive correlation between working memory capacity (WMC) and mental arithmetic. Such a finding could lead to such statements as "the greater someone's WMC, the greater their capacity for performing mental arithmetic". Consider the type of data that is collected to perform such a correlational analysis. To examine the WMC/mental arithmetic relationship, for instance, a researcher need only obtain a measure of WMC and a measure of mental arithmetic performance from each person in a sample. Thus, each person would contribute a pair of numbers to the calculation of the correlation estimate. On the basis of the whole sample of such pairs, the extent to which the two variables are related could be determined. Thus, some sort of relationship between the variables might be discovered (if one exists), such that as one variable increases in value, there is some concomitant variation in the other variable, either up or down. Typically this would suggest that a systematic relationship between the two variables has been discovered, which could be used to characterise the original data set, or possibly to make predictions about the performance of other samples. It is important to remember that, although the correlation that is derived from the analysis to describe the data set is a function that characterises the whole data set, each individual has only contributed one data point in that data set. Nothing about the data from one individual tells the researcher anything about the overall relationship between the two variables. It is only when data from many individuals are combined is the relationship revealed. But this strategy reflects an ergodic assumption; that each individual reflects the operation of the same functional relationship between the two variables, a mechanism by which a change in one variable leads to a change in the other variable. An implication of such an assumption is that, in the WMC/mental arithmetic example, if someone could somehow manage to increase their WMC, their mental arithmetic performance would improve. Alternatively, if someone's available WMC capacity was compromised by something (e.g., fatigue, performing an additional task), their mental arithmetic performance would be reduced. Regardless of whether it is possible to alter one's WMC, this implication is dubious because, as every undergraduate psychology student knows, correlations do not necessarily imply causal relationships. And yet, why would we combine individual pairs of data to examine correlations unless we believed that they all reflected the existence of a general relationship between two variables?

One of the main reasons for combining the data from many people is that it is efficient to do so in terms of time. The entire data set can be obtained at one point in time. This is far more efficient than trying to study a smaller number of people over many occasions (Van Geert & de Ruiter, 2022, p.201). For example, consider the commonly noted relationship between Aging and Choice Reaction Time (CRT). There is good evidence that CRT is associated with Age, such that the older a person is, the longer is their CRT (Dykiert et al., 2012; Woods et al., 2015). This relationship matches our intuitions and observations of the elderly as being generally slower than their younger counterparts, which no doubt informed the design of the Bargh et al. (1996) study mentioned above. Much of the evidence for this relationship is found through the types of correlations we are discussing. That is, very little involves studying someone through their lifespan to determine whether their personal CRT slows as they get older. And yet, despite the lack of evidence related to how individuals change with age, researchers are still tempted to explain the correlation by invoking age-related changes in certain physiological processes that in turn have the effect of increasing CRT (Hardwick et al., 2022). The assumption underlying this conclusion is that, in the absence of data from individuals that show a slowing of CRT as each of them ages, data from many individuals at various ages will suffice. The problem with this assumption is that it requires each of the pairs of Age–CRT values to be a good estimate of the overall relationship between Age and CRT, and this in turn assumes there is one such overall relationship and that each person contributing an Age–CRT data pair is somehow a reflection of that overall relationship. If they were not assumed to be a reflection of that relationship, then there would be no justification for combining their data with other people. In short, a correlation coefficient is used to "join the dots" between independent individuals to reach a conclusion that somehow unites the individuals. Thus, the combination of data from many people to calculate a correlation value requires the assumption that the group of people share something in common.

This could be a common cognitive mechanism that underlies a particular behaviour or attribute (e.g., CRT), or it could be a personality type (more on this below).

A Worked Example

Some of the issues just identified with the use of correlation in psychology are illustrated well in a study published by Strack et al. (1988). This study was designed to test some hypotheses about how responses to questions may be influenced by responses made to prior questions. The following example was provided by Strack et al. to illustrate their argument (p. 431):

Person A: How are things going with your dating life?
Person B: Not too good.
Person A: And how is your life going in general?
Person B: (answer)

Without going too much into the underlying theoretical issues, Strack et al. hypothesised that the order in which these questions are presented to someone has a large influence on how they will respond to the questions. That is, for various psycholinguistic reasons, being asked to evaluate something specific (e.g., dating) will have an influence on a subsequent evaluation of something general (e.g., life), and this influence will be stronger than that from being asked about something general before being asked about something specific. Thus, Strack et al. predicted that there would be a high correlation between how Person B would respond to both questions if they were presented in the above order; however, this correlation would be reduced if the questions were posed in the reverse order.

To test these predictions, Strack et al. performed an experiment in which people were assigned to one of three conditions. The first condition (we will label this condition "Specific-General") involved being posed the above questions in the above order. Participants were asked to respond to each question on an 11-point scale that ranged from "not so happy" to "extremely happy". The second condition ("General-Specific") involved the questions being posed in the opposite order. There was a third condition, but this will not be described here, other than to say that Strack et al. predicted a correlation between responses to the two questions would be somewhere in between those of the other two conditions.

The first thing to note about this study is that it is a controlled experiment. That is, all participants were randomly allocated to condition and were treated the same way except for the order in which they were presented the questions. The assumptions underlying this design, and the inherent problems associated with these assumptions, are as we have outlined earlier in this chapter.

The main reason for presenting this example here is the manner in which Strack et al. analysed the data and the interpretations they reported following these analyses. Each person in the study contributed two responses, which were both ratings on an 11-point scale. Strack et al. calculated correlations between these ratings. Three correlations were calculated, one for each condition. The values of these correlations were as predicted (i.e., Specific-General > condition 3 > General-Specific). Strack et al. interpreted this finding in the following manner:

> On the one hand, answering a specific question makes specific information more accessible for use in answering a subsequent general question. As a consequence of the information

> priming, the answer to the general question becomes more similar to the answer to the previous specific question (i.e. assimilation). On the other hand, answering a specific question marks this information as 'given' and precludes its use when answering a general question in the same communicative context according to the logic of conversation. In an attempt to be informative, respondents are likely to answer the general question in terms of its features that depart from the features of the specific question. As a consequence, the assimilation effect is attenuated.
>
> *(p. 438)*

Let's unpack the logic that underlies this interpretation, but focus on the interpretation of the correlations, rather than the supposed effects related to question order. Strack et al. have interpreted the correlation result in each condition as the degree to which the response to the first presented question has some influence over the response to the second question. When there was a positive correlation, as there was for the two experimental conditions, this reflected the fact that people who gave high ratings for their first question were more likely to give high ratings for the second question, and low first question raters were likely to give low second question ratings. There is no issue with this interpretation of the data. This pattern is what the correlation coefficient measures. The issue, however, concerns the interpretations that come next.

Strack et al.'s interpretation, quoted above, describes a cognitive mechanism that operates within each of the participants. All that changes for each person in a particular condition is their evaluation of aspects of their lives. That is, if they were in Specific-General condition, and they rated their dating life as being extremely happy, the cognitive mechanism would operate such that they would be likely to give a high happiness rating for the rest of their life, and vice-versa if they evaluated their dating life as not so happy. Our concern is how Strack et al. managed to leap to this type of interpretation from the data they collected. We leave aside the issues we have already identified with the type of experimental design used by Strack et al. Instead, we focus just on the correlational analysis performed within each condition.

The data Strack et al. analysed were pairs of rating values. Each participant in a group only contributed one pair. The correlation calculated for a condition considered the whole set of such pairs collected from the participants in that condition. Strack et al.'s hypothesis concerns how a rating provided in response to one question will influence the rating provided to a subsequent question. Specifically, if a person gives a high rating to the first question, they are likely to give a high rating to the second question. But if they give a low rating to the first question, they will give a low rating to the second question. Now, Strack et al. only ever observed people give one rating to the first question, and one rating to the second question. Thus, Strack et al. observed a trend across all observations such that as ratings to the first question increased, so too did ratings to the second question. However, although Strack et al. did not actually observe behaviour reflecting this trend in the performance of any one individual, they assumed that this trend would be observed in the behaviour of an individual if it were possible to observe such a thing. That is, although Strack et al. only analysed data based on one observation per individual, they found a trend amongst these observations that they assumed would be found if all the data points had been contributed by one individual. This assumption then enables Strack et al. to make an inference about what must be happening inside the head of each individual. But is such an inference justified? The inference is only justified if the assumption that *the trend* would be observed in each individual is justified. No data was reported to support such an assumption, and indeed, the researchers say nothing about this assumption, revealing they may not have even considered the fact that it was the basis for their theoretical inferences.

The assumption that relationships revealed by correlations would describe the behaviours of individuals if they were observed under the right conditions is implicit in any explanation of a correlation that has a causal flavour. Strack et al.'s hypothesis about the psychological mechanisms operating when people respond to their questions has a clear causal flavour. From the outset, they claimed their study was designed so "that (it) examined the way in which individuals use information when making global judgments" (p. 430). They are explicitly proposing mechanisms underlying this use of information that operate in the heads of individuals. Nonetheless, it would not be possible to make inferences about how "individuals use information when making global judgements" in their paradigm by only recording Person B's ratings to the above questions. Information about high and low ratings to both questions is required to establish a relationship. Instead of attempting to observe the relationship in the behaviour of an individual, Strack et al. assumed they could approximate the necessary information by observing lots of individuals acting as Person B. The rationale underlying this assumption is that when faced with these questions, each individual's responses are produced by the same psychological mechanism so that each set of ratings they provide contributes to the trend in the data that suggests the relationship is reflective of the operations of this mechanism.

No justification for this assumption is provided by Strack et al. Indeed, as mentioned above, the assumption is implicit in their logic. It could be that they and others would argue that this assumption is not inherent in their analyses and interpretations. But how else can the calculating of a correlation in such a situation be justified? The logic is the same as we presented in relation to the Aggregation Delusion. The only reason for combining data from many individuals, and in the Strack et al. example this is pairs of ratings, is because researchers believe that each data point is a reflection of some shared psychological mechanism. After all, Strack et al. stated in their Introduction that they were interested in how individuals processed information. That is, they were interested in the cognitive processes that operate inside the heads of individuals when they respond to the presented questions. Ultimately, Strack et al. were theorising about a process that each individual shares. They could not observe the operation of this process in each person – this would require observing an individual at many levels of the rating variables – so they observed each individual once, at a specific level of the rating variables, and thought they could estimate the trend underlying changes in these variables on the basis of the group data. Ultimately, then, they were trying to get a handle on individual psychological processes by observing aggregated group data. This is not a valid method, for all the reasons we have discussed earlier in the book. But perhaps this conundrum can be more easily understood with an example where such an approach does make sense.

The "Correlation Machine"

Imagine discovering a machine that you had not seen before. A hose is connected at one end, and a tap is at the other, with some fluid pouring out of the tap. In the middle of the machine is a dial, with the numbers 1–10 around the dial. You turn the dial to different numbers, and you notice that there is a change in the rate of flow of the fluid from the tap. After a few observations, you are confident that, as the dial is turned to higher numbers, the flow becomes much stronger. There is no great mystery about what is going on here. Each setting of the dial is related to some mechanism inside the machine that directly affects the size of some aperture within the machine through which the fluid flows. The greater this aperture, the more fluid can pass, and so a stronger flow rate occurs at the tap. Observing a number of such pairs of dial settings and flow rates was sufficient information to enable you to put the pieces of the puzzle together to discern the overall relationship between these two variables. This strategy made sense because each dial setting that is paired with a particular flow rate reflects the same underlying mechanism operating in the machine. Our desire to observe such relationships in humans probably explains the typical approach to examining correlations illustrated by the Strack et al. study. The problem, of course, is that there is no guarantee that the data pairs contributed by individuals in a sample reflect the same underlying mechanism. And if they do not, there is no rationale for combining them in a correlational analysis. Any attempt to do so will just produce misleading conclusions about the degree to which two variables are related when we have not actually had the opportunity to manipulate the variables in the way that would be necessary to make such claims.

The Correlation Delusion describes the belief that a correlation between two variables can say something about a causal mechanism operating within individuals. Given that such a correlation comes from only one data point per individual (i.e., one value on each of the variables), the correlation can only reflect something at the group level. Interpreting the correlation as saying something about the individuals is to apply the correlation to the wrong scale. The correlation belongs at the group level but is being applied at the person level. This misapplication of correlations can give rise to Simpson's paradox, whereby a pattern of results observed at the group level is different or even reversed when observed in sub-groups or individuals within the group. In Chapter 2 we described an example of this paradox. Hamaker (2012) reported that the relationship between typing speed and accuracy is different depending on whether the focus is within (it is positive) or between (it is negative) individuals. In the latter case, each individual contributes one measure of their typing speed and one measure of their typing accuracy, and the group's data is combined in the calculation of a correlation coefficient. The overall trend is such that faster typing is associated with fewer errors (i.e., higher accuracy). This can be explained easily as a reflection of differences in typing skill – the people in the group were probably of different levels of typing skill such that the experts were both fast and accurate whereas the less proficient were both slower and more error-prone. Importantly though, this relationship cannot be used to understand what happens at the level of an individual. Indeed this relationship predicts the opposite of what occurs when an individual is asked to type at increasingly faster speeds. The between-individuals relationship predicts fewer errors, but in fact, more errors are observed. The within-individuals relationship is explained by a different mechanism than the expertise one used to explain the between-individuals relationship. Instead, something like a speed-accuracy trade-off would be invoked to explain how an individual's accuracy is affected by their typing speed. Indeed, no matter what level of expertise an individual is at, such a trade-off would be observed. The takeaway message here, though, is that the correlation obtained by observing pairs of data from many individuals cannot be used to draw inferences about what underlies the behaviour of each of those individuals.

The typing speed example provides a clear illustration of the limits of what can be concluded about correlations between variables. In particular, the origin of the data that is aggregated in a correlation coefficient determines the types of conclusions that are justified by an observed correlation. In calculating a correlation, when the data pairs come from different individuals, what is a legitimate inference from this type of data? It cannot be anything about within-person mechanisms, as no within-person effects are observed. The best it can offer is inferences about between-person mechanisms or relationships. If the data comes from one individual, any correlations observed between variables in that person's data can be interpreted in terms of mechanisms that exist in that person. In contrast, when the data comes from many individuals, and a correlation is observed, conclusions about what underlies that correlation are restricted to the group level. In the typing example, the expertise explanation is an example of a group-level explanation: the individuals might be assumed to vary in their level of typing expertise, which in turn affected the speed and accuracy of their typing behaviour. Importantly, the expertise explanation cannot be verified in such data without some independent measure of the typists' expertise. To be completely confident of the validity of the expertise explanation, it would be necessary to observe how typing behaviour changes as typing expertise increases. This would require a longitudinal study of individual performance, which would provide the within-individual data that could reveal within-individual mechanisms underlying the acquisition of expertise.

Most of this chapter has dealt with experimental designs. Experimental and correlational research designs are often portrayed as distinct forms of methodology, but they are closer than this characterisation suggests. The Strack et al. example worked through above to illustrate the Correlation Delusion had an experimental design despite it using correlation as an important part of the analysis method. Nonetheless, correlation is used in a vast amount of psychology research that is not experimental in design. Many studies in psychology have utilised cross-sectional designs (i.e., where data is collected from individuals at one point in time) and measurements on multiple variables, to determine whether knowledge of one set of variables can predict or account for performance on a different set of variables (e.g., regression analysis, discriminant function analysis, mediation/moderation analysis). Another significant proportion of research in psychology looks at the relationships between multiple manifest variables to determine whether there are hidden, or latent, variables that can explain performance on the manifest variables (e.g., factor analysis, principal component analysis). This latter approach is central to the development of tests designed to measure abilities (e.g., intelligence), psychological disorders (e.g., depression, anxiety, alexithymia), and personality.

Given that correlation is fundamental to all of these types of designs and analysis techniques, and the issues we have identified with interpreting correlational information, one might expect us to suggest methods relying on correlation are necessarily questionable. We would not go this far, however, given the questions we have raised about correlation, and aggregation in general, we would advise anyone utilising such methods to question the assumptions underlying these methods. In particular, what is the justification for using relatively small amounts of data from each individual in a sample to draw conclusions about relationships between variables that are assumed to operate at the level of each individual? For instance, consider a multiple regression analysis that produces an equation that predicts performance on one variable (e.g., university GPA) on the basis of a combination of performances on a set of other variables (e.g., SES, secondary school GPA, IQ). An underlying assumption of this analysis is that each individual in the analysed sample has contributed a set of data on all of the variables that reflects the relationship between the variables described by the prediction equation. That is, the prediction equation describes a relationship between variables that exists within each individual in the sample, and takes the same form within each individual. We have to assume this; otherwise there is no justification for combining the data from many individuals to undertake the analysis. Of course, we expect people to vary in their performance on each variable – this quantitative variance is a necessary element in the calculation of a correlation coefficient. But if we were prepared to accept that for some individuals in the sample, SES was irrelevant, or that secondary school was the only important predictor variable, then there would be no justification for combining the data from such individuals with the data from individuals where all three predictor variables were important. To undertake the regression analysis, and indeed all correlational analyses, we must start with the assumption that all individuals contributing data are reflections of the same underlying relationship. That is, they are all apples, and not apples, oranges, bananas, or dogs. Very rarely is such an assumption stated, or tested. And yet, if it is violated, as will be the case in non-ergodic samples, the rationale for a correlational analysis disappears, giving rise to major cracks in the edifice of correlation-based analysis techniques (Van Geert & de Ruiter, 2022, p. 201).

A great deal of psychology research that uses correlational techniques draws conclusions about psychological entities (e.g., personality types) that are shared by individuals in their samples, and beyond the samples (Beck & Jackson, 2022). There is research though that indicates such correlational structures observed in group data do not correspond well to the structures observed within the individuals constituting those groups (Fisher et al., 2018; Molenaar, 2004). Furthermore, work by Arnulf et al. (2024) suggests correlations between items in psychological tests reflect semantic relationships between the words and phrases in those items, not psychological ones. The mathematical process of correlation can only deal with the numbers at hand, and these are just as likely to indicate something about the objects (i.e., items and their semantic meanings) as they could about psychological entities (e.g., personality types, disorders). As Lykken (1991, p.18) says, "Just because we can rank people on some dimension does not mean that there is some isomorphic entity or process in each of their brains that determines their score".

In this chapter we have discussed three delusions that emerge from the Aggregation Delusion and inattention to the scale of measurement and theorising. These delusions collectively call into question the validity of the analyses typically performed in psychology research, not so much in terms of problems with the statistical techniques used, but in how these techniques have been used to address questions of interest to psychology. Psychology's lack of awareness of these delusions has led to interpretations of data that are not warranted by the nature of the research designs that produce the data. These invalid interpretations have unfortunately engendered another set of delusions, which is the topic of the next chapter.

4

THE DELUSIONS OF PERVASIVENESS, GENERALISATION, AND SPECIFICITY

In the previous chapter we outlined some issues with Bargh et al.'s (1996) Experiment 2. In a subsequent description of Bargh et al.'s experiment, Kahneman (2011) extrapolates the Florida effect to the readers of his book, suggesting that reading the paragraphs in which the Bargh et al. experiment is described would have "primed you as well. If you had needed to stand up to get a glass of water, you would have been slightly slower than usual to rise from your chair" (pp. 53–54). By making this leap from the Bargh et al. experiment to a prediction about "your" behaviour, Kahneman is suggesting that what Bargh et al. discovered is a phenomenon that exists in us all. Such a claim is not valid, on a number of grounds. Some were identified in Chapter 3 with respect to the validity of the result and the conclusion that followed. Another issue is the Delusion of Group Comparison. The problem at the core of this delusion is clearly observed in experiments with designs such as that used by Bargh et al., where one group, the experimental group, is exposed to the experimental "treatment" (priming), and another group, the control group, does not experience this treatment (no priming). A difference in behaviour between the two groups is required to indicate the existence of an effect. Importantly, then, the effect is not directly observed in the behaviour of any individual in the experiment. It is only inferred from a difference in overall performance between the average results of the experimental group and the average results of the control group. This raises an important question: if we do not observe the effect directly in the behaviour of a person, does it really exist? If we do not observe situations where our manipulations actually change a person's behaviour, how can we make predictions about changes in a person's behaviour like that made by Kahneman? The answer is we cannot, certainly not without many caveats (e.g., the effect *may* be observed in *some* people). Unfortunately, the typical behaviour of psychology researchers is to overlook these caveats, and to proudly expound the universality of their observed effects. This has significantly contributed to the Great Psychology Delusion.

In this chapter we consider several inferential steps that are typical of psychology research and the conclusions often reported by researchers, such as Kahneman's above suggestion. We highlight areas of concern with these inferences, and how they demonstrate three more delusions, that of pervasiveness, generalisation, and specificity, delusions which some have stubbornly

DOI: 10.4324/9781003503873-5

refused to acknowledge. These related delusions refer to the extent to which the conclusions drawn from the results of typical quantitative work in psychological research cannot actually be supported by the kind of evidence that typical work produces.

When psychologists conduct research, they are rarely only interested in the behaviours of just those people whose behaviours they measure in their experiments and quasi-experiments. Proper to a scientific endeavour, but rarely explicitly articulated, is an interest in uncovering general principles that govern behaviour and experience. We can see evidence of this commitment to generality, or universalism, in the Discussion sections of research reports, where conclusions are often framed in quite general terms such as "under condition X, people do Y" (Speelman & McGann, 2020; Van Geert & de Ruiter, 2022, pp. 125–135). Alas, such conclusions are deluded. In the hope of providing a clear illustration of why such conclusions are delusional, we present two scenarios that demonstrate how the problem manifests in many common research practices.

Scenario 1: What Can an Experiment Tell us About Real-world Behaviour?

Imagine we were trying to discover a method for studying new learning material that would improve both comprehension and retention. Let's say that we wanted to compare a new study technique with a more traditional method. The standard approach to exploring this issue would be to conduct an experiment. Participants in the experiment would be recruited, typically from a university undergraduate population, on the assumption that university students are fairly representative of the general population and so whatever we observe with them should generalise well.

The participants would then be randomly allocated to one of the two experimental conditions. Both groups would be exposed to some material that they are unlikely to have experienced before, let's say a recorded lecture on the history of Mesopotamia. Afterwards, the groups could be given a quiz on the material. After the quiz, one group would be given a transcript of the lecture and asked to study the material with a traditional method, such as reading and re-reading it, for 30 minutes. The second group would also be given the transcript but would be instructed to study the material according to the new technique, also for 30 minutes. At the end of the study period, both groups would then be given the quiz again.

To determine whether the two study techniques had different effects on the ability to perform on the quiz, we could calculate a difference score for each person, comparing their result on the first quiz to their result on the second quiz. Typically, the difference scores for the two groups would be compared with some form of Null Hypothesis Significance Test (NHST), such as a t test. Other analysis methods could also be used, such as a mixed design analysis of variance (ANOVA) with study technique as a between-subjects variable, and quiz (first vs. second) as a within-subjects variable. In this case, an interaction between the two variables would indicate that the two techniques differed in their effect on learning (the relevant F value and the aforementioned t value are arithmetically related: $t^2 = F$). Of course, there are Bayesian alternatives to these sorts of analyses (e.g., Nathoo & Masson, 2016), and many other techniques that would examine the data in a myriad of ways. They would all share the one fundamental aim, however, and that is to try to detect whether performance in the two conditions was different.

Imagine that the statistical analyses of these data all indicated that the new study technique was associated with a greater improvement on quiz performance than the traditional technique. How would psychologists typically report such a result in a journal paper or a conference presentation? Following presentation of all of the statistical information and a general summary of the results at the beginning of the Discussion, we would expect to see or hear something like the following: "*The new study technique led to better learning than the traditional study technique*".

Usually when the conclusion has been stated, there is scope for some discussion of what the result means, practically and/or theoretically. In this case the researcher could expound on how the new study technique could be adopted in the classroom to help students learn more effectively. The researcher might also feel confident about commenting on the status of some theory about how memory works, and that the new study technique supports a central claim of the theory because it exploited a cognitive mechanism that is described by the theory. It is in this sort of discussion where the major problems for sample-based experimental psychology emerge. The fashion is not only to extrapolate the results of an experiment to a wider population – the result found in the sample should also be found in the population – but also to the individuals in that population. That is, the effect observed in the experiment should be observable in each individual. In this case that would mean that every person in the population would be better off studying with the new technique than with the traditional technique. Underlying these conclusions is an implicit logic, untested by the experiment in question, that each person has the same cognitive mechanism operating in their memory that the new study technique exploits.

Initially, the reader might claim that we have gone too far with this characterisation of experimental protocol; that no one claims that experimental results apply to everyone in a population. This is true, but we would argue that what is equally true is that almost no one makes claims, or offers any analysis, about the extent to which generalisations can apply to the individuals within the population. That is, what proportion of the population can be described by the results of any particular experiment?

In the scenario just described, within the sample of those students who used the new study technique, it is quite possible that some participants' performance was unaffected, or even became worse. This complexity and texture in the behaviour of individuals is suppressed by the use of tests of mean difference, and by typical results reporting procedures that provide little to no information regarding this texture and variability in the data.

With respect to this hypothetical experiment, it is valid to say that if we conducted another study on a similar sample from the same population, we could expect to see the same sort of overall effect (notwithstanding the replication issues that have been much publicised recently – Ferguson, 2015 – as well as the statistical limits on replication identified by Cumming, 2008). It is not, however, valid to say that if someone wanted to study some new material, they would be better off utilising the new study technique. Because collections of human beings are not ergodic, we have very little evidence about individual behaviour at all.

For example, imagine an educational psychologist read an account of our experiment with the conclusions presented above. She might interpret the results as advice she could apply to students at her school. Imagine that a teacher at the school has identified a few students who appear to have difficulties learning the material he is covering in his class. On the basis of the conclusions from our experiment, the psychologist decides to advise the students about the new study technique. What are the chances that this will be a successful strategy, and the students' academic performance in that class will improve? Even if their initial problems with studying were based solely on the inadequacy of the traditional study technique (i.e., we are ignoring possible social, economic, behavioural, cognitive, etc. issues), there is nothing in the results of the experiment that would enable us to estimate the probability that adopting the new study technique would result in improved performance. The best that we could hope for is that the overall performance of this new sample might improve, but we should not be confident that every person in the sample will improve. The reason is that the experiment only provided information about samples.

Maybe if the norm in psychological research was to report individual data, such as the number of people in one condition who out-performed members of the other condition, the educational psychologist could estimate the likelihood that the students she was dealing with would improve. But even that would, no doubt, fall short of her expectations of applying a new study technique. Surely her aim would be to help all of the students, not just to increase the average performance of the group. Judging by the modally occurring forms of research practice in experimental research, it would seem that psychology has settled for the latter, even though we profess to being able to provide direction on the former. One of the outcomes of this fact is the strained relationship, and often cynicism, that exists in applied domains of practice, such as education, for the outcomes of academic research, which are seen as generally neither conclusive, nor practical (Broekkamp & van Hout-Wolters, 2007; Ijzerman et al., 2020). This may reflect insufficient attention to the existence of moderating variables that can define sub-groups who may respond differently. The method of analysis we outline in Chapter 9 has the potential to simplify searching for such variables.

The failure of the ergodicity assumption not only means that analyses based on measurements of samples alone provide very little information about individuals, it forces us to recognise, and call into question, a further assumption underlying much of contemporary research in cognitive psychology – that we all have the same cognitive system.

It is common in cognitive psychology to propose mechanistic models of cognitive processes as explanations for why experimental conditions resulted in particular types of performance. Unfortunately, testing such models on the average performance of samples is only testing whether the sample possesses such a set of processes. The modellers would presumably like to suggest that their models provide an explanation for the performance of each individual in the experiment, as if each individual has a set of cognitive processes as described by the model (Grice et al., 2017; Kroupin et al., 2024; Richters, 2021). As indicated above, researchers rarely report the extent to which individual performance is consistent with sample-level effects, and so it is not possible to evaluate whether such models are good descriptions of individual cognition.

Certainly, if researchers did report such information, it would be clear that not everyone in a sample exhibits the same performance pattern as the sample, and indeed some may even exhibit the opposite pattern (e.g., Grice et al., 2017; Molenaar, 2004; Molenaar & Campbell, 2009; Speelman & McGann, 2013), a result that would count against a general model of cognition. We suspect that such an outcome would be written off as "experimental error", and the typical justification for use of a large sample is precisely to reduce error. But such an attitude reflects the assumption that everyone shares the same cognitive apparatus, and our experiments are designed to examine this through the noise that is inherent in human data. The methods we use to undertake this examination are not only based on this assumption, but they are designed to reinforce it. As a result, these methods are not conducive to exploring an alternative state of affairs, such as, for instance, the possibility that humans develop idiosyncratic cognitive processes as a result of adapting to their world (Kroupin et al., 2024; Lykken, 1991; Molenaar, 2008a; Speelman & Kirsner, 2005; Van Orden et al., 2003). This limitation of our analysis methods is illustrated in the next scenario.

Scenario 2: How Pervasive is a Significant Effect?

Let us consider in greater detail the situation where a sample-level effect is not revealed in the performance of all individuals in the sample. To explore this situation, we generated some hypothetical data to simulate a scenario where a sample of 50 people performed a test on two occasions. Imagine that we are interested in whether the scores increase from the first test to the second test (i.e., the scores improve). To simulate such a scenario, we used Microsoft Excel to generate 50 random numbers between 1 and 100 to act as difference scores (i.e., test 2 – test 1). These difference scores are presented in Table 4.1 as Set A.

The fact that all numbers in Set A are positive indicates that all participants improved on test 2 compared to their performance on test 1. Clearly, some participants improved to a greater extent than others. Straightforwardly though, as indicated by a t test that was performed to test the null hypothesis that there was no improvement, a significant improvement was detected.

Consider now the other data sets presented in Table 4.1. Each one is derived from Set A. For instance, the scores of the first 10 people in B are 20 less than the first 10 in A. The next 30 people (i.e., columns 2–4) in B have the same scores as the people in these columns in A. The final 10 people in B are 20 more than the final 10 in A. Sets C and D have been derived similarly, but the differences are 40 and 60, respectively. Sets B, C, and D were derived in this way to ensure that the mean improvement scores were the same as in A. That is, the average improvement in all sets was the same. Indeed, t tests for each set returned statistically significant

TABLE 4.1 Data sets discussed in Scenario 2

Data Set																			
Set A					*Set B*					*Set C*					*Set D*				
57	78	81	57	6	37	78	81	57	26	17	78	81	57	46	−3	78	81	57	66
77	89	53	52	70	57	89	53	52	90	37	89	53	52	110	17	89	53	52	130
31	43	61	25	37	11	43	61	25	57	−9	43	61	25	77	−29	43	61	25	97
42	70	98	10	80	22	70	98	10	100	2	70	98	10	120	−18	70	98	10	140
76	16	33	65	100	56	16	33	65	120	36	16	33	65	140	16	16	33	65	160
39	98	62	24	99	19	98	62	24	119	−1	98	62	24	139	−21	98	62	24	159
81	59	54	91	33	61	59	54	91	53	41	59	54	91	73	21	59	54	91	93
45	46	28	49	1	25	46	28	49	21	5	46	28	49	41	−15	46	28	49	61
77	76	40	78	79	57	76	40	78	99	37	76	40	78	119	17	76	40	78	139
23	44	81	55	99	3	44	81	55	119	−17	44	81	55	139	−37	44	81	55	159
Mean		57.36					57.36					57.36					57.36		
SD		26.36					30.07					37.94					47.97		
t		15.38					13.49					10.69					8.45		
p		<.001					<.001					<.001					<.001		

Notes

1 Data Set A is 50 numbers generated randomly with the constraint that the range be 1–100.

2 Data Set B is the same as Data Set A except the first column of numbers is smaller by 20, and the fifth column of numbers is larger by 20. The same pattern of difference exists between Data Sets B and C, and between Data Sets C and D.

3 All data sets are normal according to Kolmogorov–Smirnov (p>.05) and Shapiro–Wilk (p>.05) statistics.

results, indicating that there was a significant improvement in each set. Furthermore, 95% confidence intervals around these mean improvement values are a long way from overlapping with the value that would indicate no improvement (i.e., zero) (see Figure 4.1). And yet, careful inspection of each set indicates that improvement is not uniform across the sets (see Figure 4.2).

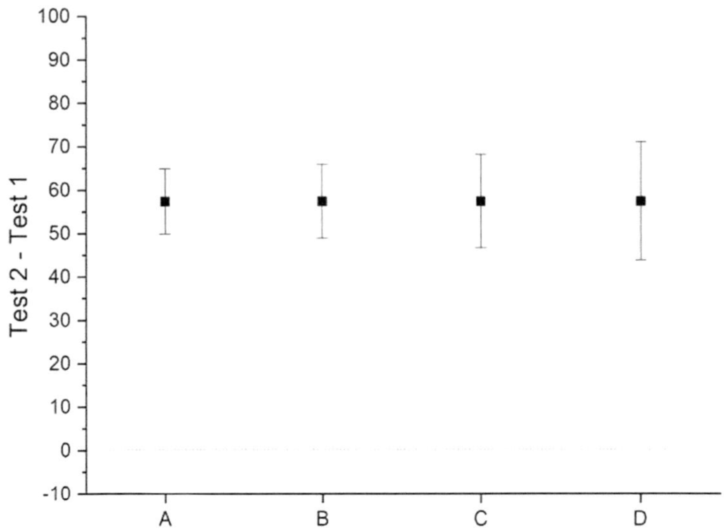

FIGURE 4.1 A graph of the mean values and their 95% confidence intervals for the hypothetical data presented in Table 4.1.

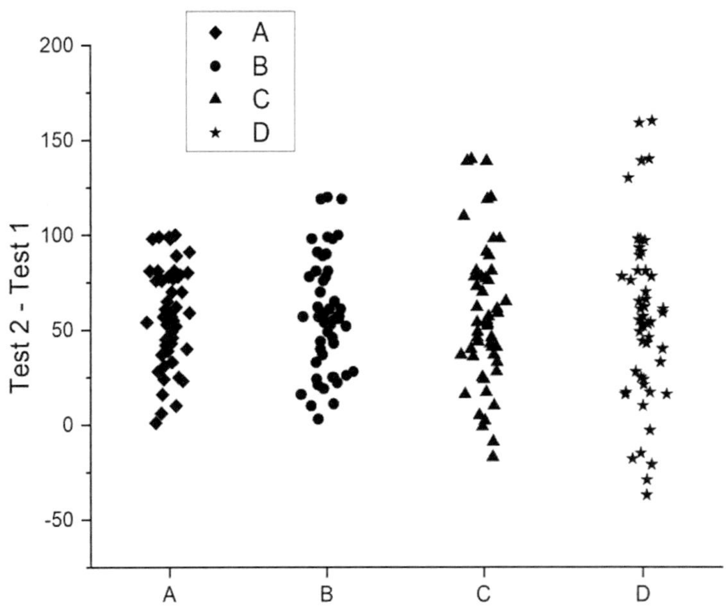

FIGURE 4.2 A graph of the hypothetical data presented in Table 4.1.

Where there is ubiquitous improvement in Sets A and B, in Set C some people show a worsening of performance, and others show an extreme amount of improvement. This pattern is magnified in Set D.

The point of this scenario is to demonstrate that, when we use NHSTs or similar tests to analyse our data at the sample level, an effect that is very large in extent in some individuals can outweigh the null or opposite effects in others, and this can result in an overall effect at the sample level (without this simply being a result of one or two notable outliers). That is, a large effect may exist in some individuals, but others can demonstrate quite a different effect or no effect. Nonetheless, we venture to suggest that many researchers would conclude similar things about each data set and its associated analysis if they had any one of the sets as the outcome of their own experiment, and that is that they have detected a general effect of the independent variable (i.e., test 1 vs. test 2). All of these data sets might return similar outcomes from significance testing (i.e., reject the null hypothesis), but which one leads to greater confidence that the effect exists? Sets A and B surely would give us more confidence that we have observed a *universal* effect. Sets C and D suggest the effect may have caveats (i.e., it only exists in certain people).

As researchers, we are not usually in the position of being able to compare experimental outcomes such as those presented in this scenario. Instead, we only have one sample to explore, and so we usually base our judgements about an effect on some common indicators about the sample. For instance, we might explore the data to ensure that the distribution of scores is normal (it is in all of the sets presented here – see information provided in Table 4.1) and, once satisfied, continue on to an inferential statistics test of some sort. When the test suggests rejecting the null hypothesis, we would probably be satisfied that a test effect had been observed. We might, however, be interested in the size of the effect.

Although the size of the effects in Sets A to D varies because of the different variances in each sample, they all exceed 1 standard deviation, which is usually considered a large effect. So, many researchers would likely conclude the same thing regardless of which data set they had at their disposal, which is that an overall effect was observed. The common approach to analysis of relying on aggregating statistics can result in situations such as those in Sets C and D being overlooked. At the very least, our standard reporting techniques and modes of discussion of results suppress a reader's ability to make these judgements for themselves and are dependent on the researchers noticing them and explicitly choosing to include them in their presentation of the experiments.

In response to the example provided above, one reviewer of an earlier version of this scenario claimed that we seem to "ignore the fact that statistical tests are often accompanied by effect size measures, which reflect how much overlap exists between groups". As should be obvious from the example, we are fully aware that effect size measures are traditionally reported, and that they provide some information about overlap between groups, but this is our point exactly. Such measures only reveal information about group overlap, and nothing about overlap between individuals within groups. Effect size measures are summary statistics just like the mean and variance and so reflect group characteristics and can be largely insensitive to dramatic differences amongst individuals as seen in Sets C and D above. Presenting information about individual performance in a figure such as Figure 4.2 is far more effective in conveying overlap between individuals within groups than standard effect size measures. Similar arguments were made many years ago by Tukey (1977).

The Pervasiveness Delusion

To many readers these points are nothing new. We have already noted that psychologists are carefully examining the limitations of our research methods and statistics (Gigerenzer, 2004; Lakens, 2021; Simmons et al., 2011). More specifically, the issues concerning ergodicity and conflict between individual and group levels of analysis have a substantive existing literature as we have already noted (Fisher et al., 2018; Hamaker, 2012; Logie, 2018; Molenaar, 2004, 2008a; Molenaar & Campbell, 2009; Rose, 2016). What is perhaps most concerning to us is that this literature has had very little impact. Some researchers may well be aware of the issue but feel it is not a problem because it is well-accepted that sample-level effects are not demonstrated in every individual but are demonstrated in most people. In this case, we should ask how do they know this? Establishing that most people in a sample behave the same way is rarely reported in journal papers – descriptive statistics rarely include this level of detail (though it would be simple to do so, and the analysis method we present in Chapter 9 provides one way for doing this). Certainly, there is no clear definition of "most".

It would appear that researchers in sample-based experimental psychology are often unaware of this conundrum. It is common to read conclusions in reports of psychological experiments like the following: "…people integrate ensemble information about the group average expression when they make judgments of individual faces' expressions" (Griffiths et al., 2018, p. 311, Abstract). In this particular instance, it is not clearly stated what is meant by "people"? Does this mean "all people"? Or are the authors more realistic and mean "most people"? But again, how can researchers be confident that they have observed something that exists in the majority? And more specifically, does this mean 90%, or 80%, or just over 50%?

We recently reported a study of the prevalence of this type of behaviour in contemporary psychological research (Speelman et al., 2024). That is, using analysis methods, such as NHSTs, that are based on aggregated values (i.e., the sample means) of group behaviours, to make inferences about individuals. As we have mentioned several times, such inferences are possibly erroneous because groups of humans rarely, if ever, constitute an ergodic system. To assume ergodicity without checking is to commit the "ergodic fallacy". We analysed three highly cited "Q1" journals in the fields of clinical, educational, and cognitive psychology for statements that indicated this error. As hypothesised, the ergodic fallacy was found in the vast majority (over 88%) of the papers investigated. We also hypothesised that the prevalence of this error would be highest in cognitive psychology papers because this field typically assesses theoretical claims about universal cognitive mechanisms, whereas clinical and educational psychology are more concerned with empirically supported interventions. This hypothesis was also supported by our results. Nonetheless, the prevalence of the ergodic fallacy was still high in all fields.

Aggregate statistics provide little to no evidence for patterns of behaviour of individual members of the sample, let alone the broader population from which that sample of individual people is selected. Relying on such statistics to generate conclusions about individuals is thus another form of delusional research practice.

> ***The Pervasiveness Delusion:*** The assumption that an effect observed in an experiment or quasi experiment, which is revealed by aggregating data from a group of individuals, is pervasive amongst the individuals of that group (i.e., it applies to all/most/a majority of the individuals).

When there has been some statistically significant effect observed, it is not the fashion to report the number of people in the study that showed the effect. So, researchers are generalising from a sample-level effect to "people". It is problematically unclear as to precisely how such claims should be parsed, and if it is intended to imply numerous "individual people", then it is simply not supported by the kinds of evidence typical to published research reports. With respect to the data depicted in Figures 4.1 and 4.2, Set A would justify a statement such as "people improve under these circumstances", whereas Set D would not justify such a statement.

Some authors have recently tackled the relationship between individual level and sample-level effects. To this end, for example, Miller and Schwarz (2018) have proposed interrogating null results in ANOVA designs more closely to determine whether the null effect exists in all participants, or whether some people in the sample show an effect. This approach has also been advocated by Smith and Little (2018). Miller and Schwarz describe a new method for examining interactions in ANOVAs to achieve this goal, whereas Smith and Little propose a small-n approach in which the number of people showing an effect is an explicit object of investigation. Although both approaches are suggestions in what we think is the right direction, these authors focused on null results. But what of non-null results, which are the majority of those published (Ferguson, 2015; Ioannidis et al., 2014; Nosek et al., 2012; Smaldino & McElreath, 2016)? We reiterate that it is just as important to examine carefully the pattern of individual effects underlying any sample-level effect.

The Generalisation Delusion

If the Pervasiveness Delusion is not enough of a problem, once researchers feel confident about extrapolating an average behaviour to the individuals in their observed sample, the nature of inferential statistics provides an avenue for generalising the results found with the sample to the population from which the sample was recruited. Inferential statistics are explicitly designed to tell us something about a population by studying a sample from that population. Estimating the mean height of the population of humans by measuring the height of many humans from across the globe is an example of the standard use of statistics. We have no issue with this exercise. A problem results, however, when the inferences go beyond the average value, or whatever parameter is in focus, to individual members of the population.

The Pervasiveness Delusion provides researchers with licence to assume that average behaviour in their sample provides some indication of how the individuals in the sample behaved. As we reported in Speelman et al. (2024), it is also common to see researchers extrapolate from this assumption to a conclusion that "people" exhibit this behaviour. That is, they extend the sample finding to a statement about the parent population, but not just about the average behaviour of the population, but also about the behaviour of members of that population. But just as there is nothing about a mean effect that enables inferences about whether the effect occurred in each individual in a sample, an estimate of an average population effect tells us nothing about the extent to which individuals in the population exhibit the effect (Kroupin et al., 2024). To believe otherwise is delusional.

The Generalisation Delusion: The belief that an inference about an average population effect extends to the members of that population.

The Pervasiveness Delusion and the Generalisation Delusion work hand in hand. The tradition in experimental psychology is that if an experiment produces the finding that average performance was consistent with the existence of a particular effect (e.g., the Serial Position Effect), this will lead to the conclusion that the individuals in the experiment also exhibited this effect (the Pervasiveness Delusion), which will then lead to the conclusion that this effect is a general feature of human cognition (the Generalisation Delusion). And to make matters worse, claims about such general features of cognition lead to further erroneous thinking.

The Specificity Delusion

Once an experimental finding based on a sample has ended up as the basis for a general feature of cognition, which applies to all, or, at least, the majority of members of humanity, it is a small step to then assume this feature applies to the next person one encounters. It is this logic that is the basis of Kahneman's (2011) suggestion that the reader of his book will be subject to the Florida effect by the mere act of reading the relevant section of the book. And, of course, the same logic underlies any attempt to take experimental findings and apply them to some real-world context, particularly when the focus is on changing something about individuals. But the hope that the average performance in an experiment will translate to predictions about an individual's behaviour, via the inferences about sample individuals' behaviour and population individuals' behaviour, is a forlorn one (Valsiner, 2019; Van Geert & de Ruiter, 2022, pp. 200–202).

> ***The Specificity Delusion:*** When one believes that aggregate statistics enable conclusions of universal principles of behaviour, and this belief leads to predictions about individual behaviour.

As implied already, the three delusions outlined in this chapter are intimately connected, in that a belief in one enables belief in the others (see also the ensemble-to-individual fallacy described

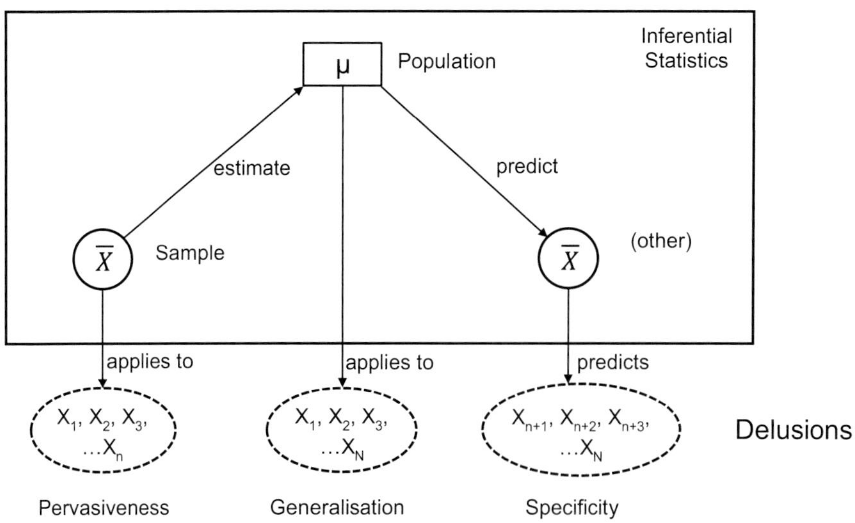

FIGURE 4.3 The relationship between delusions associated with conclusions based on inferential statistics.

by Van Geert & de Ruiter, 2022, p. 149). This relationship is represented in Figure 4.3, where inferential thinking in psychological research is characterised as comprising three major steps, each of which may involve delusional thinking:

1. Finding an effect in a group-based experiment leads to the conclusion that the group exhibited the effect. This is the beginning of a slippery slide to concluding that everyone/majority/most of the group showed the effect (the Pervasiveness Delusion).
2. The conclusion that a group effect has been observed leads to another conclusion that this effect is a characteristic of each member/individual of the population from which the sample (group) was recruited (the Generalisation Delusion).
3. The conclusion that this effect is a general/universal feature of the population means this feature should be expected in each new member of that population that is encountered (the Specificity Delusion).

Implications

We turn now to some implications of the delusions presented in this chapter. There are many implications, but we focus on a few that will feature when we present some potential ways to address the delusions inherent in current psychological research practice.

Psychology as an Actuarial Science?

The Pervasiveness Delusion makes us insensitive to the differences between quantifiers in our claims. In interpreting research results we must be more cautious about the specificity of our claims, and to a certain extent their scale. What quantifiers do we intend to use? We should be explicit about this. When we say "people do X", what do we mean by "people"? "Some", "many", "most", or "all"? Do we mean that "a" person will behave in a particular way? Most psychologists will recoil from such a strong claim. We have all learned to hedge carefully and to promise little when it comes to the specificity of our predictions. And yet, as discussed above, as researchers we are seemingly willing to couch our conclusions in terms that are easily interpreted as applying to people in general with the obvious implications of such conclusions.

Do we then simply mean that *samples* will have certain characteristics, with no suggestion as to the actions of individual people? Even this move is problematic (for separate reasons described most recently by Yarkoni (2022) and which we will turn to later), but it is at least in keeping with the statistical methods in play. However, if this is really the case, we would have nothing to say to applied disciplines. Nothing reported by research would have implications or value for those who work not with the groups or samples, but with individual clients, students, or patients. Surely this isn't what researchers mean.

Some openly admit that psychology can never provide clear predictions about individual behaviour because it is a science that enables actuarial predictions rather than clinical ones (Lykken, 1991; Stanovich, 2013). The best that can be provided is some estimate of the probability of a person behaving in a certain manner under certain circumstances. For example, a person has a 70% chance of exhibiting behaviour X when they are faced with situation Y. Stanovich states that "virtually all of the facts and relationships that have been uncovered by the science of psychology are stated in terms of probabilities" (p. 155). If this is true, then it might be a useful lesson that could drive change in the types of misleading prescriptions psychologists and other human scientists are prone to in reporting conclusions from their research (Boutron, 2020;

Reynolds-Vaughn et al., 2020). We, however, take issue with this statement. It is not the case that most psychological research is stated in terms of probabilities that would enable a statistical prediction of a behavioural outcome.

Such predictions can be derived from sample-level results of research, but only if the results have been analysed and reported in a particular way. If the research involves a comparison between samples in terms of some measure on a scale, and the conclusions are based on a statistically significant difference between the samples on that measure, then such a result can tell us nothing about the likelihood of someone exhibiting a specific behaviour. A p value that follows from an NHST, for instance, is in no way connected with the probability associated with an actuarial prediction. What is required in order to make such actuarial predictions is for the original research to have determined how many people in the sample exhibited the specific behaviour under one set of conditions compared to the number that demonstrated that behaviour under another (control) set of conditions. A great deal of sample-based experimental psychology research fails to consider this question. Researchers seem to assume that all that is necessary to enable the actuarial predictions mentioned above is to demonstrate a significant difference on some measure of behaviour. On the contrary, what is required is, first, some defined point on that measure that represents the "target" behaviour, and second, a simple count of the number of people in the various experimental and control groups that exhibit this behaviour, and those that do not.

So, if actuarial prediction is the highest ambition for the science of sample-based experimental psychology (and it may well be that actuaries, or perhaps meteorologists should be used as models of good practice for psychology), at present the field falls far short of even this mark. This is because the basic nature of sample-based experimental psychology research is aimed at producing sample-based generalisations that cannot be construed as probabilistic outcomes. A wholesale revision of experimental psychology research methods is required in order to produce results that may enable more principled predictions. We outline some methods in later chapters that we think go some way to addressing these issues.

A Special Case of the Generalisation Delusion

Without specifying the quantifiers in our conclusions, we implicitly suggest that a particular pattern of behaviour is pervasive, that it is present across people and across circumstances in keeping with the conditions studied in the research. This is not the case, as explained at length by Yarkoni (2022).

Yarkoni's (2022, see also 2020) exploration of the limits of knowledge made available via evidence derived from the most commonly used statistical techniques in psychology makes for quite grim reading. Yarkoni (2022) details the fragility of the inferences that psychologists tend to make when interpreting the implications of their experiments. On the one hand, the kinds of models typically reported provide only very limited evidence for effects or outcomes – specific only to the particular sample, the particular stimuli, the particular conditions in play during the study in question. Tightly constrained, with little support for generalisation to more people, other stimuli, other circumstances. On the other hand, even modest additional sources of noise or variation in the measured variable eradicate the confidence with which any conclusion can be drawn even there. Psychologists, Yarkoni (2022) suggests, must choose between a straightjacket of impractically narrow conclusions and a mess of uninformatively general ones.

Additionally, in a blog-post response to one of his critics, Yarkoni (2020) examines the fallacious logic that underpins generalist conclusions from inferential statistics. That is, even if done well, or approached with a disciplined and focused intention to deductively test a theory rather than inductively inform ourselves what the phenomena are, the limitations of the allowable conclusions are fatal to the typical intentions of psychological researchers.

We can't Judge Pervasiveness without Knowing What we're Looking for

It is frequently the case that the very phenomena described by researchers are only sought and discovered under statistical analysis. Null-hypothesis significance tests are deployed, and effect size estimates interpreted, to inform us if something is "there". The expectation and belief is that patterns of behaviour are so subtle, and the manifestations of them so noisy, that only through the clarifying (dichotomising!) lenses of the NHST can we perceive the presence or absence of a particular phenomenon. These subtle findings orient our future behaviour, in the hope that we can then refine our search for things worth knowing about how people's actions are organised. Rarely if ever are the actions of individual participants reported, analysed, or interpreted. That makes it impossible to count individual people and their behaviour, unless we are much more specific, up front, about the particular pattern of behaviour in which we are interested, specific enough so that we could simply count the number of times it occurs in a given observed situation.

To the extent that we want to understand how common a particular pattern of behaviour is, it should be trivial to find out: there are few things easier to do than to count the frequency of something when you know what you are looking for.

So, all we need to do is to be clear what it is we are looking for. This is not an esoteric, abstract methodological point, it is the very fundamental character of scientific enterprise.

Getting Our Scale Right

The delusions presented in this chapter, like many of the problems that we have addressed so far, are a manifestation of a scalar slippage, the scale of our descriptions and explanations slipping between that of the behaviour, person, and population with deceptive ease. In studying the behaviour we are studying the person, in studying the population, we are studying the person. But neither of these things is true (Van Geert & de Ruiter, 2022, pp. 200–202).

What we see instead is a gaping void where our understanding of the person should be. This is a product of focusing our observational lens at a particular scale, and our analytic lens at another, with no connecting tissue. This connecting tissue is stunningly the very stuff of psychology – individual human minds. The delusions of pervasiveness, generalisation, and specificity lead us to a realisation that a disturbingly large proportion of contemporary psychological science is empty of the kinds of things in which psychology is ostensibly most interested.

Denying Nihilism

Despairing readers might feel, at this point, as though they have had something stolen from them. Is all of existing psychological research worthless? Is human behaviour a heaving mass of random actions, impossible to describe, understand, or predict with any reasonable accuracy?

Reader, as we noted in our opening chapter, despite our criticisms of the psychological sciences as they are frequently carried out at present, we are optimists. The discerning reader might rightly scoff at the nihilistic view that behaviour is meaningless and unpredictable, indicating very simply the richness and complexity of human society. If there is one characteristic of human behaviour that we can be certain of, it is that it is organised, often in intricate and complexly inter-meshing ways. We will have more to say about this clear fact of organisation, and its implications for the sciences of behaviour and experience, in later chapters. For now, we can simply recognise that this organisation is a clear illustration that the phenomena proper to the discipline of psychology are not meaningless – just many of our current descriptions of them. The systematicity and clarity of those descriptions play a crucial role in the scientific endeavour, and we turn to those descriptions now and ask about how well psychological researchers tend to cope with the task of developing and refining theories.

5

THE SIMPLICITY DELUSION

Theorising in Psychology is Hard

Like many delusions, those affecting researchers in various psychological sciences betray certain logical inconsistencies. The last three chapters have attempted to articulate some of those inconsistencies, to cast them in stark terms that make them just a little bit easier to recognise. What we have seen is a lack of clarity, indeed a lack of discipline, in how the subject matter of that research is characterised.

When do we seek to understand behaviour, and the systems that generate behaviour? When do we seek to understand people, and their characteristics? When do we seek to understand populations, and their distributions, trends, and tendencies? Mainstream discourse and research methods of psychological research drift between these perspectives, and the focus of our attention as researchers is often unclear as a result.

In this chapter we will examine how this lack of clarity and discipline in understanding our own intentions as a scientific community sabotages a crucial means by which scientific progress is achieved – the development of theories.

Theory is the formal structuring of our knowledge according to our best understanding of the phenomena in which we are interested. The advancement of scientific knowledge is largely a matter of the development and refinement of theories of different kinds, such that we are able to ever better coordinate our own actions with the world that we experience.

In the previous three chapters we have focused on the ways in which our uses of widespread numerical methods are symptomatic of unclear, and we believe problematic, conceptions of the subject matter of psychological research. What is hopefully clear from those discussions is that what grants the methods we use in research their validity, and enables the interpretation of results from analyses, are the theories we have about the phenomena. Where that theory is poorly articulated, or the methods in question not calibrated to the descriptions of phenomena inherent within the theory, confusion results.

There is a tight feedback loop between theory and data. Our best current understanding enables us to formulate research questions and determines what kinds of data are relevant

DOI: 10.4324/9781003503873-6

to answering those questions. Where the array of methods available to be deployed are only appropriate for one particular form of phenomenon (say, a group or population) but tend to trump the use of other potential research methods on other phenomena (behaviours or persons, for instance), then this feedback loop is broken, and the results of experiments or other forms of research cannot improve our theories in a progressive manner.

When things are working well in scientific practice theories follow data, which in turn follow theories. Observations and measurements of the world inform our understanding of it. Theories follow data. That understanding then orients us, indicates to what aspects of the world we should pay attention and what new observations and measurements we make. Every observation, even in our most open-minded states, is formed or constrained by prior understanding. Data follow theories. Around and around we go. For this process to be *cumulative* in some way, for our knowledge to progress, in the manner which makes scientific practice such a powerful way of engaging practically with the world, theory and data must be properly calibrated to one another. What is more, different kinds of theories have different purposes and guide research in different kinds of ways.

The current circumstance in which we find psychological research is that theories are poorly specified, such that we slide without noticing between descriptions of behaviours, persons, and groups. This results in very poor guidance on choices of research and analytic methods. Indeed, to a significant extent decisions regarding methodology are a product of professional tradition rather than appropriateness to the task (Green, 2015; Gigerenzer, 2004; Stam, 2004). We constrain ourselves to asking questions in a very narrow range of ways, and as a group of professionals, we have become blind to the necessity for a diversity of research methods and forms of theory.

We thus meet a key delusion that we will see plays a role in the frustrating disorientation of our scientific endeavours, the Simplicity Delusion.

> ***The Simplicity Delusion:*** The belief or assumption that behaviour and experience are simple enough to be broken down into basic parts and understood using existing conceptual frameworks.

There are two facets to this delusion, one related to our understanding, and one related to our scientific subject matter. The first regards the seemingly easy comprehensibility of psychology's subject matter and the siren song of what, in 1890, William James warned of as the "'psychologist's fallacy '*par excellence*". Our capacity as human beings to make sense of human beings results in delusions of comprehension – thinking that we understand something as a scientist, when all that we are really doing is making sense of it as a person with our own much more limited and immediate perspective. For scientific practice in psychology, this results in a very poor tradition of theory building, and a generally poor professional understanding of theory in general. We will discuss these things in the following section.

The second facet to the Simplicity Delusion relates to the issues of *complexity*, and the ways in which we should conceive of and approach phenomena that demonstrate certain forms of complexity. We will address evidence relating to this concept of complexity later in the chapter. We turn first, however, to the means by which we turn numbers into data, and data into understanding – the fundamental set of scientific tools we call theories.

The Simplicity Delusion and the Psychologist's Fallacy

To observe, measure, and record something requires us to be able to perceive it, and to perceive something effectively we must first be oriented towards it. In the broad sweep of scientific activity, theories are a crucial part of how we orient ourselves properly with respect to our subject matter. Theories pick out what events, objects, and relationships in the world matter to our focus of interest. They identify what is likely and unlikely, credible and incredible, ordinary and extraordinary.

Concern about theory building in psychology is decades old. Its most famous early articulation is that of Paul Meehl (1978; but this wasn't even his first warning, see Meehl, 1967). He lamented "the slow progress of soft psychology" and identified a range of hefty challenges that must be overcome to have hope of successful theory development. The list of 20 items makes for uncomfortable reading even to a modern audience, and it is not coincidental that this paper has been cited in previous chapters of this book. Several of the difficulties Meehl identifies we have already addressed, but among those that apply particularly to the expression and refinement of theory development is the necessity of "open concepts" in our accounts of behaviour. Open concepts are those which play a role in the theoretical account but are not themselves finely specified by operationalisation or essential criteria. Classic examples of such open concepts are diagnostic categories, which are in a process of continuous change (as evidenced by every revision of the Diagnostic and Statistical Manual of Mental Disorders (DSM) and International Classification of Disease (ICD)), with varying relationships to symptoms or other indicators, as our broader theories evolve. The truth of the matter of course is that there are precious few concepts that can be stably defined in the manner that Meehl would like. Meehl recognises that the complexity of psychological subject matter means that it is almost impossible to avoid some dependence on such open concepts. The question for us is how we might discipline such use.

One of the major problems of relying on open concepts in our scientific practice is that the crucial orienting role is left incomplete, and the result is a problem about which psychologists have been warned since at least the work of William James. James described the "psychologist's fallacy", the tendency for a psychologist to encounter and interpret psychological phenomena not in terms of their relationships to other events, objects, and relationships in the world, but in terms of what they mean to the psychologist themselves – their "common sense" and general human response to other people, their behaviours, their expressions, and utterances. James (1890, p. 196) puts it like this:

> The *great* snare of the psychologist is the *confusion of his own standpoint with that of the mental fact* about which he is making his report. I shall hereafter call this the 'psychologist's fallacy' *par excellence*... The psychologist, as we remarked above, stands outside of the mental state he speaks of. Both itself and its object are objects for him. Now when it is a *cognitive* state (percept, thought, concept, etc.), he ordinarily has no other way of naming it than as the thought, percept, etc., *of that object.* He himself, meanwhile, knowing the self-same object in *his* way, gets easily led to suppose that the thought, which is *of* it, knows it in the same way in which he knows it, although this is often very far from being the case. The most fictitious puzzles have been introduced into our science by this means.

The danger, as we see it, is that as a person encountering and examining the behaviour and experience of other people, the researcher has little hope of neutrality in their perceptions and observations. Even disciplined caution is difficult to maintain. While it is certainly possible for psychologists to train our perspectives, to vary our attitudes and interpretations of our data, without theories to scaffold such training, the most likely result is that we bring a host of intuitions and habits to bear that derive not from systematic observations but from other domains that shape our normal "everyday" conceptions of people; our cultural, religious, and civic backgrounds. In the majority of cases of human action, there is a seductive, immediate meaningfulness to what people do. On the one hand, there are important lessons to learn here – that people are not arbitrary, that their behaviour is structured across a range of scales in ways that can be identified and investigated. On the other, the practised ease with which we make sense of others can delude us with a perceived simplicity of the system or the processes involved (Valsiner, 2019).

The decades since Meehl's observations of theory in psychology have offered significant opportunity for development in this regard, though alas we are more likely to find in the literature recurring calls to sharpen our theorising, than reports of progress in doing so. There are repeated warnings that what psychologists seem to accept as theories are little more than gestures towards scientific practice (Dar, 1987; Gigerenzer, 1998a; Lykken, 1991), or what Gerd Gigerenzer (1998a) terms "surrogates for theories". Gigerenzer lists four such surrogates: one-word explanations, re-description, muddy dichotomies, and data fitting. We might more critically term such moves as Potemkin theories, facades that provide the veneer of theory, but hiding a barrenness behind.

One-word explanations are labels given to a phenomenon as though the label itself provided some kind of explanatory power. These are titles to patterns in our observations of people's behaviour, but in and of themselves offer little beyond that. Gigerenzer's examples are all drawn from cognitive psychology: *availability*, *representativeness*, *anchoring*. While the phenomena they name can be reliably evinced in laboratory conditions, and often pointed to in real-world settings, decades of research have not offered much beyond their existence, certainly little to warrant claims of explanation and understanding other than speculative "just so" stories. Availability, for instance, is sometimes explained by the means of accessibility or excitability of mental representations, but without a clearly articulated account of "mental representation", this is no better than a theoretical promissory note.

Re-description is a more committed form of the same bait-and-switch, in which we seem to be offered an explanation but in fact are really presented with a description of the phenomenon in slightly different terms. Gigerenzer provides the example of the use of diagrams in aiding problem-solving as being described as making solutions "salient", or "transparent" to the solver – which really just restates the fact that they help the solver see the solution without offering a theoretical account as to how that aid occurs.

We might try to avoid over-simplification by offering contrasts, setting one form of explanation off against another. Psychology is replete with these "muddy dichotomies", as Gigerenzer (1998a) has them – "nature vs nurture", "serial vs parallel", "implicit vs explicit", "person vs situation", "System 1 vs System 2". Setting up such frameworks provides the appearance that the choice in question is clearly articulated, though inevitably such dichotomies are choices between two of what Meehl would call open concepts. Just as inevitably, the sensible among us claim that any phenomenon involves "both", though precisely what such an enlightened view actually means would require an explicit theoretical position that remains elusive.

We will address Gigerenzer's final point – data fitting – a little later on. For now, we might look at evidence of the continuing struggle of psychological science with this uncertainty around theoretical concepts and their relationships in the decades since these concerns were first given such strident expression.

Alas, dear reader, things are not looking good.

Joanne Hale and her colleagues (Hale et al., 2020) have plied immense effort to formalising and then creating a database of 76 theories of behaviour change in psychology. Using a technique called an "ontology-based modelling system" (OBMS), Hale et al. took each of their target theories, identified the constructs (theoretical concepts) which played operative roles within the theory, and then organised and connected them based on the relationships described by the theory (five of them were too poorly specified to diagram). Their intention in the use of OBMS was to identify, across a range of theories, a shared collection of referred-to constructs that would specify the collection of things that exist for each theory. By making clear what kinds of things existed within each theory, the points at which they overlapped could be mapped. Such a shared foundation of existing things would provide a field on which differences between theories could be articulated, and on which predictive and explanatory power can be comparatively evaluated. The result is a prospect for much more coherent, systematic evaluation of theories against each other, and against the evidence, offering quicker and more efficient progress.

Across the theories they reviewed (remember, these are all theories of behaviour change, and therefore ostensibly addressing at least related phenomena), they found a total of 1290 constructs, of which *1028 were unique and did not appear in any other theory*. It is hard to express just how bad this news is for the state of theorising in psychology. Watkins (1984) famously quipped that psychologists would sooner use each other's toothbrushes than each other's theories; Hale et al. appear to reinforce that claim with quantified evidence.

Hale et al.'s (2020) work is part of a broader discussion of the crisis of theory in psychology over the past few years. The literature on these considerations tends to focus on theories' variability (Szollosi & Donkin, 2019, 2021), logical coherence (Muthukrishan & Henrich, 2019; Oberauer & Lewandowsky, 2019), and adequate explication (Guest & Martin, 2021; Guest, 2024). Indeed, there are fundamental questions regarding what counts as a theory, and the relationship that exists between theory, empirical work, and practice (Buzbas & Devezer, 2023; Devezer et al., 2019; Gigerenzer, 1998a, 2024; Trafimow, 2025; van Rooij & Baggio, 2020, 2021).

The long history and present seeming extravagance of bad theorising in psychology would appear to invite the question: Do we just suck at this? To this blunt query, we would offer a nuanced response. What is clear is that it is important that we take steps to improve our practices in theorising just as we progress in other areas of reform in the psychological and behavioural sciences. But it is also clear, and has been so since Meehl's list of challenges (if not before), that one of the main reasons psychology struggles with bad theories is because constructing good theories in psychology is particularly hard.

We have already noted in Chapter 3 how the complexities associated with experimental control make effective causal inference unusually difficult for psychological scientists. Even the "gold standard" of the randomised controlled trial, while useful for public health and other population-level inferences, cannot quite support the understanding of causality needed for refined theory development (Eronen, 2020, 2024).

What allows physicists, chemists, and others to be confident in their discussions of the invisible is the reliability and potency of their theories, theories that enable the careful construction and evaluation of apparatuses, and the interpretation of experiences and observations made using those apparatuses. Often formalised in ways that allow not just reliable, but precise deduction and prediction, theories in other sciences are a scaffold that keeps practice in those disciplines critically accountable.

Good Theories make Data Meaningful

In 1973, Alan Newell, one of the foremost figures in the development of cognitive psychology and cognitive science, wrote what is now a classic review of a symposium held at Carnegie-Mellon University in May of that year. In the piece, entitled "You Can't Play 20 Questions With Nature and Win", Newell was both optimistic and uncertain. Optimistic because, as he saw it, the papers presented were demonstrations of excellent methodological rigour and care, and they also all seemed to relate to one another under the general umbrella of an information-processing conception of psychology, something still maturing at the time.

His principal concerns, however, related to the ways in which the different papers were framed around different phenomena, and that despite the seeming thematic relatedness there was no clear way in which they might be brought into direct contact with one another, no way in which they offered insight or relevance directly to one another. Newell cast his mind forward 30 years, wondering whether, if research continued as it seemed to be going, there was a prospect of an encompassing theory of psychology. Here, his optimism seems to falter (though he was far from despairing).

For our present purposes, it seems apt to note that one of Newell's particular concerns was the fact that researchers could develop carefully designed, rigorous, and excellently conducted experiments which nevertheless provided little by way of cumulative insight, because it was not clear that the specific tasks being investigated were achieved by participants through the use of some stable set of shared underlying cognitive resources that all participants shared.

> To put this in general terms again, our task in psychology is first to discover that structure which is fixed and invariant so that we can theoretically infer the method [Method is the reliably occuring means by which information is processed by participants in a given task]. Given the goal of the subject and the task environment which he faces, we can generate the (small) collection of methods that are likely to be used by him to perform the task (given his processing limits). Then, by means of careful design of the experiments or by suitable *post-hoc* analysis of the subject's performance we can settle what method he did indeed use. Without such a framework within which to work, the generation of new methods, hence new explanations, for old phenomena, will go on *ad nauseum*. There will be no discipline for it, as there is none now.
>
> *(Newell, 1973, p. 14)*

In his desire for a bigger picture, Newell had a specific form of information processing paradigm in mind, with which we need not agree to recognise the generality of his concerns. Given the diversity of potential ways in which a person can achieve a given end, we need not only describe what they do, but what the principle of variation of different ways of doing it are. To even begin this task at the very least requires a systematic understanding of the range and pattern of such variations in real cases.

Newell is very clearly expressing the need for a carefully articulated theory in guiding our research questions and methods, and warns of the risks of proceeding in an atheoretical manner, or with theories that are too "local" to the phenomena being examined in each set of experiments. If our research is organised by phenomenon, rather than an explicit and more encompassing description of the subject matter of our science, then work is doomed to be piecemeal, inconsistent, and possibly incommensurable. While he proposes an information theoretic approach (specifically, he suggests we consider the problem as a programming one, of control structures engaging particular routines), the broad framework for how to orient scientific enterprise so that it can be cumulative, to progress in some sense, is one that does not rely on commitment to that particular theory. But it *does* rely on a shared commitment to *some* systematic and disciplined theory.

There is More Than One Kind of Theory, and More Than One Kind of Research

In that 1973 paper, Newell is at pains to emphasise just how good the different experiments are that he is reviewing. They are carefully constructed, well conducted, and the analyses properly and critically undertaken. It is this brilliance that has Newell proclaim his optimism and satisfaction with the direction of psychological science. His concerns are at a different level, the extent to which the experiments might fit together, and assembled into a general model of psychology, or psychological phenomena. Newell does not expressly identify this as implying two different forms of theory – one local and specific that addresses questions of causation and mechanism, another more global, addressing questions of organisation and principles of variation of the subject matter of the field more generally. His perspective does implicitly hint at such a division of theoretical labour, though. These different kinds of theories arise from somewhat different forms of data production and analysis and are evaluated by different criteria, serving these distinct but complementary functions in orienting or guiding our research questions and designs. In seeking to better appreciate these differences, we can turn to a figure outside of the field of psychological science, but whom perhaps we might allow as having a reasonably strong grasp on the process of theory development.

In 1919, in a letter to *The Times of London*, Albert Einstein distinguished between two different kinds of scientific theory. Some are what he termed "theories of principle". We suggest this first kind of theory is what is required to address Newell's concerns (though we should note that Newell himself did not put it this way). Theories of principle are those generalisations from observations that are elegant, accurate, and useful descriptions of the natural world captured in those observations. Einstein (1919) notes that Newton's theory of universal gravitation and his own theories of special and general relativity fall into this category. Theories of principle do not provide accounts of mechanisms, and therefore *causation*. Newton explicitly denied any attempt to provide a description of the mechanism by which gravity has its effects. Theories of principle do not begin from a specified set of hypothesised components but rather are developed on the basis of abductively identified principles. Those principles provide systematic descriptions of a phenomenon, a means of accurately characterising the patterns of results that are found in observations and measurements. They don't include any account of the mechanisms by which those patterns come to be. As such, from these principles, descriptions of other key facets of the world can be derived. From a diversity of observations, the scientist conjectures key relationships that characterise the phenomena of interest, and with those conjectures fixed as principles, further details can be analytically deduced (Holton, 1979). They are effective insofar as they are pure, logical, and secure in their foundation in empirical data (Einstein, 1919).

The special and general theories of relativity fix the speed of light, not on the basis of an explanation for why it is how it is, but on the basis that multiple empirical demonstrations show it to have the value that it does. Having identified this fact as one of a set of basic principles, however, Einstein was able to get a surprising amount of work done. He noticed that a number of different facts were related in ways that no one else had and provided explicitly specified ways of characterising those relationships – again, without providing an account of the mechanisms by which those relationships came to be. The theory of relativity, for instance, famously predicts changes in mass and a slowing of time as bodies accelerate, limited by the speed of light. There is no mention made of the means by which mass and time change. Their relationship is captured by the theory in a way that has allowed for more than a century of accurate predictions, with no account as to precisely how it all works. The "how" of relativity remains an outstanding challenge for physicists, but it is a challenge with very clearly defined parameters.

Causal explanation must go beyond the description of how the world is. Indeed, even being able to make accurate predictions is not enough to be able to say that we have identified the causal mechanisms by which something happens. Causal explanation requires Einstein's second kind of theory, what he refers to as "constructive theories". These are models of reality constructed from simple propositions concerning hypothesised components. Constructive theories introduce a set of hypothesised elements and the mechanisms by which those elements interact. Einstein's go-to example for this was the kinetic theory of gases, which explained the relationship between pressure and temperature of a gas in a container through the motion of its component molecules. We understand a phenomenon when we have a constructive theory which encompasses it, and the theory enables an effective coordination of our actions with the phenomena in question (accurate prediction, and perhaps some form of control). We can see that insofar as this is the case, then the development of effective, useful, and comprehensive constructive theory is crucial work of a mature science.

There is plenty of discussion of theory in psychological science, though no real recognition that there might be different kinds of theories, serving different purposes, and therefore having different relationships to data.

Most discussion in the literature would seem to focus on hypothesised components and the means by which they might give rise to behaviour observed in controlled conditions. The repudiation of a simplistic behaviourist attitude that many of us learn in our undergraduate studies ensures that we are distrustful of anything that purports to be a theory but does *not* involve reference to unobserved underlying mechanisms.

The variant characteristics of the two kinds of theory identified by Einstein give them different strengths and different roles to play in the development of our knowledge. A better understanding of these differences will help us see both the value of them, and the implications that they hold for how we go about producing data to inform them.

Complementary Theories Supporting Advancement of Knowledge

Felline (2011) describes theories of principle as "structural explanations" in that they capture the "structural" aspects of the phenomena of interest. A structural explanation is a model which explains the behaviour of some part of the system in terms of its relationships to other parts of the system, without necessarily specifying how those relationships arise from the properties of the parts themselves (see also Lange, 2014). That is to say that theories of principle provide accounts of the relationships and patterns that exist in descriptions of the world, rather than descriptions of the mechanisms that give rise to those relationships. They offer these descriptions, however, in the formal terms of the scientific discipline (in Einstein's case, those terms are substantially mathematical). The perception and understanding of these patterns might arise from extensive observations and tabulations of data, introducing new concepts and ways of thinking that help organise existing observations (as in the case of Newton's theory of universal gravitation). They might re-orient the scientific community around these new patterns, in response to challenges or confusions regarding them (as was the case with Einstein's theory of relativity).

In focusing on the structural aspects of things, theories of principle make few ontological commitments (or as few as possible). Some (perhaps Einstein included; Balashov & Jansson, 2003, p. 332) consider theories of principle to be the inferior form of theory – they provide description more than explanation. But we should not underestimate the importance of that role in systematic, precise, and disciplined description.

Having identified the principles on the basis of patterns in the observed phenomena, predictions that follow from those principles can be deduced. These predictions are means of assessing the theory's effectiveness as a description of the patterns of stability and variation in phenomena. Indeed, Einstein's letter to *The Times* was prompted by the so-called Eddington Experiment. The Eddington Experiment, organised by Arthur Stanley Eddington and Frank Watson Dyson, involved measurements of starlight deflection made during a solar eclipse on either side of the Atlantic (Brazil on the west and Principe on the east). The measurements were to test predictions made by Einstein as early as 1911, and which were posited as direct tests of general relativity in 1915.

A final, and perhaps most important, role for theories of principle is in specifying the relationships between chosen components of an observed system in the formal terms of the discipline. By doing so, theories of principle impose constraints on constructive theories (Einstein, 1919; Flores, 1999).

If the theory of principle is a good one, then any constructive theory in the domain will have to encompass it and should not make any predictions that violate those principles. In this way, the theory of principle becomes the representative of natural settings within experimental laboratory work. The theory of principle can help identify research questions, set research agendas, and, by setting constraints, support the evaluation of competing constructive theories. Einstein's own theory of general relativity has performed such functions within the domain of cosmological physics for the better part of a century (once it came to be accepted by the scientific community at large).

Good theories of principle are therefore somewhat the more stable of the two kinds, not being beholden to the specific ontological or mechanistic commitments required of constructive theories (Felline, 2011; Balashov & Jansson, 2003, suggest this is partly what drew Einstein to the form of theory which he considered technically inferior). Constructive theories, however, provide descriptions and explanations at a higher degree of resolution more in tune with the highest aspirations of science. Bluntly summarising, Balashov and Jansson (2003) claim that constructive theories are about the underlying reality, while theories of principle are about the phenomena.

This complementary relationship between theories of principle and constructive theories offers a division of labour in science that can play an important role in structuring and coordinating diverse research agendas. Theories of principle, where shown to be accurate in their descriptions of the world, provide an agreed set of criteria by which otherwise varied constructive approaches can be assessed, an arena within which they can be compared directly. The theory of principle is the formalised surrogate of the natural world used to inform and evaluate studies in controlled environments.

In having different roles to play in scientific practice, the different kinds of theory have somewhat different criteria by which they should be judged, and also, crucially, different relationships to data. It is this latter aspect in particular that we argue holds some important implications for the priorities of contemporary psychological research.

Different Kinds of Theories have Different Relationships with Data

As noted above, Einstein describes theories of principle as being evaluated by the soundness of their logic, coherence, and the security of their foundation in data. This foundation in data is worth dwelling on for a moment.

Einstein describes the principles being first identified in a conjecture born of familiarity with the "multiplicity" of sense experience. Theories of principle are thus developed abductively. The data which inspire such leaps of intuition are varied, general. Einstein wants to, as much as possible, encompass the "totality of sense experiences" (Holton, 1979, p. 313; see also Einstein in Schilpp, 1949). The variety and generality of these data are crucial. For the integrating conjecture that is vital to Einstein's formation of a theory to have validity, it must attempt to encompass this totality.

We have already noted that a theory of principle should make as few ontological commitments as possible. Though observations or measurements that are wholly theory-free are impossible, each prior theoretical commitment means that a constructive theory (whether implicit or explicit) already plays a role in its structure. Each such commitment narrows the field of experience that can possibly be encompassed by the theory when developed. Laboratory practice is perforce structured by prior theory – every decision made with regard to method, material, and measurement represents the researcher's informed perspective. Opportunities for serendipity and surprise are far from eliminated but they are by definition limited by controlled settings. The totality and multiplicity with which the researcher engages in a form of "free play" (Einstein in Schilpp, 1949, p. 7) is constrained in advance.

For a theory of principle to be broadly valid, then, it must draw not only on data drawn from the laboratory, but also from less structured, though still disciplined, observations of phenomena "in the wild". Einstein for his part had a wealth of relevant information available to him, both from the laboratory and from the observations of the natural movements of heavenly and earthly bodies. His theories made sense of a "labyrinth of sense impressions", a "totality of empirical fact" (Holton, 1979, p. 313, citing Einstein, 1954). This might be something we can easily imagine of Einstein; it's something of a tall order for the rest of us. Nevertheless, we see here a call not only to ambition, but to a re-balancing of our scientific practices, particularly our data production techniques, in order to facilitate the development of better theories of principle. In the context of the wide-ranging disciplinary discussion on the professional practices of research psychologists, our methods, and approaches, it behoves us to recognise that the prescriptions for improvements in scientific practice will depend on the question of "improvements for what purpose?". Where a need for different forms of theoretical progress is identified, then different kinds of data will need to be produced accordingly, and the more explicit and aware we are of these different aspirations, the better we will manage them.

An Empirical Defence – Maybe we Don't Always Need Theory

Even before the era of "big data", there was an apparent faith among many psychologists that if we get the research and analytic methods right, then theory would take care of itself. At first blush, it seems entirely appropriate as a scientific practice that we be led by empirical work. Identifying reliable foci for research is a quintessential part of scientific practice. The first step towards strong theory is, after all, the cataloguing of things about which to theorise. What is more, if we consistently measure and record the behaviour of those things, we can use well-understood tools to map the relationships between them in a direct, empirical manner.

Though it is difficult to find people directly espousing such a view, the intense focus on the identification and cataloguing of "effects" in the study of psychology and behaviour speaks to the extent to which this kind of logic is in play (Stephen & van Orden, 2012, p. 95). By implication, scientific reform should be targeted primarily at empirical methods and analytic techniques. Where these are made valid and dependable, the thinking seems to go, so valid and dependable characterisations of the facts of the matter will follow. Fix the data, and the theories will take care of themselves.

In the past decade, and particularly in the past few years, as various technologies under the umbrella of "AI" have become rampant, we see an increasing lean towards this empirical way of thinking, as though theoretical problems can be smoothed away with enough data. Sufficient amounts of data will not only provide a reassurance of generalisability or precision but will enable a near-direct observation of even immensely complex relationships between variables, doing away with the need to use theories to guide or structure our measurements.

This empirical defence against the weakness of our theories, both in the general truffle-hunting mode of effects-driven research and in the more opaque though impressive "AI"-driven computational modelling, represents instances of that fourth surrogate for theory listed by Gigerenzer (1998a): data fitting.

In his analysis, Gigerenzer notes that since the earliest days of the discipline, psychology has relied on statistical and computational methods to identify relationships of various forms between variables. Whether through factor analysis, regression models, multidimensional scaling, or lately, artificial neural network models, powerful mathematical tools have been developed and deployed to the purpose of modelling data.

Reviewing the use of statistics, and in particular regression modelling, in psychological research, statistician David Freedman (1985) lamented the manner in which such mathematical tools are deployed without sufficient theoretical constraint in the social sciences. The result is not modelling of the principles or causal processes which give rise to particular observations. Rather it is a host of calculations which are models of the data themselves. The necessary weakness in such an *ad-hoc*, *post-hoc* approach to model building is that as soon as the data change, as they must, the model is no longer accurate. The result is the cluttered, and nonsensical landscape of ontologies and relationships summarised by Hale et al. (2020).

Freedman (1985) spends some time contrasting statistics-first approaches to theorising with the prolonged, intensive efforts of Kepler to develop a theory of planetary motion. Kepler's motivation was not to model the extensive observational data of his mentor Tycho Brahe, but to capture the inherent principles that resulted in the data. We have noted, too, the major theories of Newton and Einstein as examples of principles that organise records and enable predictions so well. It may seem to the pessimistic reader that we are advocating a kind of hero- or heroine-worship, as though we must spin our wheels until some genius arrives. Surely the great power of new tools is that they enable those of us not gifted with individual, world-altering insights, to approach such enlightenment slowly and systematically.

We vehemently agree with this position, and we reject wholeheartedly a despairing wait for some theoretical messiah. Nevertheless, this view does not absolve us of the need to use these tools carefully, and to use the *right* tools for the jobs at hand. Freedman puts it elegantly:

> Estimating coefficients by least squares before the basic variables have been understood is like using a scalpel to clear a path through the jungle.
>
> *(Freedman, 1985, p. 352)*

Being able to decide on what the right tools are involves orienting ourselves effectively to the task at hand. The job of orienting ourselves is one of the most crucial that good theories perform, and without them, we risk a basic misperceiving of the phenomena in which we are interested. Problematically, when the things that we are paying attention to are complex, messy, and tangled – the kind of "jungle" that Freedman notes – we risk making sense of noise, like hearing voices in static, or seeing shapes in clouds. This scientific pareidolia is a particular risk for psychologists, whose scientific subject matter is the stuff of our daily lives even away from work. Something we will need as we move forward is a clear-eyed understanding of just how complex our subject matter is.

Consistent in our Variability

Underlying the Simplicity Delusion, as has been the case with so much of what we have discussed this far, is the fact that people, and their psychologies, are widely variable. Let's begin with a quick bit of mental arithmetic. Take a moment to add together the two numbers 47 and 36. Reflect on the process that you used to get the result.

As a bit of homework, ask a few friends to do the same – add the same two numbers together, and then explain in detail what processes they went through in their heads in order to do so. You might be surprised by just how many ways there are to do this, and how widely variant the techniques are.

Some people begin with the tens, adding the 40 and 30. Among these, a few will then stack the units on top – first the 7, then the 6. Others will add the units and put 13 together with the 70.

Some people will spot the potential for a nice round number and borrow 3 from the 36 to make the 47 into 50 and then make the quick and simple addition of the remaining 33.

Some will add the whole 6 to 47 and then stack on the 30. Others will be even more idiosyncratic. You might even do it differently yourself in different circumstances.

The point is not that the variations are endless (they aren't), but that they are much wider than we are likely to realise before actually doing the work of checking. This is an illustration of what is a surprisingly general point – that there are often many ways to get a given cognitive job done, and not only will different people do things differently, but even the same person might do things differently in different circumstances. (Try 23 and 67 – do you use the same procedure as before?)

This toy example helps us orient ourselves to the fact that it is very easy to underestimate the ways in which psychology can vary. Once we begin to explore this variety, we can find cases where processes differ from case to case within a person; in habits and routines from person to person; and also in ways of behaving from community to community. Many aspects of behavioural or cognitive organisation that we can easily take for granted as stable, simple, and reliable are more variable than we think, *even where the outcomes are relatively stable*. The underlying processes are therefore necessarily more complex than our standing assumptions might allow us to admit.

We have noted repeatedly in the past few chapters that much of psychological science is grounded in an assumption that there is a shared, universal human cognitive endowment underlying behaviour. Some of the founders of cognitive psychology, Herbert Simon (1973) and our friend Alan Newell (1990), were careful to define cognitive systems in such a way as to support this possibility, setting the parameters of cognitive research in terms that facilitated the decomposition of cognition into stable, recognisable components (Stephen & van Orden, 2012).

Nevertheless, variation has bedevilled cognitive psychology. For instance, people have proven to adopt widely varying strategies for reasoning about syllogisms (Bucciarelli & Johnson-Laird, 1999) and shown dramatically variable performance in basic working memory tasks based on practice and experience (e.g., Ericsson & Chase, 1982). Critical thinking skills appear to follow domain-specific skills rather than be a generalisable process of reasoning (Monteiro et al., 2020). How quickly people recognise words depends on the context of non-words in which they are presented (degree of similarity to the target words), suggesting that the context plays a significant role in the perception of words, not just the characteristics of the target stimuli (Stone & van Orden, 1993; van Orden et al., 1999).

Underpinning such cognitive variability is the extensive plasticity of neural development. The brain is not a static organ, and while there are some broad similarities between people, we find quite a bit of evidence of differences both big and small based on development differences and habitual practices. Maguire et al. (2000) found a relationship between extent of navigational experience and the size of the hippocampus in London black-cab drivers, while Silva et al. (2018) review a range of evidence that in blind people, what is traditionally "visual" cortex becomes more active during auditory tasks (this is more pronounced in those who become blind earlier in life). This offers some corroboration for the more dramatic finding, though in non-human animals, that ferrets who had neo-natal neurosurgery to form connections between the optic nerves and primary auditory cortex developed retinotopic maps in areas of cortex most typically associated with coordination of auditory tasks (Roe et al., 1990). Indeed, plasticity is not just a phenomenon of the early developing brain but appears to remain possible in mature brains also (Fuchs & Flügge, 2014; Schwaber et al., 1993; though see Voss et al., 2017, for discussion that even neuroplasticity is variable across individuals and the life-span). Change over time would appear to be fundamental to the brain's *raison d'être*.

The habitual circumstances in which we find ourselves therefore likely have a strong shaping influence on the ways in which we approach activities. Merlin Donald (2001) suggests what he calls "deep enculturation" as a formative process by which the values and routines of a given community will tend to lead to a certain level of consistency within groups, but also variation between groups, in the ways in which quite basic, and what are sometimes taken to be fundamental, tasks are performed. Through these shaping constraints on plastic brains, we will see variations in what might otherwise be considered quite fundamental cognitive functions. Nisbett et al. (2001) survey a wide range of research to argue that Western (European and North American) participants in various cognitive tasks exhibit tendencies towards analytical (part-to-whole) orientations to activities which lead to patterns in attention, reasoning, categorisation, and more that is at variance with holistic (whole-to-part) orientations of East Asian (primarily Chinese and Japanese participants). Segall et al. (1963), meanwhile, note that susceptibility to visual illusions (specifically the Muller-Lyer and Sander Parallelogram) appears to vary between groups with different cultural backgrounds.

We acknowledge that almost all of the just-cited research is conducted within precisely the kinds of mean-based orientation which we criticise. We have no doubt that these generalisations tend to underplay the extent to which there is variability within cultures (indeed, culture is a notoriously difficult concept to make specific enough to operationalise). The point, however, is not to make generalisations about cultural differences, but more simply to highlight that what in some circumstances appear to be basic or fundamental characteristics of cognitive functioning may be a dynamic process held in relative stability by a number of social, cultural, developmental, and ultimately professional scientific forces tuned to make them so.

The importance of recognising this variability has perhaps been most famously articulated by Henrich et al. (2010) through their introduction of the acronym WEIRD (Western, Educated, Industrialised, Rich, Democratic) to describe the vast majority of participants in published behavioural research. Like Nisbett et al. (2001), Henrich et al. survey research demonstrating a much wider variability in the ways in which behavioural tasks are done, across social, cognitive, and other categories, than might have been expected based on the general principles of the mainstream scientific discourse at the time. Their work suggested an otherwise unsuspected variety of behaviour, perhaps underpinned by an equally unsuspected complexity or malleability of basic psychological processes. (While Nisbett et al. place a strong emphasis on different social dynamics, Henrich et al. also argue that wider factors such as environmental variation likely play a role.) At the time of writing, the paper introducing the WEIRDness of psychological research has been cited more than 6000 times, indicating a real sensitivity to the issue within the behavioural research community.

A decade later, alas, things have not much improved. Thalmayer et al. (2021, following up on a similar analysis by Arnett, 2008) present evidence that contemporary published research in the "top" (note: all English-speaking) journals can still only be argued to include representation from approximately 11% of the global population. We wholeheartedly support the many calls for wider representation among researchers and participants in psychological research. Positive developments such as the organisation of the Psychological Science Accelerator (Jarke et al., 2022; Moshontz et al., 2018) will certainly help in this regard.

Our concern with the Simplicity Delusion, however, is not just one of representation. The variability of psychological phenomena points to a contingency in their organisation that we must take care to acknowledge and incorporate into our thinking.

The past few decades have seen an increasing range of research addressing the dynamic organisation of behaviour. Exploring the extensive body of work on detailed variability of cognitive performance in skill development, Speelman and Kirsner (2005) drew the conclusion that the cognitive system is best conceived not as a general computational device but rather as a self-organising dynamical system arranged from micro-gestural (rather than modular) elements in mutual feedback. In doing so, they joined with a diverse group of researchers investigating psychology not as representational computation, but as self-organising networks of feedback processes (Kelso, 1995; Thelen & Smith, 1994; van Gelder, 1995; van Gelder & Port, 1995; van Orden et al., 2005).

We will explore the positive account of dynamical cognitive science as one of several pathways available to an improved psychology in Part II. For now, we argue that work in this area, which explicitly addresses behaviour as a complex phenomenon, illustrates the unreliability of assumptions of simplicity common to much research. Working so frequently with only surrogates for theory, psychologists build on intuitions and assumptions inherited from culture and civic life, in doing so falling prey to the psychologist's fallacy. This is often manifested in the form of an assumption that what are considered "higher" cognitive processes break down into more basic processes in much the same way that an engineer might design a system, component by component. Pinker (1997), for instance, summarises cognitive science as an effort to "reverse engineer the brain", but this approach too often involves an assumption that the brain is the sole locus of cognitive activity, and that it is organised in some way along the same kind of lines as a human engineer would build a mechanism to get the job done.

The still somewhat niche domain of psychological research conducted under the rubric of dynamical systems theory suggests otherwise. Approaching something as a dynamical system is a rather agnostic way of going about things. While it involves the assumption that the system in question (e.g., the organisation of behavioural response) is time-dependent in that what it does at one time affects what it does next, it does not make an assumption as to what the organisation of its components is like. The components in question may be very simple – none of them doing anything even remotely like the overall system does, in much the same way that what neurons, muscles, and skeletons do individually is nothing like the performance of an experimental psychology task. The feedback between these components over time, though, can have quite dramatic effects resulting in complex organised activity. That complexity can be immense, dynamic, and has potentially huge implications for how to do behavioural science.

We will explore the potential implications for theory and method in psychology later. For now, we simply want to address the question as to whether there is evidence that behaviour really is a complex dynamical system of this kind. Crucially, dynamical systems theory focuses not on averages, but on variability (Stephen & van Orden, 2012). Where more common psychological research methods see variation around the mean as noise, dynamical systems methods see it as texture to be explored. There are a number of potential hints for us to follow, but here we will focus on two signatures in variation in data sets that are indicative of the presence of complex dynamical systems: bifurcations, and multifractality.

A bifurcation is a tipping point, a sudden change in the way a system is working, a qualitative shift. Imagine a key modulation in a musical tune, or a shift in rhythm – the whole system transitions from one mode of operation to another. All of the components involved end up in new relationships, the whole system is at least slightly, and often dramatically, reorganised. Stephen and van Orden (2012) note that bifurcations can be "local", such as when a person corrects themselves in the middle of making an error, or global, such as when their overall approach to a task changes.

As an example of local bifurcation, they offer Spivey's (2008) work on mouse tracking in word identification tasks. The setup is simple: a person hears a word spoken and must move the pointer from a starting position in the bottom centre of a screen to one of two images in the top corners. The two targets might be very different – "bottle" and "airplane", say, or they might share an opening syllable, such as "carrot" and "carriage". Across a number of studies, Spivey and his colleagues showed that people don't wait until the word is completely spoken before starting to move – they get straight to it. The simple task is not broken down into discrete steps – first hear the word, then recognise it, then move to the correct target. When there is no potential confusion between targets, the mouse tracks are typically fairly straight. Where there is uncertainty (in the "carrot" vs. "carriage" example), the track can waver and cross back upon itself as it is moving. The behavioural response is not an all-or-nothing thing, it is a complex thing that can be reorganised on the fly, and the local, within-action reorganisations can be recognised clearly in the data.

Global bifurcations involve not just a revision of an on-going action, but a shift in the approach to the task entirely. Stephen et al. (2009) presented people with diagrams of interlocking gears and asked, given the direction of turn of a starting gear, to indicate the direction of turn of a target gear. Tracking eye and finger movements, they showed that people shift suddenly from tracing movements in the diagram to realising that a solution can be found by just counting the intervening gears (even numbers will turn the same way, odd, the opposite). Crucially, the insight was preceded by a signature increase in variability in the behaviour system (the measure they used was a calculation of entropy of eye movements, but the details there are not essential for us here). It is as though the whole behavioural system shifted into a less stable state briefly before re-organising completely. The cognitive change is something that rippled as a bifurcation across all aspects of participants' activity, affecting eye fixations and hand movements, a hint at the complex character of the person responding to the experimental situation.

The second signature of complexity, multifractality, is a little more complicated to explain, though the general implication is straightforward enough. Over long periods of time, a complex system's state at one time is affected by its states at previous times, often in quite pervasive but subtle ways. Roughly speaking this is the result of feedback happening between processes that work at different timescales. Think of neuron firings in cycles of tens of milliseconds, and muscle movements in the hundreds of milliseconds to seconds, to experimental tasks in the tens of seconds to minutes, and even longer situations of an hour and more. All of these things can affect one another, and the result is that the variability of a given measurement of the whole system will correlate with itself over different time periods. The mathematical tools of dynamical systems theory allow for calculation of this self-influence ("autocorrelation") relationship. It turns out that not only is multifractality present in times series of behavioural phenomena, but it is diagnostic of healthy over unhealthy heart rhythms (Goldberger et al., 2002), and a robust indicator of an eye-openingly wide range of phenomena relevant to life and actions generally, from Magnetoencephalography (MEG) and Electroencephalography (EEG) recordings of spontaneous neural activity, to postural sway, to errors in the estimation of time intervals, reaction times in memory tasks, and finger-tapping along to a metronome (Ward & Greenwood, 2007).

Chemero (2023) argues at length that the near ubiquity of multifractality in behavioural time series data is a signature of a particular kind of complex dynamical system. This is so well documented over tens of thousands of published studies that it must begin to shift our ideas about how behaviour works. Understanding such complex systems must be done on their own terms. There are methods and analytical techniques that can be very successfully applied here, but these are without precedent in civic, religious, or other sources of "folk" or "commonsense" theories of psychology. Our intuitions are not calibrated for complex systems, and the Simplicity Delusion is very likely to see us far astray.

From Theory to Practice

A good theory needs to be disciplined. We don't get theories of principle for free. We won't get them from regression models (see Freedman, 1985), and we won't get them from big data or AI models for the same reason (van Rooij et al., 2024).

But great advances come through *both* theories of principle and constructive theories.

Though he doesn't use Einstein's specific terminology, Freedman's (1985) analysis of scientific practice makes the point that moving from theories of principle to practice is *hard* and requires moving away from intuitions. Psychologists' seeming faith that regression models or similar statistical organisation of our theorising will provide the insights we need is evidence in favour of a Simplicity Delusion (the belief that we can have a solid grasp of phenomena using our own experience without significant re-training of our intuitions) (Sievers & DeFilippis, 2022).

The point here is not in any way to be dismissive of the work of psychological researchers, nor to express the traditional physics envy of the psychological scientist. As a community, we should recognise two things about our science. First, in comparison to physics, chemistry, and other "hard" sciences, psychology is extraordinarily difficult. We are talking orders of magnitude here. Where physics has crashed up against limitations imposed by a participatory universe in which observation can fundamentally change the measurement, such problems occur at the extremes of quantum phenomena. This is the *base case* in psychological science.

What is more, the challenges of psychological science are much more urgent, immediate, and valuable than those of physics (the details are more complicated for chemistry and biology). The extraordinary achievements of physics and the engineering derived from it have granted us the privilege of the work that we do as academics. It has provided us with a world tamed by the mammoth scale of the built environment and global infrastructure that beggars belief. It has sent people to the moon and lifted our gaze to beyond the solar system. We are geeks, and as these words are being written we are witnessing, via the magic of the internet, the malfunction and near miraculously achieved recovery of the Voyager I spacecraft more than 24 billion kilometres away in interstellar space, but still transmitting a staggered, increasingly garbled goodbye more than 46 years into its journey. These things bespeak the immense value of the hard sciences. But all of them are built on a foundation of humanity, and human endeavour.

How to raise and educate children, how to organise ourselves as families, communities, and global societies. How to make sense of and effectively support learning, exploration, recovery from trauma, and humanity's diversity: these are not grand ambitions; they are constant and immediate challenges which must be overcome repeatedly for grand ambitions to be possible.

Psychological practitioners don't have the time to wait on better theories – clients' needs will not attend grand science and will not bend to accommodate bad science. Our scientific practice is riddled with delusions, and the people with whom we work will not shape themselves to fit them. In this context, practitioners work with their clients, not with weak theory, and the result is an inevitable and seemingly unbridgeable gap between research and practice.

6

THE SCIENTIST-PRACTITIONER DELUSION

Getting Out in the World

You could be forgiven for thinking that the preceding chapters are rather academic. Few things seem as dry and technical as questions of methodology and theory. It all feels very "inside baseball", a nerdy pursuit for the enthused geeks among us but of little real relevance to people in everyday life. Indeed, we believe that many psychologists perceive these debates in this way – something for the keen statisticians and methodologists to discuss in specialist journals, but not something that really has too many implications for their more concrete work. On the basis of this, we offer two observations. The first is that of the journals, books, and book chapters in which these questions have been examined, some break through into "mainstream" venues such as *American Psychologist*, *Psychological Review*, or other broad channels, but most languish in smaller niches, consulted only by us oddly critical weirdos. The second is that, despite these issues having been recognised from early in the historical development of psychological and behavioural sciences, the debates have had little impact on what we teach undergraduate students or how psychological work is actually done.

These are not merely academic concerns. In this chapter, we turn to where issues raised so far connect directly with the work of psychologists outside of academia, in what is affectionately referred to as the "real world". In some cases, where research meets work with the most vulnerable clients of applied practice, these are matters of life and death (Grubbs, 2022). Research findings ultimately reach expression in impacts upon or changes to what things get done in fields of applied endeavour or how those things are achieved.

Psychologists pride ourselves on our evidence-based approaches to the development and deployment of methods and techniques in applied settings. While other major professions have undergraduate programmes that provide them with the means of entering applied settings directly upon graduation, psychology has staunchly maintained a requirement for comfort with research methods and empirical work before a person can work directly in the field, at least for roles that include the term "psychologist".

Becoming a doctor or nurse does not first require an entire degree in biology. Becoming an engineer does not require a separate prior degree in physics. But there are no undergraduate

DOI: 10.4324/9781003503873-7

degrees in clinical, health, or educational psychology. This in itself is evidence of the fact that the science is still maturing. Matters are volatile and fast-moving as we struggle to find a core set of tenets that can be subscribed to by all of those working in the field. To be a psychological professional then is not only to be a practitioner but also still a scientist able to systematically collect data, review evidence, and maintain up-to-date expertise in a research domain, all the while working with clients in whatever capacity we apply. Or at least, that's the idea.

For many professionals working in settings of applied psychological practice, our vague or implicit characterisations of the relationship between collectives and individuals that underlie problems that we have discussed, such as the Aggregation Delusion or the Specificity Delusion, are not abstract theoretical questions. They are a continuous challenge to effective and ethical practice. On the one hand, there is a widely held commitment to evidence-based practice and often also to a scientist-practitioner model in which the professional ensures that their actions and efforts are in line with what the published research indicates are the most effective techniques. On the other hand, the inability to draw reliable inferences about individual cases from collective statistics leaves a gap that can, at present, only be bridged by intuition and personal sensitivity for a client whose individual worth and dignity are central to good practice.

In this stressful tension between the collective and the individual, with psychological research conducted at a scale that is quite different from applied psychological practice, we find the "research-practice gap". As we will see, the research-practice gap is a complex phenomenon. It has theoretical and practical but also professional facets to it. The professional aspect is most clearly articulated in the principal focus of this chapter, what we will call the Scientist-Practitioner Delusion.

The Scientist-Practitioner Delusion

Fundamental to the research-practice gap is that, 70 years on from the explicit introduction of the scientist-practitioner model (Raimy, 1950), the only thing on which both research and applied professional communities agree is that it is a good idea. Just how that idea should be implemented remains a matter of uncertainty, confusion, and contestation (Belar, 2000; Lampropolous & Spengler, 2002; Milne & Paxton, 1998; Richardson, 2009; Smedslund, 2016; Stricker, 2002). The result is that the scientist-practitioner model is more aspiration than reality (Richardson, 2009), and a rather unclear aspiration at that.

For form's sake we will refer to this as the Scientist-Practitioner Delusion, but we should be fair to all concerned: though many support it as an ideal, few believe that ideal is really implemented in common practice.

> ***The Scientist-Practitioner Delusion:*** The unjustified assumptions adopted by many practitioners that: (1) the evidence base for their practice is scientific; (2) the evidence base can be extrapolated to the individuals addressed in practice; and, (3) practice is undertaken in a scientific manner.

The first two assumptions of this delusion have been considered in great depth in earlier chapters of this book but in a way that is applicable to psychology in general. Here we will consider further sources of evidence that are peculiar to the practice domain and so reflect directly on these assumptions. Following this, we consider the small amount of evidence that exists pertaining to the third assumption.

We have noted in previous chapters that some of the problems facing psychological science are created and maintained when criteria of research quality conflict with professional incentives, expectations, and typical practice within the discipline. These structures of the profession tend to impose an inertia to practices that makes them resistant to easy reform (Nosek et al., 2012). Where two (or indeed more) such professions intersect, the challenges posed by the combination of these multiple structural constraints are more likely to multiply than cancel out.

The existing literature on the research-practice gap across a number of fields of psychological work is replete with the frustrations of professionals from both communities (e.g., Lilienfield et al., 2013; Peterson, 1991; Haefell, 2022; in clinical psychology; Broekkamp & van Hout-Walters, 2007; Christodoulu, 2014; De Leeuw et al., 2022; in education; Fernández-Álvarez et al., 2020; Lampropolous & Spengler, 2002; in psychotherapy). All agree that there is a problem, but different professional perspectives and values seem to make it difficult for each group to accommodate or often even understand the stance of the other (see also Trafimow & Osman, 2022, on applied social psychology as applied to public policy).

Researchers express frustration with the slow and uncertain manner in which insights from research are taken up in applied domains. The pace of changes in practice is typically slow and often incomplete. Researchers lament an unwillingness of practitioners to commit to evidence-based practice or empirically supported techniques for professional practice (Hargreaves, 1997; Lilienfeld et al., 2019; Stewart et al., 2012; Tavris, 2003; Teachman et al., 2012). Some researchers express concerns that this results in, for instance, clinical (Lilienfeld, 2007) or educational interventions (Christodoulu, 2014) that are more shaped by ideology, tradition, or fashion than by solid empirical evidence. The potential harm or just wasted effort and opportunity cost that can result from well-intended but inadequately informed practice is significant.

For their part, practitioners clearly express a commitment to evidence-based practice and are roundly positive about the need for empirically informed techniques and interventions (Georgiou et al., 2023; Stewart et al., 2012). Their perception of the gap, however, is one that emphasises a failure of researchers to communicate effectively in terms that are properly meaningful within the applied domain (see, for illustrations, Olson et al.'s (2024) examination of differences between laboratory and clinical contexts in understanding reasoning; Peterson's (1991) concerns about the break between scientific and clinical formulation of questions; Georgiou et al. (2023) and Broekkamp and van Hout-Walters (2007) on the incompatible perspectives in education). They also argue that evidence extant within applied settings is undervalued in research (Carter, 2002; Green, 2008; Kazdin, 2008).

This mis-calibration of research and clinical relevance was apparent in the years immediately following the introduction of the scientist-practitioner model in the 1950s; it was first introduced specifically for the domain of clinical psychology. During this time the emphasis in graduate training remained on scientific skills, with the seeming expectation that such generalisable values as critical thinking and systematic examination of evidence would prove adequate to clinical problem solving (Peterson, 1991). What appears to be the typical outcome was that graduates of such programmes were more likely to work as academics than move into clinical practice, while those who went on to work in clinical practice felt ill-prepared for the task (Peterson, 1991; Stricker & Cummings, 1992). In response to this, a movement toward distinct "professional schools" arose, where course curricula shifted the balance in favour of the cultivation of applied skills.

Though there are clearly some professionals who straddle the divide, the reality is that people working in these two facets of psychological work tend to have somewhat distinct values.

Though workers in both are motivated to provide the best possible support and service to those who need it, there is an irreducible difference of perspective that we find difficult to overcome.

One of the classic distinctions used to understand the difference in values between academic and applied psychological practice is that between nomothetic and idiographic investigations. The categories were introduced by the philosopher Wilhelm Windelband to characterise two different kinds of knowledge and, ultimately then, two different kinds of disciplines.

The nomothetic concerns generalities and universals, the search for knowledge of rules, laws, and consistencies. The idiographic concerns the specific but also the contingent – not generalities but particulars in their particularity. In psychology, the distinction is most commonly associated with one of the great figures of personality psychology, Gordon Allport (1937), who acknowledged that as scientists psychologists had an interest in both kinds of knowledge. The question was not whether we should accept one or the other as the true aim of the discipline but rather when we should adopt one or the other. In fact, Windelband's distinction had been introduced to psychological discourse as early as 1898, when Hugo Munsterberg raised the issue in a presidential address to the American Psychological Association (it would be published in 1899). Munsterberg noted how the nomothetic and idiographic seemed to address questions of what he termed the *individual* and the *overindividual*, but immediately pointed out that both of these were included in the proper subject matter of psychology. We can see, therefore, that awareness of tensions in psychology as simultaneously concerned with individuals and aggregates, and how to relate them, was present explicitly from the inception of the discipline.

For Munsterberg, the disciplinary – in fact, the epistemological – boundary that really made a difference was that between art and science. He saw art as interested in just the uniqueness of the individual, which is where the beauty of immediate experience is to be found. Science is interested in the connectedness of things – even where the focus may be on the individual, it is the individual as a manifestation of the general or the ways in which they are related to or connected with others that matter. "Wherever is full isolation of facts there is beauty, wherever truth there must be full connection" (Munsterberg, 1899, p. 15).

Just prior to this definition, though, Munsterberg makes an important point: "Life does not isolate fully and gives no complete connection" (1899, p. 15). That is, when dealing with real life, we can be neither purely artists nor scientists (at least in the stark terms that Munsterberg introduced them). We value neither just the aesthetics of experience nor just the truth of the matter. We must acknowledge and cope with both. This is a laudable articulation of the tension that exists for the psychological practitioner working with individual clients.

The individual must be the focus of intent and interest of the practising professional in all of their contingent individuality. This would seem to imply a firm commitment to idiographic knowledge. But in life the idiographic is not entirely isolated from the nomothetic; the potency of a professional's practice arises from the extent to which the two can be woven coherently together. On the one hand, psychological science appears to provide principles and interventions informed by evidence developed within a nomothetic framework. On the other hand, these interventions can only be implemented within a particular therapeutic relationship that is specific to the professional and their client, in a manner that is appropriately sensitive to the key details of the unique contingent history of the particular client.

In their practice, then, the effective, evidence-informed professional performs a kind of alchemical transformation of the general into the specific, in collaboration with their clients. To describe the process in this way perhaps sounds rather glib, but we should not underestimate it. Practitioners cannot treat their clients as generic or average but work with them to make use of methods that have been developed with groups, and iteratively tune them to address the specifics of the client's experience.

Note that this is not to say that scientific research can have no role in therapeutic decision making – quite the contrary. Stewart et al. (2012), for instance, make clear that the use of structural evidence-supported therapeutic techniques has not been found to undermine the therapeutic alliance between practitioner and client. It does mean, however, that to be fully valid, scientific knowledge needs to be developed and organised in such a way as to be coherent with the processes of individual relationship dynamics within which therapeutic work – or indeed other transformational psychological work, such as education – takes place (Green, 2008; Kazdin, 2016). Insofar as there are consistent patterns in people's behaviour and experience, those consistencies can be identified and their reliability used as a lever for professional practice to achieve important positive results. But the individuality of people means that such guidance will always be uncertain and must be judiciously managed in each case (Beck & Jackson, 2022).

It is much easier to articulate these differences in professional values than it is to overcome them. The difference in orientation entails practical distinctions in how different phenomena and experiences are weighted by the different communities. It is in these more practical matters that we see the greatest resistance by both bodies of professionals to accommodating the perspective of the other.

Practical Facets of the Research-Practice Gap

There is an important asymmetry in the dialogue between researchers and applied professionals that pertains to the research-practice gap. Criticism of practitioners by researchers is experienced by applied professionals as pressure to change. The balance of power is heavily weighted by the status of science in society, such that overcoming the research-practice gap is something that requires changes in applied practice, where intuitions, traditions, and ideologies are perceived as taking the place that evidence should play in the evaluating of interventions or the planning of therapeutic actions.

Conversely, criticism of researchers by practitioners seems to carry much less force. Some researchers do acknowledge the need to find ways to make research more practice relevant or to frame questions in ways more amenable to applied considerations (Beutler et al., 2002; Green, 2008). The greater proportion of researcher discourse, however, addresses the gap as a form of resistance to evidence-supported interventions. This resistance is a problem to be overcome or routed around through improved dissemination of research outcomes or maybe through the development of new techniques for persuasion and institutional change in the form of "implementation science".

Both practitioners and researchers believe that applied practice should change and continually develop to reduce the research-practice gap, but it seems to be mostly practitioners who seem to believe that research methods need to do the same.

Though applied workers have argued repeatedly and vehemently that the complexity and individuality of particular cases is important data that should be incorporated into our knowledge production practices, these calls are downplayed by advocates of research-driven interventions. Perhaps the clearest illustration of this is in discussions regarding evidence-based practice in clinical settings, which revolves around the differential value of probabilistic and intuitive (sometimes referred to as "holistic") judgements. Paul Meehl is once again a dominant figure in the debate here, making an early and powerful intervention (Meehl, 1954).

From early days in the systematic evaluation of clinical practices and scientific addressing of clinical concerns, practitioners raised queries as to whether the kinds of findings produced on the basis of statistics could be applied to the case of individual clients. That is, professional intuition and judgement were that there were important limits to the extent that valid clinical decisions about individuals could be derived from research on groups. In this context, Meehl[1] famously defended the relative value of probabilistic information through the analogy of a game of Russian roulette.

We might grant, he argued, that statistics cannot be used to predict the individual case. But probabilistic knowledge remains better than no knowledge at all. Given two six-shooter pistols, one loaded with one bullet and one loaded with five, and a canister spun so that the aligned chamber is random, which would we prefer to use? We cannot predict the individual case with certainty, but in a situation of uncertainty (which is *always* the case in real-life clinical settings), a bet is all we can make, so let's make the safer one. Proponents of evidence-based practice fully acknowledge that such knowledge is limited, but somewhat limited information is always better than the vagaries of gut instinct – particularly as the limitations of judgements based on clinical experience alone are not without their dangers (Dawes, 2005; Lilienfeld, 2007; Lilienfeld et al., 2019).

Put in such an uncomfortable position, we are certainly with Meehl. If we've been forced into a game of Russian roulette, we'll take the one-bullet gun, please, Paul.

Proponents of evidence-based practice in clinical psychology and psychotherapy validly rehearse this simple point: reinforcing that knowledge does not need to be absolute to be useful. What really matters is whether it is better than the alternatives (Ægisdóttir et al., 2006; Dawes, 2005; Garb & Wood, 2019). In a domain as complex and unpredictable as human psychology, any improvement in our odds is hard-earned, and the notion that statistical predictions would have to be perfect or anything close in order to supplant otherwise unstructured professional intuition is not just scientifically close-minded; it is ethically dubious. For many researchers, the evidence-based practice vs. professional judgement debate is considered closed.

We wholly support evidence-based practice in clinical settings. However, on the basis of the preceding chapters, we argue that there are important nuances to this discussion that have not seen sufficient consideration. That is to say that in the blunt terms in which the options are often put by those citing Meehl's choice of weapons, the evidence clearly favours probabilistic knowledge. The extent to which clinical resistance to this decision is represented as ideological, backward, or otherwise flatly ignorant is unhelpful and blind to important nuance. A crucial point is this: research, such as that conducted in randomised controlled trials (RCTs) as they are typically organised and reported, does not provide probabilistic knowledge of the kind described for Meehl's guns (see Lamiell, 2019, for a similar argument).

To argue that clinical decisions based on RCTs are equivalent to deciding between Meehl's guns is to fall foul of the Specificity Delusion as we described it in Chapter 4. RCTs, as they are typically reported, do not provide probabilistic knowledge of this kind – only a pervasiveness analysis (see Chapter 9) or some other means of directly enumerating the prevalence of effects within a given population can offer such insights.

This is not at all to argue that we can afford to ignore the relevant research in this area, however. Despite the constraints on logic and inference that aggregate statistics impose, there is clear and reliable evidence for the superiority of formal prediction methods over the more holistic and intuitive predictions practitioners might make on the basis of their professional experience. Perhaps the most persuasive evidence with regard to this issue is a meta-analysis conducted by Grove et al. (2000). This review study is a high-water mark in the examination of the differential value of clinical vs. what they refer to as "mechanical predictions". In this context, mechanical predictions are any process by which a professional uses a statistical process, formula, algorithm, or other formal tool for the purposes of predicting a specific outcome. By contrast, clinical judgements are more or less "everything else". These are sometimes referred to as "holistic" judgements in more recent literature (Dana & Thomas, 2006; Neumann et al., 2023) and involve the expert's broad consideration of all of the available evidence and the drawing of a conclusion based on that consideration.

Grove et al. (2000) analysed 136 studies where data allowed for direct comparisons between the accuracy of mechanical and clinical predictions (this was not always the specific research question of the study being reviewed). In their results they describe an unmistakable superiority of mechanical prediction across a number of potential forms of comparison. The data presented are clear, the analyses largely straightforward, and the overall conclusion compelling. However, it would be doing Grove et al. an injustice to claim that this strong trend was all there is to the story. Two other points in particular stand out.

The first is that a large number of studies show only a small advantage of mechanical prediction. Those showing a strong superiority for mechanical methods greatly outnumber those showing a strong advantage for a clinical approach, but a simple dismissal of clinical judgement as valueless in comparison is not warranted. Rather, the findings invite us to ask more fine-grained questions. This leads us to the second key point.

Frustratingly, Grove et al. (2000) were unable to identify any particular characteristics of the prediction tasks or tools – particular kinds of information, levels of experience of the judges, or use of particular instruments – that served to reliably make a difference to the accuracy of predictions. The sole exception to this was the use of clinical interviews, which served to *weaken* rather than strengthen clinical predictions (Grove et al., 2000, p. 24).

Given that there is some evidence that the difference in accuracy between good clinical judgement and mechanical prediction is marginal, but the specific means by which mechanical prediction is superior is unclear, we can perhaps understand practitioners' frustration that the resulting recommendation is a necessary faith in mechanical prediction, rather than more specific insight into how judgement might actually be improved (Dawes, 2005).

It is possible to venture more than this, however. It may be that much of the advantage arises merely through the fact that the mechanical process forces a level of systematicity that is otherwise too easy for us human beings to lose (even when highly experienced in a given field). Grove and Vrieze (2013) suggest such a conclusion when trying to make sense of Goldberg's (1970) finding that simple models used to predict clinicians' predictions were often more accurate than the clinicians they were supposed to be predicting. That is, intended to predict clinicians making predictions about outcomes, the simple models were often more accurate predictions of the outcomes than the clinicians were!

Dana and Thomas (2006) also suggest this significant role for systematicity, finding through experimental work that holistic judgements can be made more accurate than some forms of mechanical prediction when the relevant experiences being weighed are systematically evoked and considered. Conversely, replicating the general trend in the literature, when judges were not directed to be systematic but encouraged to be holistic in their predictions, their performance dropped below that of even simple mechanical techniques.

This tantalising indication may have something to tell us about how we can orient ourselves when it comes to shifting between idiographic and nomothetic perspectives. In the case of prediction, we have just seen that there is a clear implication for how applied practitioners and their clients can benefit from greater systematicity.

The careful and deliberate approach to observation and judgement is the very foundation of scientific practice and may in fact be at the basis of one of the other frequent criticisms by practitioners of researchers.

Along with the concern that aggregate statistics cannot provide valid insights into individuals, perhaps the most frequent concern raised by applied professionals in the literature is that the participants in research studies are often unrepresentative of clients in the real world. Where samples in research are selected to be "clean" – presenting with only specific, target diagnoses or characteristics – typical cases are complex or messy. The idiographic would seem to swamp the nomothetic.

Researchers are correct to be undeterred by such complexity, but judgements of generalisability should be grounded in a clear-eyed understanding of how representative the research sample is to the population as a whole. That is, we should have as an ambition the prospect of probabilistic or actuarial knowledge championed by Meehl, but that means producing appropriate data.

Samples of research participants are selected to cohere systematically with the theoretical framing of the research question, but there remains a great deal of work to be done to systematically survey the population as a whole and therefore to be able to properly understand the relationship between the population and that sample.

Lilienfeld et al. (2013) review various reasons for practitioners' resistance to evidence-based practice and offer suggestions as to why we should not be put off by such resistance. Some of the reasons outlined for unwillingness to engage with evidence-based practice are certainly problematic. For instance, where commitment to therapeutic techniques seems to be ideological rather than sensitive to evidence, it is a clear cause of concern. It is the case in any profession that there are examples of clinicians and therapists whose standards and practices need to be improved. As Carter (2002) notes, however, by far the most commonly described therapeutic model is the "eclectic", a fact that arises precisely because clinicians *are* sensitive to the effectiveness of individual techniques and their value for different clients and different challenges. As a result, clinicians change things up accordingly.

These real differences in how researchers and practitioners consider and work with people in the course of their professional activities are compounded by other practical facets of the research-practice gap that are much more basic. Applied professionals have identified demands on their time to be a major obstacle to their engaging fully with research (Addis, 2002; Gallo & Barlow, 2012; Stewart et al., 2012). Even academics report difficulty making time to keep up with the literature (Archer et al., 2019), and so the possibility that clinicians, educators, or other practitioners working under heavy caseloads will keep up to date seems remote.

Continuous refinements and examination of ever more fine-grained research questions exacerbate this issue, as research vocabularies become ever more technical and niche (McBeath et al., 2019). The incentive structures for researchers ultimately place a premium on channels and forums for sharing their work that are poorly accessible and ill-suited to busy psychologists in applied fields.

A striking illustration of scientific publication being unfit for the purpose of communicating with applied professionals is that of implementation science, a field whose entire *raison d'etre* is effectively to transfer knowledge between researchers and applied workers and thereby close the research-practice gap. Ironically, recent evidence suggests that what insights implementation science has produced thus far have remained almost entirely within academia and had surprisingly little impact in applied fields (Westerlund et al., 2019).

As research methods and analytical techniques have also seen continuous development, the sheer amount of knowledge required to remain abreast of new research work is challenging. The difficulty in cultivating expertise enough in both research and applied skills to embody the scientist-practitioner should not surprise us. Consistent findings regarding the limits of expertise and the difficulty in developing multiple forms of expertise would seem to militate against the likelihood that professionals could effectively straddle both domains without it being inherent in their occupational role (as an academic clinician, for instance, or a similar dual-aspect job).

We write these words fully in the knowledge that there are many examples of working professionals who *do* divide their time between research and practice. Such professionals (perhaps you are one!) strike some kind of balance between academic work and work with clients and patients, with the two often in significant overlap. Across professional schools of various kinds as well as more traditional academic institutions, the existence of researching-practitioners and clinically active researchers are a vitally important part of the ecosystem around applied psychology. We recognise the often extraordinary level of dedication, effort, and teamwork that is required to maintain such positions. However, such bridging positions have existed for the entire history of professional psychology and certainly since the development of the scientist-practitioner model. Despite the immense effort in keeping one foot in both worlds, the research-practice gap has remained stubbornly unclosed. It would seem that the distinct vocabularies and practices of the different communities prevent the two from being easily brought together even where a person develops such dual expertise. We were struck by one observation by a philosopher embedded for a prolonged period within a programme of psychiatric research. De Haan (2020, p. ix) noted that the clinicians appeared to "code switch", speaking in one manner, with one set of vocabulary relating to experience, feeling and behaviour in the clinic, while another, more brain-based, at professional conferences.

It would seem that even where research and practice come together within the work of individual psychologists, something resists closing the gap completely.

The Broken Feedback Loop

With respect to the third assumption underlying the Scientist-Practitioner Delusion, there is an important role that practitioners can play with respect to providing feedback to researchers about the evidence produced by research regarding treatment options. One of the aims of the scientist-practitioner model (Richardson, 2009) is to train new practitioners as scientists in the sense that they are capable of conducting psychological research as well as being critical consumers of others' research. In turn, they are trained as professional psychologists to approach their practice in a scientific manner, applying best practice as suggested by research in a style that respects fundamental features of the scientific method (e.g., objective and systematic observation and measurement, accurate non-biased recording of data, analysis of data). Under such circumstances, it would be expected that clinicians would notice if the methods suggested to be effective by research just did not work in practice. Unfortunately, though, we are in the dark here: clinicians may well be noticing such things, or they could be quite satisfied with the methods they have been applying, but such information is not forthcoming. The feedback loop is not routinely completed, and this may be related to incentives inherent in professional practice:

1. With respect to making accurate diagnoses of psychological problems and applying effective treatments, there are few incentives for getting it right or, at the least, getting it right most of the time. Indeed, clinicians are paid in any case.
2. Clinicians do not record the necessary data and/or make these data public. There is no incentive to do so, and this would take time away from the money-making side of the business.
3. If clinicians did record the necessary data, they would be reflecting on the effectiveness of their own practice. Although this would be valuable for the clinician, this is not conducive to objective data collection. An independent observer and record collector would be required. There are few incentives to provide such a resource.

Clinicians may feel that they are doing a good job because of all the clients who tell them they feel better. This may well be the case, but again we do not have the appropriate data to critically test this assertion. Important elements of research design we instruct our undergraduate students in suggest a few ways in which relying on clinician-reported data can lead to misleading results:

1. *Demand characteristics*: The clients who claim to be feeling better could be responding to how they think the clinician wants them to respond. Also, there is an element of self-fulfilling prophecy in the clinical setting: Clinicians expect to make a difference in their clients. Clients expect clinicians will be able to help them feel better. Expectations are heavily influential in perceptions and may explain what could amount to just placebo effects.
2. *Subject mortality*: Only those people who respond well to treatment remain in treatment. The rest discontinue treatment, leaving a bunch of satisfied people.
3. *Control conditions*: The clinical setting is not conducive to the utilisation of control conditions, where control clients would have the same experience as treatment clients, except for the therapy. We tell our students that the best way to tell if a treatment condition has an effect is to compare it with an identical condition without the treatment. The rationale is we can tell if any change observed in the treatment subjects is related to the treatment or some other time-induced change. Of course, this suggestion to engage in some form of control design ignores what we have already said about the Delusions of Experimental Control and Group Comparison. As an alternative, some form of single-subject design (e.g., extended periods of no treatment to establish stable baseline measurements with which to compare measurements during treatment periods; see Chapter 9), especially when combined with the results of other single-subject experiments, could provide a useful evaluation of the efficacy of a particular treatment method. At present, though, there appears little incentive for clinicians to adopt such a practice. Clients, insurers (Van Geert & de Ruiter, 2022, pp. 138, 141), and government health services are unlikely to want to pay for such a service either.

Thus, there is a tension between the assumptions and methods of psychological research and the reality of applied professional practice, which makes it difficult to get value from research. This results in a difficulty in implementing the scientist-practitioner model of practice, which may go some way to explain why so few practitioners actually work according to this model

(Richardson, 2009). Some practitioners adopt a far more *ad hoc* mode of practice. For example, Smedslund (2016, p. 10) suggests that

> In psychological practice,...the initial low predictability associated with interventions is handled by trying out small tentative steps at a time, and the ensuing concrete changes in a client are accepted as useful only when they are becoming sufficiently dependable over time and situation to be noticeable in ordinary everyday life.

Such an experimental approach might be considered scientific but does not conform to the scientist-practitioner model. In that model, practice is supposed to follow scientifically validated methods. Allowing individual results to dictate method suggests more of a craft than a validated form of practice. It also suggests that the apparently validated practice method cannot be applied well to real-world clients. Furthermore, this information is probably not being reported in a way that can inform the practice of others. Ultimately, then, the feedback loop between research and practice is broken, with the corollary being that the two worlds of psychological research and practice can continue in blissful ignorance of whether their work has any validity.

We have provided a number of arguments in this book for why there is little justification for using the results of scientific experiments in psychology, when they are conducted in their typical form, to inform the professional practice of psychology in applied settings. And, as disturbing as this conclusion is, there is an obvious means for determining whether the psychology profession has been misled by psychological science. There could be systematic evaluations of the effects of psychological treatments in clinical settings. Unfortunately, this seems to be rare in clinical practice (Bugatti et al., 2023; Catts et al., 2010; Halford & Frost, 2021) and yet is a seemingly essential part of the ethos behind the scientist-practitioner model. Furthermore, in the one example we could find where this has been undertaken in a practice setting (N = 1439), psychotherapy was found to reduce depressive symptoms in 51.4% of the sample, but 44.8% experienced no reliable change, and 3.8% displayed reliable deterioration in their condition (Bugatti et al., 2023). In terms of the likelihood of psychotherapy being beneficial to a person, this is an outcome similar to tossing a coin.

The Theoretical Facet of the Research-Practice Gap

Kurt Lewin famously pronounced that "There is nothing so practical as a good theory" (Lewin, 1951, p. 169). We noted in the previous chapter that there is more than one kind of theory whose differences we should be careful not to overlook and that they are practical for different purposes. Descriptive theories, particularly in the form of theories of principle, can offer structure and coherence to an otherwise messy and disparate set of observations. In doing so, they provide the means to calibrate and refine constructive, explanatory theories, which often offer the kind of predictive and controlling grasp on the real world that we look for from good science (McGann & Speelman, 2020) and from which we can derive effective practices, technologies, and interventions.

Psychology's disorganised, unstructured attempts at theory development that we surveyed in the previous chapter leave the applied fields in something of a theoretical limbo. There is little option but to snatch at prospects and concepts in a way that is frustratingly piecemeal. In the previous chapter, we touched on Hale et al.'s (2020) agonising review of theories of behaviour change – a concept central to domains such as health psychology, counselling, and psychotherapy.

Given this illustrative lack of coherence, it would again seem entirely unsurprising that the most common framework cited by working therapists for their practice is "eclectic".

Carter (2002) has argued that the variability of eclecticism is, in fact, a result of the kind of continuous results-sensitive tuning of practice quite similar to what proponents of evidence-based practice would promote. As Carter put it, the messiness of real-world experience and relationships is part of the crucial break between the universalist tendencies of basic research and the idiographic commitments of health and support services.

Psychological research too often models the data, rather than identifying the underlying principles that generate those data (Freedman, 1985). In the place of coherent and generative principles, we are left with a disparate grab-bag of theoretical positions. All that is left to allow practitioners to bridge between nomothetic and idiographic aspects of their work is professional intuition and personal sensitivity. The uniqueness and individuality of human beings ensure that specific personal relationships and experiences will always be like local weather patterns – infinitely textured and impossible to finely predict over any extended period of time.

Nevertheless, it is also true that scientific research can better serve professional practice by supporting knowledge in terms that enable the individual case to be interpretable in its details within the context of a collective landscape. As we have explored in these first chapters, the most common present research practices prevent this, obscuring the roles that individual data can play in the patterns of collective measurements and calculations, without any theoretical or analytic tools to support the exploration of possible forms of relationship between the person and the population.

Avoiding Nihilism and Dodos

A wary, or indeed weary, reader at this point might lay either one or both of two related criticisms by Lilienfeld et al. (2013). The first is an accusation of nihilism, a despairing claim that because of the complexity of our subject matter, we can have no meaningful information that is relevant to inform professional practice. The second is what they call the Dodo's Verdict: "Everybody wins and they must all have prizes", as though there were no differential value of different kinds of insight.

As we have noted before, we are optimistic and excited about the science of psychology and deny both charges.

We might take the Dodo's Verdict first, as the narrative framing of the point is an interesting one. The phrase is a reference to Alice in Wonderland, in which a number of characters take part in a race, and the verdict is a rather cowardly refusal to make a difficult or unpopular judgement, however valid it might be. Lilienfeld et al. do not make much of the concept of the *race*, but the point is nevertheless framed in rather zero-sum terms – as though the only valid result involves some sort of *win*.

But knowledge doesn't work that way. It is not something that accretes, unidimensionally, with some forms of investigation or analysis always providing "more" and some providing "less". Rather, it is often the case that knowledge is contextual, providing insight for certain pragmatic purposes under some conditions. There is no single "finish line" to the race by which we might judge the always-greater value of one piece of knowledge in all circumstances over another. There are contexts in which the outcomes of nomothetically oriented investigations will offer the greatest insight and others where professional judgement on the idiographic details will be the only effective guide. The question is not which perspective should "win", but rather how we can recognise the circumstances in which we should draw from one and when from the other, or how we can orient ourselves such that we understand one perspective with respect to the other in specific terms.

To the concerned reader, this may seem a lurch toward the other accusation – that the complexity of psychology means that knowledge is never complete, or worse, that we cannot really know anything. We note, however, that to be critically sensitive to the limitations of all the available sources of knowledge relevant to psychological work is not nihilism but good scientific practice. To argue that typical research designs and analyses do not provide the kinds of information most informative to practitioners, while also fundamentally agreeing with the value of an evidence-based practice approach, cannot be nihilism unless these things are somehow mutually exclusive. They are not.

Instead, we suggest that, given our improved sensitivity to the challenges facing scientific psychology, a bridging of the research-practice gap will involve a transformation of research practices as much as it will a change in clinical, educational, health, and other applied ones. We must look to systematically develop ways in which we might better understand how the individual and aggregate, the specific and the general, relate to one another.

The challenge of the research-practice gap concerns not only how to derive individual predictions from collective observations. There also remains the challenge of how to systematise recordings and observations of real-world cases, phenomena, and events, work that is significantly undervalued in contemporary psychological science (see Chapter 8). The result is that crucial knowledge about overall prevalence and patterns of different kinds of psychological phenomena is still in a relatively poorly developed state.

The point is not to abandon or stall evidence-based practices. Rather, the point is that to overcome the Scientist-Practitioner Delusion will require changes at both poles of that continuum. We must recognise that there is value and insight to be gained if we see the need for more systematic influence going in both directions – from research into the real world, but also from the real world into research.

Closing the Loop Between Lab and Field

Several of the criticisms of psychology's poor theoretical state concern the lack of an integrative or over-arching framework (Borsboom, 2013; Muthukrishna & Henrich, 2019; Wilson, 2011). Muthukrishna and Henrich (2019) explicitly suggest a theory that addresses mechanisms of development and change as offering such a framework, but if Einstein is correct, then this is putting the cart before the horse. The encompassing framework is more likely to be, in the first instance, a theory of principle rather than a constructive one – descriptive rather than explanatory.

Where a theory of principle is sought, it becomes important for us to understand the role and value of observations of our phenomena of interest outside of the lab, in the "psychologist-free environment of behavior" (Barker, 1968, p. 4; with recognition of the necessary irony that such attempts would involve). If we are to develop descriptive but principled accounts of the structure and pattern of relationships between key aspects of our science, we must seek these patterns in the wild before we can hope to consistently produce them in the laboratory. Where the development of a theory of principle is considered a valid and useful effort for psychology, we will have to spend more time than we have done gathering information on the naturally occurring behaviour of human beings in our natural habitat. The challenge of the research-practice gap is not only how to derive individual predictions from collective observations.

There also remains important systematic observational work that is significantly undervalued in contemporary psychological science. We take up these ideas in greater depth in Chapter 8.

We believe that a more refined understanding of different kinds of theory and their complementary roles in the development of science offers one way to articulate the importance of such efforts. Alas, our discipline's blindness to distinctions between, and distinct roles of, different kinds of theory offers a somewhat pessimistic outlook for such work to be undertaken. We believe that this leaves psychologists trying to do science with one arm tied behind their backs – addressing questions of data collection and theory building from only one aspect of a complementary set of perspectives.

Advancement of knowledge is not a unitary phenomenon, however. It is not a slow march of progress from ignorance to enlightenment. It is more like way-finding within a complex landscape of ignorance, certainty, and value; not measured on a single dimension. It is neither simply the improving accuracy of theories nor the increasing confidence in the results of statistical tests. Advancement is multidimensional, depending on the kind of understanding that theories provide and the multifarious values of these different theories for different purposes. In the previous chapter, we outlined just two different kinds of theories, but also that these different theories have different relationships with data and tend to give differential roles to different kinds of data. Calibrating our data production practices with theory is thus not a linear process but one with a feedback loop. Best methodological practice will depend on our understanding of theories, and those theories will thus shift as we continue to generate and interpret different data. We must take great care to avoid any simple hierarchy of priorities. Reforms of methodological practice must make reference to the theories that frame them, while calls for improvement in theory must similarly situate themselves within questions of method.

Having taken stock of the array of delusions that beset the behavioural sciences, which result in what we have called the Great Psychology Delusion, you would be forgiven for thinking that we are pessimists about the prospects of a scientific psychology. Happily, nothing could be further from the truth. It is a demonstration of the strength of scientific principles that we, and the long traditions of analysis within the relevant literature, are able to make these diagnoses. What is more, pointing out these problems is the necessary first step to remedying them. Through the preceding chapters we have surveyed the challenges – delusions, tempting illusions, and false leads – faced by researchers and practitioners. With a clearer perspective on the status of things, we can turn, in Part II, to survey some of the ways in which we can advance from here.

Note

1 We should note that though Meehl's parable is most often used to argue for a critical evaluation of clinical judgement, the book from which it is drawn (Meehl, 1954) does not argue for a dismissal of the importance of clinical experience – it is, rather, a careful consideration of the different domains of work in which different forms of judgement are valid and reliable. Meehl was very aware of the need for appropriate contextualising of tools with tasks.

PART II

Towards a More Successful Psychological Science

7

A PLURALISTIC PSYCHOLOGICAL SCIENCE

Let's be honest, it's been rough going to this point. Through all of the preceding chapters, we have explored deep, crucial problems with some of the most fundamental, most frequently used modes of design, analysis, and interpretation of psychological research. We have done so rather starkly, we think unflinchingly, because we feel it important to drive the point home. These are not small issues, they are not simple ones, and they are not new.

Psychologists of various stripes – clinicians, statisticians, historians, theoreticians, educational, therapeutic, and numerous kinds of researchers – have been sounding the alarm regarding most of the challenges that we have raised for some time. Often for decades. Our intention with the chapters of Part I was to gather discussion of that material in one place and demonstrate the ways that they interact. We have also attempted to make the point as plainly as we can do, to join this decades long chorus of people aiming to steady the foundations of research in behaviour and experience.

Despite these problems, we noted in Chapter 1 that we remain optimistic about the future of the psychological sciences. In this and the following chapters, we explain why.

There already exists some work examining some of the reasons for inertia with regard to reform of research practice (see, e.g., Chambers, 2017; Munafò et al., 2017; Nosek et al., 2012; Simmons et al., 2011; Wasserstein et al., 2019). Much of it is the product of institutional and professional structures. In these next few chapters, we address this point but note that it combines with and compounds significant conceptual issues around our subject matter, around the purposes and functions of our theories, and around key points of laboratory research practice. In this Part II of the book, we use these diagnoses to make some concrete suggestions as to how we can ground our scientific practice more firmly in the phenomena of our subject matter and overcome our delusions.

Looking Forward

We have argued repeatedly through the preceding chapters that a major underlying factor in the existence of the Great Psychology Delusion, and the problems that have given rise to the various

DOI: 10.4324/9781003503873-9

crises in the discipline, is that psychology's subject matter is complex. The Great Delusion – that psychology is a valid science despite it being grounded in untested and invalid assumptions – is almost unavoidable once we approach the messy tangle of different phenomena with the methods that we do.

We're not just hand waving at the difficulty of the science here, but making an explicit point regarding the manner in which psychological phenomena arise and develop in the first place. People are sensitive to what's going on around them and act accordingly. Their actions, in turn, affect what is going on, which feeds back into the person's awareness and their on-going flow of behaviour. There are numerous forms of such feedback relations, the end result of which is that it is difficult, if not impossible, to tell simple, linear stories about how psychological phenomena such as behaviour and experience are caused.

What is more, this process of feedback happens at different scales of time – from the immediate way in which movement of the eyes affects the dappling of light on the retinae, to how the movement of the body puts distance between ourselves and some things, while moving us closer to others, all the way to the manner in which the results of scientific psychological work feed into society in various ways, which in turn actually transforms the way events, organisations, and community-scale activities are arranged, making some possible actions available to members of society, while reducing or eliminating others.

We noted in Chapter 1 that our only problem with the idea that "psychology is a science" is the subtle trick done by the singular "a" in that phrase. In this second part of the book, we will outline some key steps that psychological researchers can take that will enable us to better ground and orient ourselves in relation to our subject matter. In this chapter we will raise two crucially related points – the need to be more clear about just what *is* the subject matter of our science (or sciences), and thereby making more clear just what it is we want to know. We will close the chapter with an argument that, in making these things more clear, we will come to realise that psychology needs to be more pluralistic – not "a science", but "sciences".

To address the first issue, we will turn to the question of scale and put to work the recognition, derived from the Aggregation Delusion and its corollaries, that phenomena addressed by different kinds of psychological research methods are different kinds of things, occurring at different scales.

A Question of Scale

As we begin our search for ways to work free of delusions and better ground ourselves in the reality of our subject than current mainstream practices support, a basic logical problem is that because human beings are complex, a collection of them cannot be ergodic. We are, indeed, some of the least ergodic things in the known universe. Knowing what is true of the collective offers surprisingly little information about the individual members of that collective (as we have discussed in terms of the Aggregation Delusion and its corollaries). There is a veil drawn between scales that makes conclusions drawn at one scale (the scale of the group, say) invalid, or at the very least unreliable, at another (the scale of the individual person).

It is surprisingly only recently that the very concept of scale has become the focus of explicit attention. In 2021 two works examining the issue in some depth were published (Di Caglio, 2021; Horton, 2021). These are both inter-disciplinary in character and try to tease apart how scales come to exist and how differences of scale affect the dynamics of phenomena both at their own scale, and at others. We won't get too far into the philosophical weeds here, but both authors make clear that phenomena at one scale cannot be easily mapped simply and directly onto phenomena at another. Larger scale phenomena are not merely smaller scale ones, but "more". Similarly, smaller scale phenomena are not just "shrunk" versions of larger ones. Differences of scale are differences that make a real difference.

It is perhaps trite to note that the move from the quantum to the classical domains in physics involves quite different kinds of phenomena, and concomitantly different appropriate methods of research and analysis. The tools of observation, recording, and measurement appropriate to one scale become inappropriate, even obstacles, at another – the forest comes to dominate where before we examined trees. What is an undifferentiable aggregate at one scale becomes a distinct but coherent phenomenon at another, with a different set of dynamics. The dynamics that govern the behaviour of the forest ecosystem are quite different to those of the individual trees, shrubs, fungi, and wildlife that form it. This is something that occurs in every domain – scale matters, and it cannot be casually dismissed or finessed away (DiCalgio, 2021; Horton, 2021).

To consider an example more directly relevant to psychological research, we return once more to the Aggregation Delusion. The formation and measurement of a sample of participants typically creates a "group", and researchers then work not with a collection of measurements of a given pattern of behaviour, but the statistics that are measurements of that "group" – statistics that may have no related measurement for each of the individual members of the sample. A person and a group are different scales of phenomena, and the non-ergodic nature of human beings means that there is no simple way to treat them as the same kinds of things. As we discussed extensively in Chapter 2, there is no way to sensibly relate conclusions at the scale of the group, to conclusions at the scale of the person.

Both DiCaglio (2021) and Horton (2021) warn that because of these qualitative differences between the dynamics of phenomena at different scales, to orient to a given scale necessarily implies orienting *away* from the others. We cannot coherently address two different scales of phenomena simultaneously. It would be like trying to look at the iris of a person's eye and look at their whole face *at the same time*. Indeed, it becomes a crucial methodological question as to how to mediate between theories of phenomena at different scales. We will return to this point later in the chapter. For now, it is important to recognise that the shift between phenomena at one scale and the phenomena at another cannot be done validly without great care.

We have argued repeatedly that problems such as the Aggregation Delusion and the Specificity Delusion (that conclusions about groups enable predictions of individual people's behaviour) are errors that arise because psychology has played too fast and loose with the difference between the scale of individual human beings and that of the collective. By making ourselves sensitive to differences of scale, we can realise that a sizeable portion of psychological research is conducted in a manner that is "scale-blind". A more successful psychology is one that will adopt a more explicit, deliberate approach to understanding the different scales of psychological phenomena, and carefully calibrating our accounts of the relationships between them. This means that psychology as we know it is likely to separate into more clearly distinct disciplinary endeavours, but also that we can make as an explicit ambition of psychological research the exploration of how these distinct disciplines relate to one another. A more successful psychology will be diverse but inclusive, respectful of real differences but with an aim to collaboration and coordination rather than blithely neglectful or dismissive of those differences.

Psychology, a Disoriented Science

Contemporary psychological science addresses questions at a number of different scales. A brief reflection on the matter provides at least four possible such domains in what we might take to be typical mainstream research (though as the issue of these as different scales has seen little discussion, we will find questions arising about where to draw the lines between some):

- *The physiological*; most frequently and explicitly neurological, but far from exclusively so.
- *The behavioural*; involving the measurement of individual behavioural episodes, the scale at which experimental methods are most frequently oriented.
- *The personal*; the level of individual human beings, the scale addressed most frequently by legal and civic considerations, particularly in the West; ironically probably the scale for which psychology has least developed theories or methods (Shotter, 1998; Valsiner, 1986).
- *The group*; a broad scale spanning small-group samples to populations, the most frequent level of analysis of experimental research through the use of aggregationist statistics; also the level of both method and analysis of inter-individual research.

Orientation to a scale provides for a clear focus on a given phenomenon, but what seems to be unfortunately too-frequent practice within psychological science involves the conflation of scales and the undisciplined use of the same conceptual terms across these different domains without explicit recognition of the fact. Two examples will illustrate. The first is that of cognitive psychological research on deductive reasoning (for illustration only, the same pattern can be found in a wide variety of research fields).

A common form of research as typically conducted on reasoning invites participants to endorse conclusions on the basis of presented premises (e.g., Brisson & Markovits, 2020; Espino & Byrne, 2020). Records are then taken as to the frequency of particular endorsements across a sample, and potentially other variables such as time to endorsement. We might also occasionally see such tasks carried out within an MRI machine, providing BOLD (blood-oxygen-level dependent) signal observations during performance (e.g., Coetzee & Monti, 2018).

The ostensive purpose of such studies is to illuminate the processes by which inferences are produced by a generic, or standard cognitive system, presumably shared by all of the participants (perhaps as an evolutionary inheritance). To the extent that even this broad brush outline is a fair description of the foundational logic of such research, we can see the extent to which this kind of psychological research is disoriented with respect to scale. Quite different phenomena are connected by a shared vocabulary (the same concepts are applied across different scales), but that shared vocabulary is not underpinned by a clear theory that enables us to understand what the relationships between those different phenomena are.

Let us take the four scales identified above. At the scale of *groups* of people, the data from a sample of participants (indeed, the larger the group the better) are collated, summarised, and used to produce aggregate statistics for the purposes of analyses (most frequently through the use of some implementation of the general linear model). There are a number of assumptions underlying such use of aggregate statistics that are problematic here, as we have discussed in previous chapters, but our particular focus is on the extent to which these characteristics of a group are taken to represent a process of inference, and in particular, the extent to which this process is the same thing that is broached by observations or conceptualisations that are applied at the other scales.

The same concept of "inference" can be applied as the process represented by the group statistics, the process completed by a given *person's* cognitive endowment, the process underlying the *behaviour* of pressing a response button in a given instance of task performance, and the process being captured by the recording of the *physiological* BOLD signal in an fMRI study. That this reuse of the same concept is possible is indicative of the extent to which typical discourse in the psychological sciences conflates the dynamics of phenomena across scales, is, indeed, oblivious to the distinctions between them, and applies no explicit framework for managing our understanding of their relationships.

We contend that this problem is not at all specific to the example of inference and reasoning here. Across the entire field of cognitive psychology, it is possible to see examples from decision-making, to memory, to attention illustrating the same thing. Similar patterns are discernible in some areas of social psychology (particularly attitudinal research, for instance). It is in the field of individual differences research that this has perhaps come closest to being explicitly acknowledged, in the case of James Flynn's (2007) critique of the lack of discipline around the use of the term "intelligence".

Flynn describes three domains, rather than four, and does not make the explicit link to issues of scale (though as noted, there were no developed theories of scale available to him at the time). In reviewing the manner in which research on intelligence has been conducted Flynn divides conceptualisations into three areas – the biological (the underlying neural processes involved in cognitive instantiation of intelligence), individual differences (intelligence as a dimension along which different people vary), and the social value (intelligence as virtue or ideal). Through examination of research in each field, the ways in which they relate to one another, but more importantly the ways in which they articulate and come apart when examined closely, Flynn diagnoses a confusion, a blindness to the independence of these frames of reference. The singular term "intelligence" is deployed differently in each one but then, precisely because it is a singular term, elides the unsupported conflation of one frame of reference with another leading to what Flynn refers to as "paradoxes", situations where some notion of "intelligence" is demonstrating seemingly inconsistent patterns of action.

Perhaps the clearest example of this is in the case of the "Flynn Effect", which was a rising trend in average IQ scores over the course of the twentieth century. Flynn described a paradox of measured average increases, something at the level of the group, not fitting with our perceptions of social virtue (2007, pp. 9–10), something that we experience at the level of the individual person. While the IQ tests were indicating increasing cognitive ability, there were no notable differences in the typical nuance of perception, subtleness of conversation, mathematical capability, or other indicators between generations of people. In very simple terms, there were no signs in everyday life of people getting smarter, and yet IQ tests were indicating they were.

Paradoxes such as this dissolve once the recognition of differences between concepts of intelligence are more carefully resolved and discipline is imposed on the way the term is deployed. This conceptual confusion arises when the phenomena in which we are interested are at different scales, but our theoretical and empirical orientation does not change accordingly.

Flynn (2007) resolves the paradox in this way. He points out that when examined in more detail, the rise in "overall" IQ measurements was primarily driven by large changes in just one common sub-scale of many measurement instruments. Specifically, it was increases in performance of the specific kind of abstract problem-solving that is central to the curricula of formal systems of education. Flynn therefore suggests that the Flynn effect is a product of group, social level phenomena, not personal, individual level ones (Kroupin et al., 2024 suggest something similar, couched in terms of changes of environment). From this perspective, the "paradox" is really just a conceptual confusion produced by the use of the same term applied to phenomena from different scalar domains. Flynn refers to this as a form of "conceptual imperialism", in which a concept developed within one domain is applied uncritically in another.

There are a host of ways in which psychological research suffers from a lack of conceptual clarity (see Danziger, 1994; Popov, 2023; Yarkoni, 2022). What we present here is one of the ways in which we can diagnose and begin to ameliorate that conceptual confusion, by taking the first steps to orient ourselves reliably.

How Psychology has Implicitly Coped with Scale

A scale-blind science will continue to encounter crucial differences that it cannot adequately conceptualise, theorise, and investigate. Unable to address scalar differences explicitly, psychological science can only encounter and cope with them implicitly. We suggest that to date, psychological scientists encounter and cope with scalar differences in three key ways.

The first, and perhaps most common, is a reductionist philosophy of science. This is an approach that assumes a foundational or base (typically neurological) level of explanation from which the patterns of phenomena at all higher scales can in principle be derived, even if it is difficult or impossible in practice. Such a reductionist mindset is usually present where people equate psychological phenomena with the brain – some examples are the use of terms such as "mind-brain", or in cases where people describe psychological phenomena such as decisions, inferences, attitudes, or social encounters as really being about "something happening in your brain".

There are two outcomes of a reductionist mindset for professional psychologists that seem positive but are deceptive. The first is an explanatory satisfaction when a neurological story is presented as underlying a given psychological phenomenon. Brain narratives feel scientific and compelling. For example, "you feel good in that situation because you are experiencing a rush of dopamine". They can be observed and recorded through techniques that constrain the ways in which interpretations can be made and have the feel of something objective or neutral.

The second, perhaps more operative, outcome is that it collapses scalar differences. Behavioural, personal, and group-level phenomena are conceived as simply aggregates, complex collections, of biological (or neurological) events. A reductionist perspective is therefore an implicit claim that scalar differences do not exist. While happenings at other scales might be useful descriptions or summaries of what is going on, the real action is in the meat of body and brain.

A second, more reflective but also rather rare approach to scalar difference is given explicit articulation by Borsboom et al. (2009). These authors argue that phenomena at the scale of inter-individual differences in populations supervene on individual behaviour and its biological underpinnings. The concept of supervenience can be tricky to grasp, but it is one that explicitly addresses the looseness of the connections between related phenomena at different scales. In terms that we have been considering, it is a concept that recognises that group phenomena depend upon individual people, but it is nevertheless not the same as those individual people. In the jargon, the relationship of supervenience means that phenomena of populations depend on the behaviour of individuals, but that events at the higher scales are "multiply realisable". There are many (perhaps a great many) different ways in which the same higher-level phenomenon can be instantiated by things at smaller scales.

Think of a sports team – the existence of the team supervenes on the participation and behaviour of all of the members of the team, but through substitutions during play, or departures and arrivals of different members of the team over time, the phenomenon of the *team* is realised in many different ways at different times.

To think more in terms of a person's behaviour, it is possible that the same bodily motion can be achieved through a wide array of underlying patterns of neural activity. Or it may be that the same group-level phenomenon can sometimes be achieved by a number of different behaviour-level events. Sometimes a nod is as good as a wink.

Moving into the domain of cognitive psychology, Borsboom et al. (2009) provide as illustration the example of chess expertise, as measured by the international standard metric of the Elo-rating. Players of similar levels of skill will win games against weaker opponents and lose games against stronger ones, with a similar frequency. Their playing techniques, however, may vary widely – that is, there is always many more than one way to perform at a given level of skill. Indeed, it is a crucial failure of the Aggregation Delusion that we are blinded to such differences which are a fundamental characteristic of human activity (remember our example of mental arithmetic in Chapter 5). The very notion of *technique* (inherent in any discussion of skill) and the experience of different accents of native speakers in the pronunciation of a language are instances of multiple valid realisations that are familiar to all of us, simply not typically discussed in such terms.

The recognition of these implications of supervenience and multiple realisability leads Borsboom et al. (2009) to a pessimism regarding the integration of psychology as a coherent discipline. The explanatory asymmetry between intra-individual processes and inter-individual differences means that the two disciplines of psychology are ultimately just asking questions about different things.

Given the lack of simple reducibility across scales argued for in depth by DiCaglio (2021) and Horton (2021) that we have endorsed here, and in keeping with the analysis offered by Borsboom et al. (2009), it would seem that we should just allow the two different aspects of psychology to de-couple from one another and be done with it. This view, however, is made rather tricky by the third, implicit, and much more problematic manner in which psychological science has tended to encounter scalar differences. That is as context effects.

By "context effects" here, we refer to the broad, varied kinds of phenomena across different sub-fields of psychology that result in the complex web of interactions bemoaned by Cronbach (1975). When people do things, what matters is not simply the specific stimuli or movements involved, but the whole situation. Repeatedly we find that if we observe and measure specific behaviours (including similar tasks, or experimental conditions) in different circumstances, we get different results (Cronbach, 1975, provides some nice examples; see also, e.g., Feldman Barrett et al., 2010; Kagan, 2012). What context effects tell us is that interaction between scales is not simply the reductionist one by which we have "bottom-up" influence on happenings, nor are the distinct dynamics of higher scales entirely independent of the lower, such that sciences of different scales can afford to be wholly ignorant of what goes on between them. Instead, complex feedback relations exist between scales that cannot be ignored.

We are not saying that all context effects are scalar phenomena – that is an empirical question that would first need to do the impressive task of getting psychologists to agree on how to identify a context effect. We *are*, however, saying that many things described as context effects are implicitly identifying the interaction between things at different scales, such as the same bodily motion (e.g., a smile), can be an encouragement, a reinforcement, a threat, or a flirtation, depending on the overall structure and flow of the situation in which it arises.

Being Scale-aware

In order to avoid the kinds of slippage and conceptual imperialism that arise due to scale-blindness, it will become necessary for psychological scientists to cultivate some new standards of practice and habits of thought. Primarily, this will be simple forms of reflection that enable us to orient ourselves effectively and reliably with regard to the scales and context of phenomena with which we are working.

The most direct form of reflection will involve thinking carefully about, and identifying explicitly, the phenomena in which we are interested. What will a single case of such phenomena look like and how would we recognise it as such? Is it a pattern of neural activity, a movement of the body, the completion of a single meaningful action in a defined context or situation, or something else? (We explore this point in much greater depth in Chapter 9.)

A more demanding question will be how we can definitively recognise a single case of the phenomenon in which we are interested. This is of course our old friend "operational definition" – listing the specific physical actions we undertake in order to identify a particular phenomenon.

This question might be better worded as "What is the finest grain of resolution at which I can identify the phenomenon in which I am interested?" For example, it might be that, given the definition with which I am working, I cannot identify a single case of my phenomenon of interest in a single human being, but only in a mean difference between groups. In these circumstances I have helped myself identify the scale at which I am working, regardless of the scale at which I *thought* I was working.

The point here is not that one scale is more important or more valid than another, but rather that for different purposes, different scales will provide different kinds of information. These different kinds of information can, and should, be separately investigated for their value in guiding policy, action, and evaluation. However, insights at one scale do not validly transfer to another without significant effort, and so it will be necessary to explicate the ways in which theories at one scale interact or interface with theories at the other. Indeed, there may be some occasions where no such interaction can be systematically articulated. That is, until we have a much better understanding of scalar differences and their relationship, it is possible that there will be some phenomena that can *only* be investigated at one scale and can never be related to others. This is an open empirical question. For example, the two atomic constituents of water – hydrogen and oxygen – are both highly combustible gases; however, this property tells us nothing about the wetness of water when they are combined (Gernigon et al., 2023, p. 3). Similarly, we would learn little about a computer's operating system by analysing the activity of its circuits (Jonas & Kording, 2017). By analogy it might be folly to try to understand human behaviour by interpreting neural firing.

What is certainly true is that the methods we use to investigate any aspect of psychology must be properly attuned to that particular aspect. The running theme in all of this is that psychologists of different stripes need to be much clearer about their interests, the specifics of their subject matter, and the scale at which they are working. We thus come to the vital importance of being clear about what it is we want to know, and using the right tools to do so.

Being Clear About What we Want to Know

Daniël Lakens (2021) has raised this question, though in the more narrowly defined scope of the critical examination of contemporary statistical methods. We believe that the general thrust of his argument has a much broader validity, however. Ultimately it is not the methods at fault, but the researchers. In particular, Lakens suggests that psychologists can only find the right tools if we better clarify what it is that we want to know.

Defending the much maligned p-value, he has claimed that what has led the psychological research community into the muddle fuss regarding statistics in which we find ourselves is that the tool is being forced into service for roles it was never designed. As the most valuable currency for publication, and therefore career progression, the system of professional incentives is to forage for significant p-values, regardless as to whether these are the most appropriate indicators of research success. Gird Gigerenzer (1998a, 2024) refers to this as "statistical rituals", with the purpose not of drawing inferences but rather in order to sanctify research results. In such circumstances, it is easy to understand people's misapplication of these tools. As the American politician Upton Sinclair so famously put it, "It is difficult to get a man [sic] to understand something, when his salary depends upon his not understanding it!" (Sinclair, 1934, p. 19, column 3).

Gigerenzer argues similarly to Lakens, therefore, that much of statistical practice has little to do with the role the p-value plays in valid statistical inference. Lakens suggests that psychologists better consider, and make more explicit, what it is that they want to know. It is only in clearly and effectively formulating the research question that we can evaluate the available tools and select the one most appropriate for the task.

Olivia Guest and Andrea Martin (2021) take it a step further to demarcate an explicit process of conceptualisation that helps ensure that questions, and hypotheses being tested in experiments, are fully and effectively articulated. Specifically using computational modelling as a framework for considering the different steps from initial conceptualisation to refinement and final expression of a testable hypothesis, they provide a set of guidelines to improve theory building and disciplined question formulation.

We see in Figure 7.1 that the process begins with a general framework, within which a theory is identified, which should then be specified in formal terms in order to make its various tenets explicit and therefore accountable. This formalised model is then implemented computationally in order to provide the basis for expression of a hypothesis in operationalised terms. Data are produced and the hypothesis is tested accordingly.

Guest and Martin's (2021) framework is focused on computational thinking and hypothesis testing, but the overall shape of their system is more general. Indeed, most readers will recognise the "funnel" structure which is often taught as good practice in report introduction writing, and which resonates importantly with the natural processes of perception. If we approach an object from a distance, say, a small building on top of a hill we are climbing, we first see the object within the context of the overall landscape, and very basic aspects of it – its contour or shape, some sense of its size, and perhaps an overall colour. As we continue our approach, this initial perception is refined – first particulars of contour such as orientation of its faces, or broad features such as doors and windows, and then finer details of texture such as materials and finish on the walls, handles, and locks on the door. Perception of finer points arises already within the context of the on-going perception of, and orientation towards, the broader features.

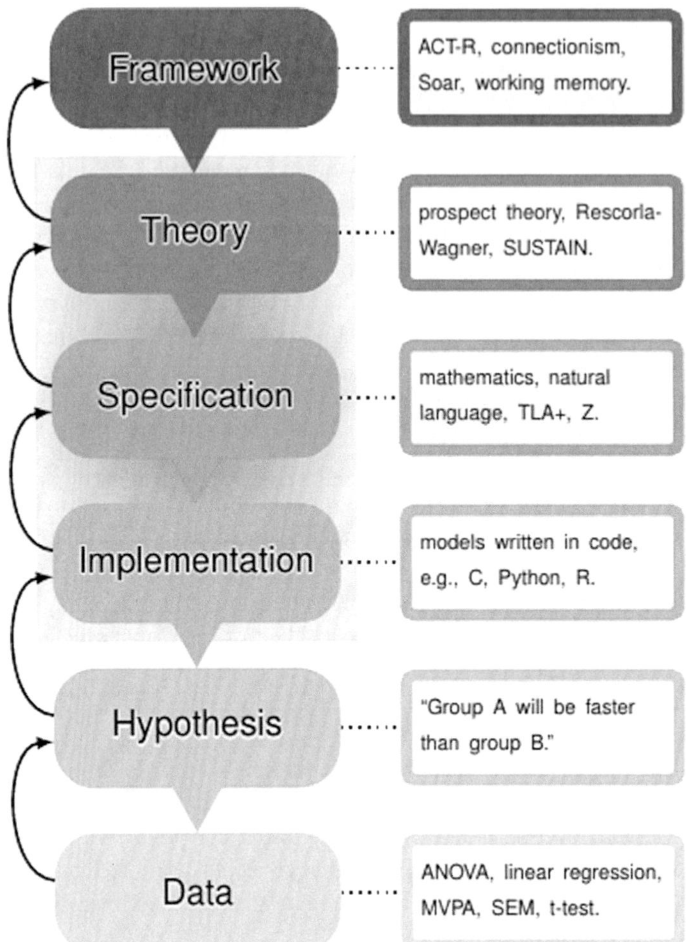

FIGURE 7.1 An example of how computational specification can be used to discipline research question formulation according to Guest and Martin (2021).

Applying this analogy to the formulation of research questions, we have argued above that we should begin by explaining at what scale are the phenomena in which we are interested. In doing so, we can make clear to ourselves what the constraints on our theorising will be – what kinds of objects or events can be involved. With this landscape of concepts in mind, we can turn to theoretical frameworks, and the further specification of particular models where appropriate. In many cases our knowledge or understanding of the phenomena, or indeed our research purposes, may not allow for or need a model or hypothesis specification. Such questions do not apply to much qualitative work. Clarity regarding the phenomena of interest and the scale of observations is still necessary, however.

Articulating these specifics for research agendas will not, in most cases, be a simple linear sequence of steps. Our initial description of the scale in which we are working might change as we refine and more finely express the research questions, which in turn might affect what theoretical frameworks we think will be most productive of new insights. That reflective process, and the need to be explicit in our articulations not just of operationalised variables, but the theoretical and scalar context in which the overall research question has been developed, is the point.

Being explicit about all of these things performs several important professional functions. Firstly, as Guest and Martin (2021) and Lakens (2021) argue, being clearer about the form of our models and hypotheses, and the kinds of evidence that are therefore relevant, rather than jumping to the detailed formulation in a specific experiment or statistical test, will help discipline our thinking. This is a reform of practice in psychological research that would facilitate improvement in the conceptualisation of theory as well as the conduct of methods of data production and analyses.

Secondly, the current organisation of our profession essentially places a massively unbalanced status on the use of particular forms of analytical tools that means much research is straight-jacketed into a very small number of potential forms (NHST being the most popular). There has always been some resistance to this of course, but other analytic approaches have nothing like the status and weight of those mainstream statistical methods. In the coming chapters we will add our voice to arguments that these more marginalised approaches need to be expanded and substantially mainstreamed as part of a more general critical awareness of what kinds of evidence fit the kinds of questions we really want to ask.

The point is not to "ban" these popular methods, but to stop suppressing others such that a wide range of questions and a wider range of relevant tools are deployed. Making the broader frameworks and models of our practice more explicit will facilitate the vital re-balancing of value for different forms of research – different kinds of questions, and different kinds of answers.

The changes in professional practice that we are advocating here are, like many of the reforms that have been mooted in recent times, not difficult to accomplish in principle for individual psychologists. It is true many will find it difficult to change their habits and to reassess not just others' work but their own. A great challenge to action by individual researchers will be in the inertia in the incentive structures of institutions, professional bodies, and scientific communities that militate against such change in practices.

Using less frequently utilised tools provides challenges to the publication process both in terms of peer review (are there experts who can evaluate it properly?) and readership. Some of this problem is systemic and can only be addressed over time through changes to training curricula, but the first part of it has to be addressed through culture, and in particular through the cultivation of a greater appreciation for and comfort with scientific diversity.

A Federation of Psychologies

At first glance, the diversity of scales across which psychological phenomena fall might seem daunting, or even fatal. Borsboom et al. (2009), on reviewing the evidence that the phenomena of Cronbach's "correlational psychology" are fundamentally distinct from those of the "experimentalists", seem to reach such a conclusion.

> [S]ometimes science progresses by showing that a dreamed route of progress is blocked...Our suggestion in the present work is that the integration of intra-individual and inter-individual research programs may be exactly such a case: a dreamed route of progress that is really a dead end street.
>
> *(Borsboom et al., 2009, p. 94)*

This is an important point, and certainly we have some sympathy with these authors' frustrations. Is it the case, then, that we should simply allow different domains of psychology to go their separate ways and have little or nothing to do with one another? We don't think so. We agree with Borsboom et al. that a simple "integration" (in the sense of a reductionist consilience) is not on the cards, but the reader should not take this to imply that these different endeavours have nothing to offer one another.

Examining in fine-grained detail examples from physics, chemistry, and psychiatry, the historian and philosopher of science Hasok Chang has argued that it is the case across the board that effective, progressive science is a pluralistic undertaking. That is, during any given period within a scientific discipline, there is more than one, perhaps several, ontologies – different categories of things that are taken to be real – around which different systems of scientific practice are organised (questions asked, tools deployed, methods of analysis brought to bear). Perhaps the simplest example is that of classical and quantum physics. Heisenberg described both Newtonian and quantum mechanics as "closed theories", each internally coherent, but entirely incompatible. Both of these forms of "real" are used effectively in different domains. But Chang explores examples of working pluralism in other fields too, in the areas of temperature (Chang, 2004), and our understanding of the chemistry of water (Chang, 2012). In a delightful passage worth quoting at length, he describes how a pluralistic physics is essential in complex cases:

> A nice cutting-edge high-tech example of such integration is the global positioning system (GPS): by means of satellites kept in place by Newtonian physics, and atomic clocks ruled by quantum mechanics and corrected by special and general relativity, this system maps the spherical surface of the round earth on a geocentric grid (or rather, a geostatic field), and gives advice to people on the ground from a flat-earth point of view.
>
> *(Chang, 2012, p.266)*

That is to say that pluralism in practice is not an esoteric or niche point, it seems to be a common and important part in making progress in science.

Sometimes these different perspectives on the phenomena in question directly impact on one another, and in doing so our understanding of those phenomena can change over time. In contrast to the non-interacting, closed theories described by Heisenberg, Chang (2022) refers to this as *interactive pluralism.* The different approaches to the science interact in interesting and sometimes very productive ways.

In science, as in so many areas of life, diversity is a feature, not a bug; variety is a strength, monoculture, a vulnerability.

The mistake is to assume that, or try to force, all of these different ideas into a single system of practices, insisting that there is a single "correct" way in which to conduct science. Science has never been a unified, singular process (Dupré, 1993; Richardson, 2006). It is not organised around a single set of precepts, nor even around the frequently invoked conception of "the Scientific Method", running its loop from theoretical question or problem, to hypothesis, experiment, results, and back to theory. Scientific research involves a complex, even messy, collection of practices. This messiness, though, is often a benefit, not a problem.

Between the extremes of an ideal consilient unity and a fatalistic isolation of different domains, there lie intermediate positions that it is worthwhile to cultivate. It is helpful to do so deliberately, reflectively, rather than by accident. If our aim is to make sense of the diversity of facets of psychological phenomena, perhaps the more productive model will not be one of integration, but rather something more like federation.

In a federated psychological science, different areas of psychology can operate within their own set of practices. There are certainly requirements that researchers be clear and careful in their theory building and conceptualisation. But it is not necessary that researchers in every field use precisely the same concepts. Federation doesn't require a wholesale transformation of goals, but a reflective stance that recognises the necessarily limited nature of the results within a given field of work.

The aim of this reflection on and recognition of the limits of one's own knowledge, the constrained character of results and findings, is to foster sensitivity to potential alternative approaches, and the cross-pollination between distinct perspectives. Chang (2017, 2022) argues persuasively that progressive science *requires* this kind of diversity, even in the case where one theoretical framework is notably more effective and productive than competing alternatives, pluralistic sciences are more effective at avoiding "local minima". A local minimum in this case is a tempting perception that a phenomenon or domain is "solved" when more comprehensive or deeper explanations are potentially available from other perspectives.

Psychology does not lack for a diversity of ontologies or viewpoints. What it *does* seem to miss is a valued forum or medium within which these different viewpoints can cross-pollinate, and an awareness of their own limited nature. What is missing is not some magical correct "method" that psychologists must all adopt. No, what we need is *much* harder to achieve (remembering Sinclair's dictum cited above) – an effective social and political reorganisation of the profession.

A federated approach to psychology would involve some proportion of time being spent in explicit inter-speciality communication and reflection with regard to the place of one's own work within the larger federation of psychological sciences. This is both particularly important and particularly likely during the early career, where habits of a professional lifetime are laid down, but important for more senior researchers both to recognise the limits of their own viewpoint and to mentor and foster such communication and reflection within their teams. (Dewsbury (2009) makes a similar argument with regard to the role of theoretical psychology.)

As we have noted above, the greatest challenge in making progress is not in developing effective reflective practices to manage this, but in the political and social processes of collective action needed to achieve it. The inertia of institutional structures and professional incentives require effective collective action to be overcome. It will require leadership from those in more senior positions, not just within schools of psychology, but the wider circumstances of universities and colleges, as well as funding bodies and policy makers, and also advocacy, subversion, and occasionally rebellion from those in more junior positions.

Hoffman et al. (2022) note some of the risks associated with explicit attempts to bridge domains of research practice through the creation of new structures and positions. Their focus is more broad – looking at attempts at integration across disciplines, rather than on cross-pollination between sub-fields of a discipline – but many of the same dynamics apply. Effective communication between specialist domains cannot be left just to "integration specialists", both because such specialists may become as enclosed and insular as other groups, but also because communication requires all researchers to be sensitive and responsive to potential relevant influence, or opportunities for insight from other fields. The point is not to create a small group of elite "generalists" who do the work of integration, but to create a broad culture of open-mindedness within which occasional links and points of mutual influences can arise, perhaps supported by specialists in facilitating such integrative, or cross-pollination activities. Lyall (2019) notes that once a researcher has become fully inducted into the disciplinary practices of their field, it becomes immensely difficult to break those habits, if appropriate reflective habits are not cultivated from early on. We should not underestimate the challenges that this implies for our need to persuade current senior researchers in reform efforts.

More Concrete Steps

In many ways, the Great Psychology Delusion is a statement about how and why the dominance of a narrow range of practices in psychological science is a problematic, perhaps even toxic, organisation of our collective endeavour. The monocultural perspective that obscures the diversity and complexity of scales, experience, and individuality of our subject matter limits the extent and effectiveness of progress and imposes upon us problems such as the research–practice gap across several fields of professional work. Getting over the Delusion is less about everyone adopting the single correct set of tools, than it is a re-balancing of our values, and the relative influence of disparate investigative and explanatory approaches.

The federalist model that we are suggesting here is one which insists that we simultaneously recognise the necessarily limited, partial character of our knowledge and sees that as an opportunity, not a condemnation. In Chapter 1 we stated that we will not attempt to make an argument for a One True Psychology. What we can do, however, is argue for the value of a pluralistic one. While there is no simple model to follow in order to achieve this shift in professional organisation, a few relatively clear steps are immediately apparent.

Funding bodies should adjust their awarding models to deliberately foster pluralism in practice. Perhaps the simplest means of doing this is to earmark a portion of funding for non-mainstream approaches in research. There are already some efforts in this direction underway in some areas of science, and it would not be difficult to extend these models. The U.S. National Institutes of Health (NIH) Director's Pioneer Award Program is explicitly intended to fund innovative, paradigm-challenging projects of research (National Institutes of Health, 2024). In the United Kingdom, the Engineering and Physical Sciences Research Council includes a stream for "Transformative Research" with the aim of encouraging non-mainstream approaches, to "create new sub-fields", and "cause paradigm shifts" (UK Research & Innovation, 2021). These funding priorities (both of them relatively modest in terms of their body's overall funding budget) are special priorities explicitly intended to support innovative or creative programmes of research. Such beginnings could be extended by explicitly endorsing and rewarding multi-team projects involving complementary, or even competitive endeavours between groups with different theoretical viewpoints on a more routine basis.

Academic and administrative leaders in research institutions (particularly in higher education institutions) can promote pluralism by requiring schools above a given size to deliberately hire from across a range of perspectives. We should note that many schools already have such practice, where qualitative researchers are often sought to balance strong quantitative representation among staff. Further steps can be taken at the level of the school or institution, however. Promotion within departments, particularly to higher positions, might require evidence of inter-specialism, inter-perspectival actions. While there is likely to be value in such inter-perspectival actions being new forms of research, the fostering of inter-specialism dialogue need not be only in formal terms of team collaborations. Conferences, postgraduate programme development and other means can all be effective in facilitating cross-pollination.

Professional organisations, who bestow awards, make statements and policies regarding best practice in a discipline can review and revise the criteria for awards and the wording of policies.

To repeat, the point is not to claim that there is a single best way to organise the community of psychological scientists to optimise progress. Rather, the point is that given science is driven by ignorance, the organisation of our collective endeavour is not something it is possible to optimise. There is no golden mean, or single stable configuration of effort and practice that will ensure the most productive outcomes for our science. We can, however, be more explicit, reflective, and disciplined about our scientific goals and adapt our actions accordingly, not just in periods of reformist fervour, but as an inherent part of our standard practice. What we can do is learn from our own history, and the history of other sciences, in identifying values and characteristics of practice that tend to promote progress.

8

TAKING STOCK OF THE RESEARCH TOOLBOX

The Wide Landscape of Psychological Science

One of the great benefits of shaking ourselves loose of the delusions that have caused such confusion and frustration for the psychological sciences is a greater appreciation for the wide and varied landscape of psychological phenomena and the methods we can use to explore that landscape. Psychology's diversity and pluralism is not something for the future, though. As we have previously noted, there are already a plethora of methods and approaches deployed by researchers of different stripes. The point is not to identify just one approach or one set of methods and argue that "this one is the right one" that every psychological researcher must master. Rather, we must better appreciate the value of collaborations amidst differences. Finding better ways to balance the interplay between different research methods and their outcomes, without aiming for an ill-considered hegemony of a single framework or narrow set of research techniques.

To prevent ourselves from becoming lost anew amid this rich domain of work, in the previous chapter, we introduced a few general principles that we should bear in mind. We should maintain an explicit awareness of how observations at different scales relate to one another and avoid abstractions (statistical or otherwise) that muddy our perceptions of those relationships. In this chapter, we will explore a few different methods that have already been developed and are successfully deployed by psychological researchers. In doing so, we aim to make clear that effective techniques already exist that are in keeping with the principles we have set out but which are at present perhaps too confined within subfields (either by the perceptions of mainstream aggregate-focused researchers or by the ideological standpoints of those niche researchers themselves). Greater advantage can be taken of opportunities for interaction and collaboration between researchers across these subfields.

The toolbox of psychological research is better stocked, with more varied implements, than a typical undergraduate or even most postgraduate curricula would have us believe. In saying this, we are not simply referring to the seemingly intractable schism between qualitative and quantitative methods and the Jets vs. Sharks mentality adopted by advocates of each (ignoring

DOI: 10.4324/9781003503873-10

the pleas for mixed-method enlightenment of those Marias and Tonys optimistically caught in the middle of the analytical dance-off).

What we will explore in this chapter and the next are a range of methods. Some of these are relatively obscure techniques, but ones whose validity and worth are nevertheless well-established – what we will see as a form of natural history for psychology. Some are more widely known and used but still perhaps too narrowly cast, with the potential for greater value than is typically recognised. Various qualitative methods, for instance, have much greater potential than even some of their proponents frequently present. Others are scale-aware (or explicitly scale-agnostic) methods of quantitative analysis that have presented exciting and impressive successes in recent years. Our intention is not to provide an exhaustive list of valid methods (we repeat that we have no interest in doing so and would find it counter-productive to foreclose the issue). Rather, our point is that being more scale-aware and keeping the relationships between individual agents, group phenomena, or sub-personal processes clearly in view is possible across the range of circumstances in which we work as researchers. As we will see, a resultant theme that ties the various methodological approaches addressed in this chapter is that of ecosystems and ecologies and the need to undertake research, particularly in the early stages of getting to grips with a phenomenon, in terms that maintain the ecological relationships and the entanglements with the context of our subject matter.

Though there are unique aspects to psychological sciences that we should not underestimate, we can also look to other sciences to see how such diversity of methods is managed. As we will also see, psychology's struggles with how to balance the valuing of different research techniques are far from unusual. Even in the more established disciplines whose credentials are not questioned, science is never a fixed and stable thing. The values, standards, and ambitions of research are always being negotiated.

Surveying Across Scales – The Need for More Natural History of Psychology

An instructive example of such negotiations which has some useful implications for our own explorations here concerns the place of "natural history" within the field of biology. As with so many phrases, the term "natural history" has no single definition with universal consensus in the literature, though there is general agreement in broad terms. Researchers, for instance, speak of a "kind of close, scrupulous observation of nature" (Wilcove & Eisner, 2000, B24), or "the observation and description of the natural world" (Tewksbury et al., 2014, p. 300), or "a practice of intentional, focused attentiveness and receptivity to the more-than-human world, guided by honesty and accuracy" (Fleischner, 2011, pp. 5–6). This broad consensus on the general form of it, however, comes in a context of uncertainty regarding its role within the scientific practice of biologists in the modern era and the fear that its place is being lost despite both historical and current significance.

Bates (1950/2014, p. 7) describes natural history as "the study of life at the level of the individual – of what plants and animals do, how they react to each other and their environment, how they are organized into larger groupings like populations and communities". Bates' description clearly places the practice of natural history in a role that involves the consideration of phenomena across scales. The result is a key interest in patterns and relationships, particularly between individuals and their environments. Wilcove and Eisner (2000, B24) note natural history as involving a "close observation of organisms – their origins, their evolution, their behaviour, and their relationships with other species". Tewksbury et al. (2014, p. 300) note that the study of "organisms and their linkages to the environment being central" is crucial to the idea. Sunderland, Klitz, and Yoshihara (2012, p. 826) point out that though natural history is often associated with simply the collection of specimens, field notes on context, prevalence, behaviour, surrounding vegetation, weather, and landscape are crucial to the naturalist's practice. The surrounding habitat is considered an essential component of the description of the animal (even if it is a little harder to transport back to the specimen cupboard).

Natural history is a rich practice that provides descriptions of the broader contours and structures within which more mechanistic theories of biological processes are framed. Bartholomew (1986, pp. 326–327) claims that "information provided by natural history will always be the touchstone for synthesis (biological significance)", arguing that it is only in the context offered from natural historical accounts that knowledge becomes biological, as opposed to chemical or physical. As biological research has been increasingly structured (and not coincidentally, funded) by questions of genetics, biochemistry, and pharmacology, so natural history has declined in status and been squeezed out of over-stuffed curricula (Barrows et al., 2016; Noss, 1996; Wilcove & Eisner, 2000). Callaghan et al. (2018) have argued that it is only the cross-scale perspective of natural history that can help us understand the inter-relationship between the sweeping impacts of climate change and the individual animals of different species being affected (they refer to this perspective as a need for an "unnatural history", p. 475). Sunderland et al. (2012) argue that natural history and the various experimental and theoretical wings of the biological sciences (molecular biology, physiology, morphology, theoretical biology, and many others) are mutually dependent, each providing insights, questions, and validity checks for the other.

Among natural history's various aspects, given our discussion of the development of theories of principle (see Chapter 5), we might focus on two key points:

1. The cataloguing of prevalences and event frequencies in the natural world;
2. The identifying of relationships among different kinds of events and between organisms and their environments in natural settings.

A range of extant methods might be involved in these two undertakings – from narrative descriptions to imaging of various kinds, video or audio recording, or the use of observational checklists and similar structured surveys of natural settings. This disciplining of observations forms the backbone of the process of formalisation of descriptions of the phenomena that are essential to the development of a theory of principle for a given domain, as Einstein (1919) has described it. This is not to say that such theories are built only from observations of the natural world. We noted in Chapter 5 that both Einstein and Newton, for example, also drew from more controlled observations. The richness of naturalistic data is vital, however. As Heft (2018) argues, natural history requires not just an open-minded, descriptive mode but an ecosystems perspective, one that explicitly records the event or specimen in context in a way that retains important data about the relationship between the phenomenon of interest and the web of related phenomena in which it naturally occurs. While we agree with Heft, it is worth noting that the concept of the ecosystem itself is one of biology's theories of principle, a descriptive and organising concept that helps structure other investigations. It was derived and refined over time by a series of biologists, most notably Humboldt (Anderson, 2017; Wulf, 2015), but refined by a number of subsequent researchers, typically on the basis of yet more data produced through the process of natural history.

At present, the discipline of psychology largely lacks such naturalistic data (Flake et al., 2022). In the typical story, many of us learn as undergraduates that the proper founding of the discipline is taken to be the dedication of laboratory space on either side of the Atlantic in the late 1870s, and there has been a strong emphasis on observation in carefully controlled settings ever since. As we discussed in Chapter 1, historians of psychology have noted that psychologists have standardised around methods that typically value laboratory investigations over work in natural settings (Danziger, 1994; Green, 2015; Stam, 2004). This has been to the extent that Danziger (1994, p. 45) describes developments in the early decades of the discipline as a "repudiation of Wundt", who argued vehemently for the need for balance between controlled and naturalistic observations through the practices of what he termed *Völkerpsychologie* (often translated as cultural or folk psychology).

The definition of psychology by the founding of laboratories sets the discipline apart from other sciences, where natural history and laboratory practice wove in and out of one another as their methods developed (Anderson, 2017). Indeed, they continue to do so, even as some researchers raise concerns that the emphasis has swung too far away from naturalistic observation (Bartholomew, 1986; Sunderland, Klitz, & Yoshihara, 2012). The same cannot be said of psychology, which appears to have more or less skipped what we might call the "butterfly collection" phase of its scientific development in our haste to identify ourselves as a properly experimental science (Barker, 1968).

Heft (2001, 2018) and Morris (2009) point out that though there are some exceptions to this general rule, field work of the kind that can be termed natural history remains rare and not very influential within psychological research. This is not to suggest that it does not occur at all, but its role within the discipline is under-valued and unsystematic. Such research tends to be conducted within already rich theoretical frameworks and has little systematic role in the identification of patterns and relationships proper to natural history (Heft, 2018).

True to the historical development of the science, a large proportion of psychological researchers begin their careers in the laboratory and tend to stay there. Where research is conducted in natural settings, it is often in the form of intervention or implementation science, such that the kinds of aims served by the activities of natural history cannot be achieved (Heft, 2018). The result is a dearth of naturalistic observation and very limited amounts of data that can characterise phenomena in the "real world" or allow us to explore patterns and consistencies that might arise in such data. Without adequate systematic data relating to natural settings, it becomes next to impossible to develop systematic and coherent theories of principle (Debrouwere & Rosseel, 2022; Eronen & Bringmann, 2021). This in turn means that our theoretical sophistication and scientific practice remain weaker than they could and should be. There are no general patterns and models that might "put manners" on laboratory practice and keep them closely connected to more naturally occurring behaviour "in the wild" of what we affectionately consider the daily lives of "normal" people (in all of our fantastic diversity). This unmooring of experimental work from real-world ecologies of behaviour and experience, and the lack of constraint on both hypotheses and interpretations of experiments that result, is precisely the concern we discussed in relation to Alan Newell's (1973) review of the possible future of cognitive psychology.

A natural history of psychology is difficult, but there are some significant positive examples available for us to work with. Descriptive observation of human behaviour in the wild is not only possible; it is currently conducted in a number of sub-fields of the discipline in focused ways (examples abound in social psychology, developed from the work of Garfinkel, 1967, Sacks,

1992, and others; naturalistic recording is also relatively well represented in developmental studies, such as Heft, 1979, 1988, Jayaraman et al., 2015; Karasik et al., 2011; Karasik et al., 2015; Rossmanith et al., 2014, and in the study of human relationships and marriage, Gottman & Notarius, 2000).

Of course the essential value of this kind of work to comparative and non-human psychology hardly needs mentioning, but there are vital insights from animal ethology for research on human psychology too. Indeed, Barrett and Stulp (2013) revisit the seminal work of Niko Tinbergen (1963) to conclude that his arguments for the value of ethology in the study of human behaviour remain valid, as does, alas (more than 60 years later), his recognition of the need for greater engagement with that practice by psychologists. Behavioural ethology with non-human animals provides some superb examples, not just of the value of observational work in the course of systematic descriptions, but also of the ways in which it can bring into view both consistencies and variations that provide for insights difficult to achieve in any other way (see Barrett, 2009, for a wonderful example of this in the case of baboons).

The richest resource for a natural history of human behaviour conducted by psychologists is the work of Roger Barker, Louise Shedd Barker, Herbert Wright, Phil Schoggen, and their colleagues, who conducted more than 25 years of field work in a small town in rural Kansas, work that is as impressive as it is unknown.

In a reflection at the end of his career, Barker (1979) described how his life's work was steered by a singular early moment of shock, a "negative 'Aha!'" (p. 2150). This occurred when he was a young academic, as the train he was riding on stopped in numerous small towns through rural Illinois in the United States. Despite having recently gained his PhD and being an expert in human behaviour, he had little idea beyond his own common sense as to what actually happened, day in, day out, in these various places. Moving to the University of Kansas, he, Louise Shedd Barker, a zoologist, and a cadre of graduate students set up a field research station in the town of Oskaloosa (referred to in their research as "Midwest"). Over a period of twenty-five years (from 1948 to 1973, when the Midwest Psychological Field Station closed), they went from observing every activity of a small group of children to recording data on many different settings of people's activities within the public spaces of the town, as well as comprehensive assessments of the various resources the town provided for those activities. The result is a striking body of work which identifies some deeply important relationships between human behaviour and the physical and social environments in which they take place.

It is beyond what we can manage in this chapter to offer anything other than a few breadcrumbs to lead the reader to this work (see Avram et al., 2024; Barker, 1968; Heft, 2001, chapter 7; 2024; Schoggen, 1989). Years of extensive recording and cataloguing of behaviour enabled the group to identify patterns, relationships, and structures that offered significant insights into psychology. For the moment, suffice it to point out that if we have an interest in predicting behaviours and have access only to a single piece of information about a person, then by far the most valuable datum we can seek is "what setting are they in?" In an oft-used phrase to summarise the idea, "In church, people behave church; in school, people behave school". Behaviour tends to vary more within people across settings than between people within settings.

Psychological researchers have a tendency, remarked upon by Barker (1968, p. 4) and largely unchanged since, to either take complete control of the environment (through the provision of stimulus packages in blandly painted and sparely furnished laboratories) or treat the environment as being probabilistically structured, a statistical puzzle to solve. These are understandings of the relationship between people and their environments that do not survive an effort after natural history and observation of the highly structured, nested character of settings for behaviour in the human habitat.

Barker and his colleagues developed a rich body of theory derived from their observational research, one that offers substantial return on the investment in getting to know it. But it is work that has seen little replication and surprisingly sparse study by researchers outside of the original research group. We should note explicitly, however, that some of the Midwest work, particularly that with regards to the population (and under-population) of behaviour settings, has been examined by others (e.g., Wicker, 1978), but the extensive naturalistic data gathering remains an outlier in the field. This appears to have been due to a number of factors, but largely a lack of available funding and constraints of professional incentives which run counter to slow, careful, descriptive work (Scott, 2005).

The team's various publications provide extensive information on their methods of observation, recording, and analysis, all conducted in a small rural town and with an emphasis on the "molar" level of description – behaviour in its contours rather than its fine details, a decision made for reasons of practicality and to address an apparent gap in psychological research generally (Barker, 1968). These methods offer the potential for the creation of rich and important corpora of behavioural data, but only if the value and purpose of it can be imagined by psychological scientists and their funders. It is slow work, demanding substantial investments of time in particular. Modern recording technologies will no doubt allow for some work to be divided in ways it has typically not been, but only if we can manage to pick our way carefully through the ethical challenges and legal complications of doing so. It is worth remarking, though, that these are the primary obstacles for the conduct of research that can in principle be conducted with nothing more than patience, care, a notebook, and pencil.

We have noted that one purpose of natural history is to provide descriptions of the naturally occurring phenomena of a scientific domain. Natural histories enable scientists to understand the relative frequency of particular kinds of occurrences in order to evaluate how representative their controlled studies are of ordinarily occurring events (Bartholomew, 1986; Bates, 2014; and Brunswik, 1947, all make similar observations relevant to psychology). This would also mean for psychology developing a clearer picture of the diversity, the range and variability of behaviour and mental life (Debrouwere & Rosseel, 2022), something it is surprisingly difficult to do from our extant body of theory (see the preface to Barker et al., 1978, for an enlightening outlining of this issue).

Additionally, natural histories can be conducted at varying levels of description (somewhat in contrast to laboratory experiments, where the focus is on a very narrow range of temporal and spatial scales for behaviour). In doing so, they allow us to look at not just the relative frequency but the relationships in time and space between different phenomena of interest to the discipline as they occur in the environment not under the control of the psychologist.

For instance, a natural history of cognition would enable us to form descriptions, and then hypotheses, about the importance of places in the emergence and development of cognitive functions in normal settings (Barker, 1968; Klein, 1993; Schoggen, 1989; see Gastelum et al., 2024 for an interesting discussion on this with regard to reasoning). It would also enable the examination of patterns of behaviours (cognitive, social, emotional) over the course of minutes, hours, days, or longer, which could offer us opportunities to perceive, hypothesise, and ultimately test theories about relationships between different aspects of behaviour or mental activity. The anthropological work of Ed Hutchins (1995) provides a superb example of this kind of work, examining how a team of sailors manage the process of navigation. Hutchins' research provides insights into the relationship between cognitive processes, tools, settings, and social interaction that is difficult or impossible to even frame as questions before such naturalistic work has been undertaken (see also Baggs & Sanchez de Oliveira, 2024, for a useful comparison and contrast of the methods of Hutchins and the Midwest team).

The Place of Qualitative Research Methods

Natural history provides the possibility for both quantitative and qualitative analysis, but it is its maintenance of relationships and its emphasis on context and connectedness that makes it so important and full of potential.

Aspers and Cortes (2019) have argued that it is the possibility to enable exploration of alternative perspectives, at multiple grains of analysis, that best characterises qualitative research. Quantitative work involves making decisions in advance about the variables of interest. This makes a level of precision possible that is otherwise precluded by more flexible methods but depends on the validity and reliability of the measurement tools as having been finely established in advance. The pre-selection of specific variables requires that the relationships between the variables in question and other potential factors are already known or effectively modelled, lest the work be replete with confounds.

More flexible qualitative work does not eliminate that problem entirely (every method is selective in some form or another), but the greater the agency of the participants and the richer the qualitative data that are produced, then the more likely it is that important points of context or relationships that matter but are not explicitly tracked by the researchers can still show up and make themselves known when examined by the researcher or reflected on with the participants.

Aggregationist methods prevent almost any possibility of this because of their asymmetry – we go from individual cases to aggregate statistics, but we cannot go the other way. The relationships between context and particular people or behaviours are necessarily and irreversibly obscured.

Oddly, this demonstrates a limitation on aggregationist quantitative work that is often considered a hard constraint on the value of *qualitative* methods – the possibility of generalisation.

Yarkoni (2022) has made an extensive argument that the variables present in the simplest statistical models of psychological data make it next to impossible for those models to accurately make predictions about prevalences of particular cases in the population. That is to say that the crucial inference that is supposed to be offered by inferential statistics – that the pattern observed in the sample is representative of the population – cannot be depended upon because of the causal complexity and compounded sources of variability in any given psychological situation. Factors such as individual differences, research site, experimenter, instructions, laboratory testing conditions, task, and more all vary in ways that are not just potentially important but which *are not randomly distributed*.

These variables are different characteristics of the ecology of the behaviours in question, and just as relationships between the specimens of natural history and their habitats, ecological neighbours, and other networks of dependencies are crucial to understanding them, so such complex webs are crucial to understanding the emergence and progression of any given behaviour in any given situation (experiment or otherwise). Yarkoni (2022) warns that, at best, in any given psychological research project, only some very small proportion of these or other potential variables are included in the model, and for the most part, they are included as random variables, when in reality it is unlikely that these variables are random at all.

Indeed, in discussing the ecosystems of human behaviour, Barker (1978) notes that there is little real randomness at play. The environment is not probabilistically or stochastically structured. It is *meaningfully* nested at multiple scales. When moving from one behaviour setting to another, it is not a roll of the dice that you step from a classroom to a concert. Human beings organise and construct our environments and behavioural ecosystems in careful, often quite deliberate and intentional ways (Heft, 2018; see also Heft, 2014, for an argument that an ecological approach to psychology is necessarily one that addresses meaning for the behavioural agents in question).

Yarkoni (2022) did not explicitly discuss ecological thinking in terms of behaviour settings. His paper does, however, make very clear the fatal weaknesses of not addressing context and behavioural ecosystems in detail. The loss for psychological science is the generalisability of research findings, which must remain pinned to the stimuli, setting, and participants involved when the circumstances of the overall situation are not adequately represented in the theorisation, modelling, and testing of the behaviours of interest.

It is somewhat ironic that aggregationist quantitative work is limited in just this way, as it is precisely in terms of generalisation, and the prospect of generalities or universals, that the differences between the value of quantitative and qualitative work are often couched.

In our descriptions and discussions of the various delusions afflicting psychological science, our focus has been heavily on quantitative work. The Aggregation Delusion, as well as the delusions of Control, Specificity, and Correlation, would seem dependent on quantification. Readers with a strong qualitative bent may find themselves sitting smugly assured that their perceptions are unblinkered by the delusions we have otherwise diagnosed so widely. Indeed, there is justification for this view. Because much (though not all) qualitative work involves detailed recording of utterances and activities attributable to individual specific participants, there is an accountability and grain of resolution to qualitative work too often absent from the quantitative. Much more to the point, however, is the caution and humility under which qualitative work is completed. It is common for researchers to explicitly deny any prospect of generalisation or identification of underlying laws or rules governing the data produced.

Willig (2019), for instance, describes one of the major differences between quantitative and qualitative psychology as being the ambition to universalism. While quantitative psychology seems to have an aim to identify and measure universal or general aspects of psychological phenomena, qualitative researchers are explicitly more humble, sometimes going as far as to say that generalisation is not possible from qualitative work. As it happens, though, it may well be that there is reason for a little more optimism on this point.

Roald et al. (2021) critically examine our understanding of generalisation in qualitative research and conclude that it is not only possible but ubiquitous. In order to make sense of this, they identify a number of forms of generalisation (in doing so, they build on prior work by both Kvale, 1997 [cited in Roald et al., 2021] and Flyvberg, 2006).[1]

The first is naturalistic or "common sense" generalisation, in which we draw on our own past experiences in order to estimate the generality of a phenomenon – how representative it might be of typical similar events or actions. Roald et al. claim that much qualitative work is conducted and interpreted in light of such intuitive practice – indeed, it is almost impossible to suppress such perceptions.

Somewhat contrasted is analytical generalisation, which is a more systematic attempt to address the same question. Statistical generalisation is a particular example of analytical generalisation but is not its only form. There are a number of potential ways in which generality can be assessed which may not include the production and evaluation of statistics. The tabulation of descriptors and the evaluation of an observation based on key points of relevance or precision are examples. Each of these provides a means of making clear, in a manner that is systematic and comparable across examples of work, what has been included or captured in a piece of research. It then becomes possible to more analytically (though still broadly qualitatively) evaluate the variety or scope of the phenomena that have shown up in that research. We can then deliberately seek examples of phenomena or circumstances which have not been addressed by the prior work, or which have, in order to further evaluate its generality.

Roald et al. (2021) argue that not only does this mean that qualitative research can support certain kinds of generalisation, but that in some circumstances this is an explicit intention. While the number of cases described, recorded, or evoked in qualitative research tends to be much smaller than those measured in quantitative work, the selection of the sample is sometimes undertaken with the explicit intention of it being representative of a large group of similar circumstances – be it settings, events, members of a profession, or otherwise.

What is more, specific cases form the bedrock of scientific inferences in a number of ways. In the natural sciences, individual cases can be exceptions which clearly disprove rules, performing vital falsification. Case studies also show what is *possible*, even if they do not, as individual cases, offer fine-grained information on what is *probable*. Nevertheless, the building of a collection of individual cases over time provides deeply valuable information about prevalences, relationships between aspects of facets of cases, and can come to play a role in scientific case-based reasoning that is much like citation of precedent in "common law" in various legal systems (Roald et al., 2021, p. 73). Indeed, Sechrest and Sidani (1995) point out that the social science's self-consciousness about qualitative methods seems something of a quirky idiosyncrasy. Within the natural sciences, what are commonly referred to by social scientists as "mixed methods" are so much taken for granted as to be unworthy of a name or remark. In a manner that Lakens (2021) would appreciate, what matters is not what kind of analysis is applied but rather whether the data produced and analysis used provide evidence that befits the kinds of questions being asked.

We are not suggesting that qualitative work provides "the solution" to the various delusions we are trying to move past. What matters, rather, is that the richness of the resources available to psychology to produce evidence that can provide insight into the description, explanation, and prediction of behaviours not be self-defeatingly siloed into different sub-fields with little or no interaction. After all, the divide between qualitative and quantitative methods is probably not as clear as some would believe – Syed and McLean (2022) point out that Discussion sections in quantitative papers usually include a qualitative interpretation of statistical findings, and the labelling of latent factors to explain covariations between measures typically follows a naming process that is similar to the identification of themes in qualitative research. There is no place for ideological isolationism between qualitative and quantitative researchers; just care to be taken in fitting method to question appropriately.

Indeed, the virtue of qualitative methods that we are promoting here is the maintenance of a link to people and contexts so that we can orient ourselves in multiple ways via the data without losing track of phenomena because individual cases are typically (though not always) in view or accessible through such work. Aggregated works that lose that connection to individual cases are forced to be either exactly correct or leave us with no means to adequately reorient ourselves. This might be fine if our overall understanding of setting, context, and situations were more advanced, but as things stand, it is deeply unhelpful.

Valuing Numbers in Context

Our attempt to argue for a healthier balance of kinds of evidence in psychological science and our optimism that diverse and even traditionally mutually exclusive modes of investigation can be effectively used to improve our understanding may seem to some readers as a repudiation of numbers – a rejection of quantification much in line with some of the more strident manifestos traditionally attributed to qualitative researchers.

Though we have noted the value and use of natural history as a source of numerical data, and argued that qualitative work is not as inimical to quantitative research as supposed by some, our criticism of the careless use of aggregationist statistics (of either frequentist or Bayesian kind) may seem ideological and extreme.

We vehemently deny such accusations. We are very much in favour of numbers. The clarity, precision, and discipline that they impose on our characterisations of phenomena are invaluable. However, all numbers are not created equal. Their capacity to provide clarity and discipline depends not just on their character as numbers but on their position within an ecosystem of theory, measurement, and explanation – without which they are empty symbols, used to sanctify conclusions, rather than test hypotheses (Gigerenzer, 1998b; Tukey, 1969; see also Uher, 2022a, for a discussion of some common ways in which psychology assigns numerical values to behaviour and the problematic nature of these). They do not all provide evidence that can support the kinds of questions in which psychologists seem to be interested. What we need is a good place to start that orients us effectively to the phenomena of our subject matter. A place to start that helps us describe and analyse those phenomena clearly, in ways that, as Lakens (2021) suggests, give us some insight into what we really want to know.

Laboratory Situations

Our considerations of the various delusions have forced us to take a step back and look at things in context a little more. In this chapter, we have noted the potential benefit of seeing the bigger picture, describing and seeking to analyse behaviour and experience within webs of relationships, an ecosystem to which we can be oriented in ways from the broad and general, in terms perhaps of culture and anthropology, to the mid-scale of behaviour settings, to the finer grain of individual actions within those settings. Scientific practice that makes all of these scales of phenomena available to systematic description, explanation, and perhaps prediction is important, but the finest grain of understanding will remain dependent on observations and measurements in carefully controlled situations – laboratories. Reproducing behaviour or experience in a laboratory will involve not just the production of particular bodily motions or uttered sounds but the production of the crucial features of the situations in question.

Insofar as behaviours and experiences are phenomena that arise embedded within a web of relationships at different scales that give them meaning and form systems of feedback, then the most effective laboratory practices will involve some means of sampling whole "loops" – not just the start and end points of a behaviour or an experience, but the process of it within some sampled set of those loops, the feedback relationships. Not just behaviours, but whole activities.

A wide range of experimental techniques can be applied in this way. What they have in common, as Michael Spivey (2008) puts it, is a recognition of the continuous nature of behaviour. These varied techniques do less to isolate actions or discretise them such that all that can be ascertained is the connection between a stimulus and a response. Rather, there is a recording and examination of the progression of the activity. Often, this is not simply a matter of watching single responses to tasks as they unfold over milliseconds or seconds, but also how a person's actions at one time relate to and affect their actions at a later time, embedded in a variety of feedback mechanisms that characterise whole situations or settings.

Discretising responses separates them from context and breaks any analysis that might identify scalar or cross-scalar relationships. Paying attention to the whole activity and the relationships within it (changing over time and inter-connected across temporal and spatial scales as they may be) facilitates the production of precise but still contextualised data that offer insights into not just the type and frequency of behaviour but the *how* of it. This makes it much more likely that we can recognise consistencies and generalities (rather than assuming them) but also makes it easier to recognise qualitative differences in the way people go about the activity in question (Diener et al., 2022). An example from developmental psychology is illustrative here. Thelen and Smith (1994) describe research undertaken with infants as they develop the capacity to reach and grasp an object in front of them. Looking just at the task and the outcome, we see a developmental change that seems general – infants go from not being able to coordinate their actions effectively to being able to reliably complete the perceptuomotor task. In simple terms, this might be described as a common developmental milestone that is general across children. Thelen and Smith (1994), however, describe two children, Hannah and Gabriel, who both achieve this milestone but do so in qualitatively different ways. Hannah is a rather placid child, with habitually slow and gentle movements. Gabriel is more energetic, commonly making large, rapid motions. The development tasks for each, then, in order to successfully coordinate their reaching and grasping, are quite distinct. Hannah must put more *ooomph* into her actions to get the job done, while Gabriel needs to learn to tone it down. Both get to the same destination, but via different development trajectories.

Similarly, Knight and Fischer (1992) describe different means by which children learn to read. Examining not just error rates and fluency but the techniques and means by which children engage in the process, they identified three different learning pathways by which children were able to achieve reading fluency. These different learning trajectories were qualitatively different from one another and had dramatically different patterns of errors and success (one was clearly superior in this regard), but that qualitative difference would only be discerned via the focus on process and dynamics.

The dynamics of systems – how performance evolves over time in different phases of a task, how coordination between a person and their environment changes or responds to perturbations, falling apart or recovering – these provide insights into the relationship between a person and their context. Such research allows for both the identification of consistencies and variances in the performance of action. When are patterns robust to transformation or interference? When are patterns unstable and easily disrupted? When effective or satisfying, when inefficient or frustrating? Investigations framed in terms like these make available and relevant a large body of analytical and modelling tools in the form of "dynamical systems theory". Among other things, this mathematics allows for analysis of patterns of change, interaction, and coordination between components of a system (e.g., a person and their environment) and provide means for identifying cross-scalar variances as well as scale-invariant rules, and all without necessary recourse to aggregationist practices (though we should note that dynamical systems are not necessarily case-based and can be used in aggregationist ways).

Dynamical systems thinking is not an easy change of mindset for those of us used to working with more traditional experimental methods. Nevertheless, over the past few decades, it has proven to be a framework within which some of the most robust, precise, and replicable behavioural science has been undertaken (see Chemero, 2023; Favela, 2020 for some interesting overviews). The use of dynamical systems thinking has been pioneered and effectively used in fields as diverse as neuropsychology (Freeman, 1975, 1995; Shenoy et al., 2013); developmental psychology (Adolph & Hoch, 2019; Fischer & Bidell, 2006; Thelen, 1995; Thelen & Smith, 1994); cognitive psychology and psycholinguistics (Spivey, 2008; Townsend & Busemeyer, 1995; van Orden et al., 2003, 2005); social psychology (Richardson et al., 2014; Riley et al., 2011); and more (see Kelso, 1995 for a wide-ranging exploration of dynamical systems thinking within the inter-disciplinary field of cognitive science).

We noted in Chapter 5 that many of the principles of dynamical systems appear to be surprisingly general. The kind of autocorrelation over time that gives rise to the phenomenon of multifractality that we discussed briefly in that chapter is an example of this. The array of domains in which these tools have been effectively deployed, however, is strikingly broad. Patterns driven by these underlying principles have been identified not just across the breadth of psychological research but on topics as far-flung as the physics of pendula, the flickering of fireflies, the timing of heartbeats, the organisation of convection currents in heated pans of oil, the prediction and modelling of the weather, and many more. Crucially, these tools provide the means to ask questions sensibly about general underlying principles that nevertheless produce varied behaviours in differing contexts by finding ways to characterise and then analyse how the system transforms over time affected by its own history of activity – that is, in the presence of feedback.

Some of these principles exist not just across domains but also across scales. Kelty-Stephen (2024) has argued in a manner resonant with what we have said here that we must be sensitive to and cognisant of *scale-invariant* laws of dynamical systems. This is not a claim that some things happen the same across all scales, but that the same principles apply to the effects, feedback, autocorrelation, and other dynamics regardless of scale; behaviours that are quite different at different scales can nevertheless have underlying them the same dynamical principles. That such principles might be possible cannot be assessed by a scale-blind science.

As a set of principles for the framing of empirical questions and analysing the results of experiments or other controlled observations, the diverse collection of tools covered by the umbrella term of "dynamical systems theory" offers us a way to examine individual cases and explore generalities in a way that is scale-aware and appreciative of context.

These are of course not the only tools available to us. Indeed, the shift in perspective and skills needed to take full advantage is pretty daunting. There are much simpler, more basic steps that those of us with a more traditional training can take. (Young scholars take note, though; find ye some training in both ethological and/or more dynamic methods.) The question of whether a given pattern of behaviour, or a particular "effect", is a prevalent or pervasive phenomenon, an idiosyncratic one, or something that is a result of aggregation to samples and populations, is an empirical one. The means to answer that question is surprisingly straightforward and remains in keeping with the principles for research that we have set forward. In this chapter we have focused heavily on some of the ways in which research can be undertaken that maintains the connections between behaviour and the setting or context in which it takes place. In the following chapter, we continue our exploration of the rich and varied landscape of possibilities in research that are revealed to us when we shake ourselves loose of the Great Psychology Delusion, with a focus on a recognition of and working with individual cases.

Note

1 In addition to the forms described in the following paragraphs, Roald et al. (2021) also describe a "writer-reader generalisation", which is the implicit assumption that what is intended by the writer is picked and interpreted as such by the reader, something which is grounded in common-sense generalisation and whose limits should be reflected on explicitly.

9

BUILDING THE CASE FOR A MORE VALID SCIENCE

Think of a casino as having two doors. If we enter from one door, we are the House. From this perspective, we see the whole set of the games. The casino floor is a series of repeating events with varied (though generally known) probabilities. Though it is a place of chance and dynamic outcomes, it is also a place that can be known, and predicted, to a certain grain of resolution. If we operate at a scale appropriate to that grain of resolution, then we can be confident in our outcomes. Over the sweep of time, the House always wins.

If we enter the casino from the other door, things are quite different. From here, we are the gambler. We participate in first one game, one hand of cards, one spin of the wheel, then another. We experience the casino at a much finer grain of resolution, and at this scale it is a much more fraught place. There is excitement and hope, both energised by uncertainty. The trend of a game might be predictable, but each individual case is something else. The individual case is not a distribution in microcosm, it is its own thing. A single bet is as different from a game's long-term outcome as a house is from a brick, or a forest is from a tree.

The mismatch between these different perspectives on a complex environment mirrors that between different professionals engaged with human behaviour and experience. Public health and institutional policies must be set for the group, to steer or guide the overall flow of people's engagement with the settings in which those policies are applied. And while it is clear that human psychology is affected by those bigger scales and contexts, and cannot be fully understood without them, so too it is true that people are individuals, and the behaviours and experiences that we might explore in research and practice are not things that occur *in general*, but rather, are things that occur *in particulars*. Successful psychological research practice will provide data, and produce evidence, relevant to questions directed to that domain of individual people. In doing so, it will better characterise and investigate the subject matter of psychological science, but also provide a much sounder basis for the dialogue between research and professional practice.

As we noted in the previous chapter, for the most part this does not require a reinvention of the wheel. There already exist a host of relevant methods that can be brought to bear, but which don't play enough of a systematic or heavily weighted role in mainstream psychological research.

DOI: 10.4324/9781003503873-11

A properly nuanced and critical introduction to these various methods warrants entire books of their own. Our intention here is to provide enough of an overview to appreciate their potential value as providing evidence directly addressing questions that psychological researchers want answered. That is, the sciences of psychology are more likely to be valid and successful if we re-balance the respect and influence of research conducted according to these tenets. Where new analytical techniques are required, we will find that some will be more simple but more robust than many common analytical practices. In the second half of this chapter, we provide detailed explanation of a particular form of analysis which is both surprisingly straightforward, and surprisingly effective.

As a metaphor for life, there are two major limitations to the casino as we have just described it. The first is that we have presented the gambler in stark individuality – an isolated gambler making their way, game by game, across the casino floor. But we have just spent two chapters addressing the fact that we do not simply encounter the world on a moment by moment basis, entirely divorced from others. We live our lives in collaboration with others, sometimes in close connection, caught up in and moved by collective effort and experiences (see Cummins, 2018, for a fascinating exploration of these phenomena). At other times we are more self-aware and individuated, but still participating in collaborative settings most of which are governed by dynamics that are very different from the antagonism between player and House that is inherent in casinos.

The second, perhaps even more important limitation, is the role of chance and randomness. A casino is a place that is very carefully designed and built to be governed by randomness. In most countries they are closely monitored and controlled by regulators in order to ensure this. It takes great effort and care to make a person's world random, and this can only be achieved when a great deal of what makes the person who they are, and how their lives work, is stripped away and allowed to play no role. Casinos are technical places that are highly distinct from the rest of the world we live in.

Outside of casinos, as Stricker and Trierweiler (1995, p. 998) put it simply, "randomness is not random at the local level". Brunswik's (1955) original definition of ecological validity was that stimuli presented in a laboratory should occur with the same probability that they occur in the natural world, as though the natural world were a collection of random events with varying probabilities (indeed, it is often still modelled in this way). But as Heft (2014) has pointed out, within an ecosystem, while relationships may be complex they are anything but random. As we noted at length in the previous chapter, our environments have structure at multiple scales which is meaningful because together those structures make up the ecosystem in which our behaviour and experience occur.

While it is clearly true that behavioural ecology, settings, and context all shape and help give meaning to the activities in which we find ourselves, in our everyday lives it is still true that we don't enter this richer, more complex environment through the House door. More pointedly, if we find ourselves in need of the support of a professional psychologist, we are most likely to seek those services as an individual.

The Science of Clients

In Chapter 6, we explored the tensions that exist between the aggregationist perspective of most psychological research and the individual focus of applied work. The principles of research that we have proposed in Chapter 7 commit us to scientific work not just at the scale of groups and collectives, but with individual people. Many of the key phenomena of our science are not global, but local, and should be identifiable in individual cases not simply on aggregate.

Fortunately, in this case as in others that we have addressed, effective approaches are already available to be built upon. There are ways in which we can bring the needs of science and the needs of applied professionals into effective alignment. Among clinicians, as well as in other domains such as education and forensic psychology, a widespread technique to try to make sense of the individual in their context in a theory-informed and empirically-minded way is case formulation.

Case formulation is a method of recording and organising information relevant to a client of an applied professional. It evolved particularly within the domain of clinical practice, as a means of synthesising a variety of details relating to an individual case (Bruch, 2015; Turkat, 2014). There are numerous approaches to engaging in formulation, and as a result there are a range of definitions available in the literature. While there is variation, however, there is yet consensus on the broad terms.

Meyer and Turkat (1979, pp. 261–262) introduced the notion as an explanatory hypothesis that "(1) relates all of the patient's complaints to one another, (2) explains why the individual developed these difficulties, and (3) provides predictions regarding the patient's behavior given any stimulus conditions". Eells (2015, p. 15) describes it as a "process for developing a hypothesis about, and a plan to address, the causes, precipitants, and maintaining influences of a person's psychological, interpersonal, and behavioral problems in the context of that individual's culture and environment". Summarising, Bruch (2015, p. 34) offers "In other words, the formulation assumes the status of a personalized clinical theory to explain the nature and mechanism of the patient's problem". He goes on to add, however, that "...a valid formulation should also enable the clinician to make predictions about obstacles that are likely to occur during the course of treatment" (p. 35).

In formulation, the professional records details of symptoms, behaviours, experiences, and circumstances, and organises this information using available theories, forming hypotheses regarding the issues in question (Bruch, 2015). This integrative narrative forms part of the conversation with the client and helps support communication. From this perspective, then, interventions of various kinds are perceived as a form of hypothesis testing. Changes arising from actions taken are fed back into the case formulation, and the process iterated with the aim of supporting the client in overcoming challenges, alleviating distress and suffering, and fostering growth towards desired outcomes (Plutynski, 2024).

In this way, case formulation engages with the client's challenges as a scientific problem, to be approached and addressed with the attitude and methods of scientific practice. For some in therapeutic fields this makes the process undesirable – it would seem counter to the dignity of clients that they be treated as scientific puzzles, potentially objectifying people as mere "cases" rather than approached with full respect as humans that they deserve (e.g., Leiper, 2013; McClelland, 2013), possibly due to power differentials between the client and the practitioner (Grenier, 2021; McClelland, 2013). Defenders of case formulation approaches, however, argue that formulation can serve to *increase* the practitioner's empathy, by providing a scaffold for eliciting and appreciating the fullness of clients' experiences in the round – being *client* centred rather than *treatment* centred (Eells, 2015, p. 19). It is not the client, but their challenges, distress, and problems that are accounted as cases and investigated through the iterative process of formulation, intervention, and re-assessment.

This is not to suggest that case formulation as it is currently practised is a panacea for the problems associated with the research–practice gap and aggregationist research. As with any practice, case formulation is something that can be done well or done poorly, and as with the therapeutic process more generally it is difficult to evaluate (Ghaderi, 2011). There are varied methods used to undertake it, and extant suggestions for how formulation practices can be improved in a variety of ways. A tightly focussed case formulation process can constrain clients' communication rather than expand it. Ryan and Kilroe (2020) warn that some techniques put too sharp a limit on the extent to which aspects of a client's life that seem distant from their problematic experiences come to be represented in the formulation. To do formulation well, they argue, is to avoid narrowly constraining it, particularly early in the process (Ryan & Kilroe, 2020, see also the various chapters of Ryan, 2020).

There are a range of different techniques and models of formulation in use, and while we would be the last people to argue that there must be a single universal standard, more explicit discussion of and organisation around standards to improve communication and comparison would be valuable. Existing peer-reviewed journals for case sharing provide significant grounding in this regard (Fishman, 2000; Hersen, 2002).

The proponents of case formulation argue that it is demonstrably superior to simple diagnostic models, because few clients fit neatly into single diagnostic categories. A number of authors have suggested that case formulations form the basis of scientific practice within clinical or applied settings (Kraus & Behn, 2022; Stricker & Trierweiler, 1995).

Is Case Formulation Science?

Given our very brief outlining of case formulation here as a scientific process, in line with its proponents, one could be content to accept that professional practice can be effectively *scientific*, but still be wary of the extent to which such clearly idiographic work can contribute to the more progressive ambitions of *science*. Even advocates of case formulation do so in the recognition that individual cases are *messy*, not easily fitting into stable categories, with idiosyncrasies, variations, and exceptions being the norm. This messiness is a virtue because it provides for clinical sensitivity to the individual case, but might seem problematic for any hope of these practices supporting scientific activity, which is so often driven by a search for consistency.

It might be possible to see how general scientific practice can inform the local, but how is it that local science can inform the general?

Case formulations represent an example of thinking in relation to a person and their context which addresses the full loop of the interaction – in line with the principles of good experimental practice that we identified in the previous chapter in relation to dynamical approaches to understanding people's actions. In applied cases, the progression to the person's whole personal perspective and activity is in scope, and recorded at a very human scale of observation. The applied case is one that involves interventions, responses, a trajectory of the whole person-in-ecosystem over time. Case formulations therefore have some of the characteristics of natural histories, but include interventions by the practitioner-client alliance as well as developmental changes, in ways that can be made amenable to systematic review and reflection (Stricker & Trierwieler, 1995). Formulations also differ from natural histories in that they are collaborative endeavours with the subjects of the record.

Individual cases are typically messy affairs, but just as with the natural historical and behaviour settings work that we discussed in Chapter 8, where recurrences, patterns, or other regularities appear across such individual examples, they become viable targets for more fine-grained and systematic investigations. There will of course be a number of ways in which such investigations can be undertaken. It may be that a structured, controlled activity with the right characteristics can form the basis of a laboratory experiment ripe for examination with the tools of dynamical systems theory, or perhaps other investigative approaches with a more applied bent are relevant. Here we think it worthwhile to note one additional set of techniques that have decades of development behind them and that maintain that strong emphasis on the capacity to identify and track individual people and the phenomena of psychology that they present: single-case research designs.

Single-case Research Designs

Single-case research designs (which also go by alternative labels such as "N=1", "N-of-1", or "single-patient", in different contexts) involve systematically repeated recordings of particular target or dependent variables, and deliberate manipulations of an intervention or independent variable. They are therefore somewhat more focused and controlled than the more encompassing process of case formulation, though no doubt some case formulations could be counted as examples of single-case designs.

Continuous recording is crucial to the exercise, as that enables the identification of stable levels of the target variable (let's say, for example, the number of anxiety attacks) during a given period (Kazdin, 2021b; Vlaeyen et al., 2020). When a change is made (maybe a given clinical intervention such as the use of a particular self-calming technique), repeated measurements under the new regime are made until a new stable level can be identified. The individual being worked with therefore works as their own control condition (Gelman, 2018), and changes in the target variable can be evaluated through simple visual checking of a line graph or similar tool.

There are a host of different ways in which this basic format can vary, producing a rich family of single-case methods (Barlow et al., 2008; Kazdin, 2021b; see also Franklin et al., 1996; Kratochwill & Levin, 1992). Because these various forms of research design work with an individual, the possibility of confounding variables and other complexities is minimised or eliminated, while evidence for the relationship between the key variables is maximised (Kazdin, 2021a). If there is some question as to whether a change in the target variable was a result of a coincidence or something other than the intervention, a simple return to the baseline condition – removal of the intervention – will provide some clarity. What is more, repeated measurement during both baseline and intervention phases make clear whether the target variable is naturally unstable and … well, variable. This contextualises and facilitates the interpretation of any perceived change that takes place during the intervention phase.

Kazdin (2021a) laments that the terms "single" and "case" in "single-case research design" both come loaded with baggage that makes their introduction to researchers from other backgrounds often rather fraught. The word "case", for instance, is for many tightly bound up with the notion of the narrative "case study", and while such descriptions can be rich, insightful, and evocative, they often have relatively little by way of systematicity or standardisation to them. Somewhat differently, the notion of a "case" is considered by some practitioners as reductive, setting aside the humanity of the person in our care in favour of their consideration as a "case", an object of study (we noted above that the same concern is also raised for models of case formulation).

Kazdin (2021a) and others (Aydin, 2024; Normand, 2016; Vlaeyen et al., 2020), however, note that the concept of "case" is deployed not in a reductive manner, but an open one. The client is met on their own terms, and though there is a specific focus on chosen variables of interest, the concept of a case is one that encompasses them as a whole, without attempts to minimise their particularities or count them just as a member of a particular category, or instance of a given classification or diagnosis.

The singularity of single-case research is also carefully articulated by advocates of this family of methods in ways that are of interest to us here. These researchers are very clear that what matters in single-case design is that the unit of research is explicitly stated and then addressed at the level of that unit. The single-case is not always a single person – it might be a school, a hospital, a team, or a community (Kazdin, 2021a). In our present terms, the scale of observations is clearly stated up front, and interventions, observations, and measurements are consistently addressed appropriately to that scale.

All of which represents an argument for richer, more-involved engagement with a smaller number of participants, and indeed the potential for integration with any number of qualitative methods seems apparent. But this description may yet leave the reader with the same concerns about replication and generalisation as were raised with case formulation. As psychologists we are painstakingly trained to be sceptical of individuals – a science grounded only in exceptions is no science at all, and people are so diverse that a conclusion drawn on the basis of working with one might have no bearing in relation to others. If we very generously set aside that this fact has crippling implications for aggregationist approaches too, we can still perceive a strength to the slow and deliberate way in which replication and generalisation can be managed within a single-case framework. What these approaches open up is a systematic programme of generalisation based not on the production from a random sample, but from a carefully selected representative one.

A Systematic Programme of Generalisation

We briefly mentioned in Chapter 8 that qualitative work, though frequently described as providing very limited bases for generalisation, can nevertheless provide more insights regarding generality than they are often given credit for. This is because the participants in such studies can be selected for their representativeness. This is an important aspect of generalisation that has seen relatively little discussion but is unpacked in clarifying detail by Zhao (2021). In that paper she clearly articulates the logic of inference from samples and notes that confidence in generalisation does not arrive through some magical properties of random sampling, but rather from the extent to which a distribution of variables in the sample match those in the population – or simply-put, the extent to which the group of participants actually researched have characteristics or attributes in the same proportions as the overall population from which they are drawn.

Large random samples are frequently taken as an ideal because that process of sampling is taken to provide the greatest likelihood of that representativeness and has the benefit of being increasingly likely to do so as the sample size increases. Zhao (2021) notes, however, that even in cases where very large samples are involved, random sampling alone is not considered adequate. For instance, in the US National Comorbidity Survey (NCS), a stratified, multistage area probability sample was used but resulted in a group with 47.5% male participants. The NCS post-stratified their sample for the survey because a full enumeration of the population indicated

49.1% males. That is, even with large numbers, random sampling needs to be adjusted for the purposes of representativeness. In order to build up an accurate picture of prevalence of certain patterns or effects in a given population, what matters is not necessarily that participants are randomly selected, but that they are carefully selected to be representative (Zhao, 2021).

For the purposes of understanding generalisation in single-case research designs, this means that selection of participants can be made into a systematic programme for research (Normand, 2016). Every individual study represents an evaluation of the replicability of the patterns of outcomes being examined, as well as an explicit building block towards a broader evaluation of the generality of findings (see Shapiro, 1966 for a seminal articulation of this point). The set of participants can be planned and selected in the service of specific research goals, with intermediate insights and slow careful assessment of reliability being an inherent and essential part of the whole process (Normand, 2016).

Many readers may still chafe at the patience required to build up such fine-grained pictures of distributions and generalities of effects. Though gaining practice at single-case research is not difficult, when research habits and intuitions have been developed for years or decades on group-based methods, the desire for broad overviews of how pervasive certain patterns of behaviour are in a particular group or population is strong. We understand. And what is more, we have good news on this front. As it happens, it is quite possible to extend single-case research into the realms of the rich but seemingly oxymoronic multiple single-case design. In such instances the logic of repeated measurement of single individuals applies, though each case can be overlaid and patterns across cases as well as within them assessed for reliability. The point, however, is that the resolution of data all the way to individual participants is available for evaluation.

What is more, an even simpler mode of research and analysis is available, one that we believe closes the gap between single-case designs and more traditional group-based work, while still resisting aggregation. Keeping individual-participant data in frame at all times, we can examine whether a given pattern or behavioural effect is prevalent, or even pervasive in a given sample, and provide evidence that directly supports the kinds of conclusions that psychologists clearly want to make.

Testing the Pervasiveness of Psychological Effects

While we have raised in this book grave concerns about some common (though certainly not universal) practices of sample-based experimental psychology, we do not argue that sample means should be of no interest to psychology, nor that research to date does not offer us important insights. Indeed, it is quite possible that all of the raw data that have been collected to date have more to offer our research community than has been reported thus far.

There are specifics of individual variability, frequencies of individuals showing changes or effects, and other details that can provide us with a much more rounded description of the phenomena in which we are interested. But it is important to realise that averages describe systems different to the individuals that make up those systems. In order to understand them, we will not only have to study the individuals as individuals more frequently but will also need to develop a set of theoretical resources (currently unavailable for most domains, such as cognitive psychology) for understanding the relationship between the individuals and the samples in which they participate. In doing so, it will greatly improve the coherence between psychological phenomena as they occur in controlled settings, and as they occur "in the wild" (Hutchins, 1995; see also Cialdini, 2009 and McGann & Speelman, 2020).

It turns out that there may be a great deal to be gained from focussing more on intensive examination of individual behaviour. This was *de rigueur* in the early history of psychology (Danziger, 1994; Gigerenzer, 1998b) and has been a regular feature of research into perceptual processes (Smith & Little, 2018). There will still be a need for studying collections of individuals, but there must be a close focus on the data produced by each individual so as to determine the pervasiveness of particular behaviour patterns, and the possibility that differences in behaviour within a sample are more likely to be seen in particular sub-samples identifiable by some shared characteristic. Such data will better inform generalisation statements, and possible applications beyond the research field.

Large data samples will still be important. For instance, we venture to suggest that a conclusion that 80% of people demonstrate a particular effect will be far more convincing when it is derived from a sample of 500 people than if it were derived from a sample of 10 people.

Analysis of Pervasiveness

As indicated earlier, we suggest that one of the reasons why researchers who were aware of the ergodic problem may have been reluctant to move away from traditional sample-based experimental psychology designs is that they were unaware of any easily applied or understood alternative methods. Below we describe one method for addressing the ergodic problem in a subset of experimental psychology designs that researchers may find relatively straightforward to apply. The design used in the example is simple, but it reveals the required evidence for common conclusions. More complicated designs can be analysed to provide such evidence, but more sophisticated techniques are required (e.g., Bayesian Prevalence, Ince et al., 2021; McManus et al., 2023; Observation Oriented Modelling (OOM), Grice, 2011, 2015; Grice et al., 2015). The method for analysing the pervasiveness of an effect we demonstrate below can be considered a specific case of an Ordinal Pattern Analysis (OPA) (Craig & Abramson, 2018; Thorngate & Carroll, 1986). Thus, this method is not a new one, however, we present it in a simple manner to demonstrate both the need for such an approach to data analysis, and the sorts of conclusions such an analysis can enable.

For a method of data analysis to be useful it should reflect the types of conclusions that researchers generally report but often do not have the evidence to support (see Molenaar, 2008a; Thorngate & Carroll, 1986). For example, "people behave in X fashion under Y circumstances" – such a statement carries with it the implication that *most* people behave in X fashion, however, researchers rarely substantiate such an implication with relevant evidence (Speelman et al., 2024). What is required to support such statements is some indication of how many people were observed to behave in this way (Sauer, 2018). Equally useful would be some indication of how many people did not behave this way. This can be reported directly, or the number of people behaving in the target manner can be reported as a proportion of the total number of people observed. There may also be good reason to report the number of people who behaved in the opposite manner (if that makes sense in the context). Above all, this method of analysis should be a measure of the pervasiveness of the target behaviour.

To achieve the aims of the pervasiveness analysis, we need at least three things:

Precise Definitions of Behaviour

In practice, this will require more than just a clear description of the behaviour. It will often require that a precise criterion is defined whereby we can determine if the behaviour has been observed, or not. For instance, we may be interested in whether or not a person has exhibited a particular effect (e.g., the Stroop effect). To achieve the aims we have specified for the pervasiveness measure, it will be necessary to be able to decide from an individual's performance data whether that individual exhibited the effect. Traditionally psychologists make this judgement on the basis of a sample of people and make decisions about whether or not an effect was observed *in the sample*. The pervasiveness measure requires that this can be done with each individual. How this is done requires some significant thinking about what constitutes an effect, and this should include how large an effect is before we conclude that an effect has been observed. We fully acknowledge that this could be a difficult task, but we argue that such considerations will ultimately be valuable in increasing the confidence in the validity and reliability of our research results. We illustrate the types of necessary considerations below in an example.

Count the Number of People

When we have a clear definition of what constitutes the target behaviour, it is a simple matter then to count the number of people in our sample that exhibited this behaviour. Most of the time this will imply the number of people who did not show the behaviour, although sometimes it might be useful to introduce greater granularity in the counting. For example, a researcher might be interested in the number of people that exhibit a particular effect (e.g., performance on X in Condition A is better than in Condition B: $X_A > X_B$) and distinguish this number from the number that show no such effect ($X_A = X_B$) and those that show the opposite effect ($X_A < X_B$). Further, there could also be occasions where the behaviour has a variety of definitions that vary in extent (e.g., the effect is observed when the differences in performance exceed 10% vs. the effect is observed when the differences in performance exceed 20%), and so the number of people that fall into the relevant categories under the respective conditions will be required.

Define "Majority"

When we have determined the number of people in our sample that have exhibited an effect, we should then be interested in how best to characterise that number. For instance, does this number represent the "majority" of people in the sample? To answer this question requires a definition of "majority", a pre-defined proportion value corresponding to our idea of "most people". In our view, this is a value that would convince others that what we have observed is "pervasive", and presumably, worthy of theoretical and practical interest. For instance, "80% of people showing the effect" might be considered convincing evidence that "the effect exists in most people". Before we are criticised for attempting to replace one arbitrary criterion ($\alpha = .05$) with another arbitrary criterion, this 80% value could be considered a benchmark value that signals a degree of confidence that we have observed a pervasive phenomenon. That is, if the proportion of a sample that behaves in a particular manner is 80% or more, it is unlikely that many people will argue if this result is characterised as "most participants behaved in this manner". As the proportion falls below this value, however, more people are likely to take issue if the result is described as a characteristic of "most" of the sample. Thus the criterion pervasiveness value can be viewed as the degree to which an assertion about the existence of an effect is likely to be considered convincing by others. Importantly, this value should not be considered fixed and indeed is likely to change to reflect a range of factors, including the controversial nature of the claim.

At this point we would emphasise that the pervasiveness approach is presented as a more appropriate means of discovering the (near) universality of an effect. That is, it is a technique that can provide the evidence to justify the type of conclusions psychology researchers are keen to make about their research, and so is a worthy substitute for the aggregationist statistics we have criticised earlier in the book. Nonetheless, our championing of pervasiveness analyses should not be taken as an indication that effects seen in the majority are the only ones worth detecting. Discovering that only a small number of people reliably show the effects of a particular intervention would be important knowledge when considering the efficacy of the intervention. For instance, a minority of people may respond well to a particular form of therapy, but the majority do not. This does not rule out the therapy as a useful tool in counselling but simply requires us to develop a means of identifying those people for whom the therapy is effective. We pick up this point below.

Analysis of Pervasiveness: A Worked Example

Some years ago, one of us published a report of an experiment designed to test several methods for improving peoples' skill at determining whether a skin lesion is dangerous (Speelman et al., 2010). Details of the methodology and results can be found in that paper, but in essence there were five experimental conditions to which 100 participants were allocated randomly ($n = 20$). Two of these conditions involved practice at making decisions about skin lesions. The indicator of whether a condition (the *condition* variable) was effective in improving skill was the difference between performance on a Pre-test and a Post-test (the *test* variable) of making a dangerous/non-dangerous decision about a set of pictures of skin lesions. The conditions were compared in their effect on this skill by conducting ANOVAs on the accuracy (*Acc*) of, and time to make (*RT*), decisions about the lesions. In both analyses, interactions between *condition* and *test* were statistically significant, indicating that the amount of improvement observed from the Pre-test to the Post-test was related to the condition experienced in between the tests.

It is pertinent to focus on the way in which the results of this experiment were characterised in the conclusions. As reported in the paper, "The current experiment found that 30 min. of training with several hundred pictures of skin lesions can improve the ability to discriminate between dangerous and non-dangerous skin lesions by 12–15%" (Speelman et al., 2010, p. 293). An obvious question that should be asked of this conclusion is, what is the pervasiveness of this finding? Did everyone in the conditions that showed this overall level of improvement demonstrate a similar amount of improvement? And what of people in the other conditions – did they uniformly show little improvement? As was convention at the time, and, as we argue here, still the case now, no information that could be used to answer these questions was reported in the paper. This is where the pervasiveness analysis can fill the gap between the data we often routinely collect and the conclusions we usually want to make about our experiments.

The mean data values from each individual that were analysed with ANOVA in the original paper are presented in Tables 9.1 and 9.2. In Table 9.1, the Pre-test RT is compared with the Post-test RT. Positive RT difference values represent an improvement in the speed of making

TABLE 9.1 RT (*ms*) data from Speelman et al. (2010)

Participant	*Condition*	*Premean*	*Postmean*	*Diff (pre–post)*	*Participant*	*Condition*	*Premean*	*Postmean*	*Diff (pre–post)*	*Participant*	*Condition*	*Premean*	*Postmean*	*diff (pre–post)*
1	1	2013.06	832.26	1180.8	41	3	1368.06	907.16	460.9	81	5	2467.06	1695.74	771.32
2	1	2604.94	1317.04	1287.9	42	3	1904.03	741.24	1162.79	82	5	1996.35	1653.86	342.49
3	1	2648.43	2027.32	621.11	43	3	1339.48	951.54	387.94	83	5	874.71	931.93	-57.22
4	1	2345.89	1038.43	1307.46	44	3	1876.62	981.83	894.79	84	5	1286.4	920.17	366.23
5	1	2241.44	1035.26	1206.18	45	3	1680.52	1171.45	509.07	85	5	1742.49	1425.27	317.22
6	1	2435.8	784.57	1651.23	46	3	2070.37	1692.01	378.36	86	5	2006.94	2074.1	-67.16
7	1	2347.35	772.15	1575.2	47	3	1551.54	800.8	750.74	87	5	3348.83	3361.56	-12.73
8	1	1976.36	718.17	1258.19	48	3	2151.11	1225.61	925.5	88	5	1565.82	1600.44	-34.62
9	1	2591.59	1593.74	997.85	49	3	1932.1	1543.13	388.97	89	5	1936.61	1490.12	446.49
10	1	2213.02	1143.95	1069.07	50	3	3261.32	1218.78	2042.54	90	5	1699.1	1282.89	416.21
11	1	2315.94	924.17	1391.77	51	3	2446.97	1066.47	1380.5	91	5	840.17	771.62	68.55
12	1	2389.63	1291.25	1098.38	52	3	1977.76	926.58	1051.18	92	5	1621.41	1532.9	88.51
13	1	2007.84	1382.1	625.74	53	3	3109.07	1213.93	1895.14	93	5	2083.82	1881.5	202.32
14	1	2091.5	984.35	1107.15	54	3	1866.5	1362.81	503.69	94	5	1508.56	1684.86	-176.3
15	1	2729.48	1086.35	1643.13	55	3	2274.39	1658.72	615.67	95	5	1561.06	1410.25	150.81
16	1	1849.05	1237.83	611.22	56	3	2265.82	1204.99	1060.83	96	5	1676.82	2146.16	-469.34
17	1	2369.29	950.32	1418.97	57	3	1783.42	925.24	858.18	97	5	3001.33	1447.63	1553.7
18	1	2724.26	1199.57	1524.69	58	3	3534.62	1171.8	2362.82	98	5	1790.08	1275.83	514.25
19	1	2555.23	1066.91	1488.32	59	3	2428.83	1164	1264.83	99	5	1929.88	1454.15	475.73
20	1	2512.35	1356.28	1156.07	60	3	1237.35	714.32	523.03	100	5	1145.2	1196.51	-51.31
21	2	3140.15	1802.76	1337.39	61	4	2099.92	1770.96	328.96					
22	2	1645.91	2578.85	-932.94	62	4	2344.75	2166.57	178.18					
23	2	2155.22	1562.05	593.17	63	4	2842.33	2853.46	–11.13					
24	2	2483.86	1971.13	512.73	64	4	1185.57	1107.5	78.07					
25	2	1450.26	1975.1	–524.84	65	4	1861.44	2099.17	–237.73					
26	2	3029.75	2122.21	907.54	66	4	2207.76	1413.79	793.97					
27	2	2261.57	2228.38	33.19	67	4	2679.25	1499.89	1179.36					
28	2	2251.91	1712.87	539.04	68	4	3089.42	1559.58	1529.84					

(*Continued*)

TABLE 9.1 (Continued)

Participant	*Condition*	*Premean*	*Postmean*	*Diff (pre–post)*	*Participant*	*Condition*	*Premean*	*Postmean*	*Diff (pre–post)*	*Participant*	*Condition*	*Premean*	*Postmean*	*diff (pre–post)*
29	2	1804.35	1681.31	123.04	69	4	2415.24	1629.1	786.14					
30	2	2364.68	2021.7	342.98	70	4	1581.82	931.49	650.33					
31	2	2245.64	2016.78	228.86	71	4	2708.03	2694.96	13.07					
32	2	1778.43	1686.13	92.3	72	4	1017.21	1232.96	–215.75					
33	2	2783.01	1764.77	1018.24	73	4	1737.45	1510.94	226.51					
34	2	2165.08	1964.08	201	74	4	1780.16	1888.63	–108.47					
35	2	1897.53	2097.56	–200.03	75	4	1609.85	1554.2	55.65					
36	2	2084.23	2134.07	–49.84	76	4	1869.37	1193.85	675.52					
37	2	1906.34	1914.46	–8.12	77	4	1419.11	867.9	551.21					
38	2	2017.65	1693.88	323.77	78	4	2139.53	2506.74	–367.21					
39	2	2079.25	2017.6	61.65	79	4	1185.85	1627.96	–442.11					
40	2	2017.91	2016.63	1.28	80	4	2857.52	1498.24	1359.28					

TABLE 9.2 Accuracy (%) data from Speelman et al. (2010)

Participant	*Group*	*Premean*	*Postmean*	*Diff (post–pre)*	*Participant*	*Group*	*Premean*	*Postmean*	*Diff (post–pre)*	*Participant*	*Group*	*Premean*	*Postmean*	*Diff (post–pre)*
1	1	65.18	80	14.82	41	3	70	73.33	3.33	81	5	63.33	56.67	-6.66
2	1	76.67	73.33	–3.34	42	3	86.67	86.67	0	82	5	76.67	83.33	6.66
3	1	70	64.81	–5.19	43	3	76.67	86.67	10	83	5	83.33	83.33	0
4	1	82.22	70	–12.22	44	3	70	86.67	16.67	84	5	70	67.78	-2.22
5	1	79.26	73.33	–5.93	45	3	83.33	90	6.67	85	5	83.33	76.67	-6.66
6	1	63.33	93.33	30	46	3	76.67	70	-6.67	86	5	56.67	61.11	4.44
7	1	76.67	86.67	10	47	3	80	66.67	-13.33	87	5	70	80	10
8	1	65.18	80	14.82	48	3	86.67	96.67	10	88	5	73.33	75.56	2.23
9	1	72.22	75.55	3.33	49	3	56.67	82.22	25.55	89	5	73.33	73.33	0
10	1	75.18	83.33	8.15	50	3	76.67	80	3.33	90	5	66.67	60	-6.67
11	1	76.67	86.67	10	51	3	60	86.67	26.67	91	5	66.67	76.67	10
12	1	68.52	83.33	14.81	52	3	72.59	80	7.41	92	5	73.33	78.89	5.56
13	1	80	90	10	53	3	55.56	83.33	27.77	93	5	86.67	83.33	-3.34
14	1	54.81	66.67	11.86	54	3	83.33	93.33	10	94	5	90	80	-10
15	1	53.33	76.67	23.34	55	3	58.33	86.67	28.34	95	5	53.33	86.67	33.34
16	1	66.67	86.67	20	56	3	63.33	83.33	20	96	5	73.33	73.33	0
17	1	66.67	83.33	16.66	57	3	82.59	90.61	8.02	97	5	65	70	5
18	1	68.52	90	21.48	58	3	46.67	85.93	39.26	98	5	70	76.67	6.67
19	1	72.59	93.33	20.74	59	3	53.33	85.93	32.6	99	5	89.63	93.33	3.7
20	1	73.33	86.67	13.34	60	3	33.33	86.67	53.34	100	5	58.89	76.67	17.78
21	2	67.59	66.67	–0.92	61	4	82.22	79.63	-2.59					
22	2	63.33	83.33	20	62	4	43.33	60	16.67					
23	2	72.22	60	–12.22	63	4	53.33	69.26	15.93					
24	2	68.15	46.67	–21.48	64	4	76.67	86.67	10					
25	2	61.85	73.33	11.48	65	4	63.33	56.67	-6.66					
26	2	71.48	66.67	–4.81	66	4	66.67	75.41	8.74					
27	2	72.22	63.33	–8.89	67	4	68.15	65.55	-2.6					
28	2	72.96	66.67	–6.29	68	4	43.33	55.18	11.85					

(Continued)

TABLE 9.2 (Continued)

Participant	*Group*	*Premean*	*Postmean*	*Diff (post–pre)*	*Participant*	*Group*	*Premean*	*Postmean*	*Diff (post–pre)*	*Participant*	*Group*	*Premean*	*Postmean*	*Diff (post–pre)*
29	2	75.92	86.67	10.75	69	4	66.67	83.33	16.66					
30	2	78.52	70	–8.52	70	4	69.26	63.33	-5.93					
31	2	90	66.67	–23.33	71	4	73.33	82.96	9.63					
32	2	86.67	80	–6.67	72	4	80	83.33	3.33					
33	2	54.44	90	35.56	73	4	86.67	53.33	-33.34					
34	2	82.96	63.33	–19.63	74	4	90	83.33	-6.67					
35	2	86.67	76.67	–10	75	4	69.26	70	0.74					
36	2	76.67	66.67	–10	76	4	20	96.67	76.67					
37	2	83.33	83.33	0	77	4	60	70	10					
38	2	86.67	80	–6.67	78	4	70.36	81.76	11.4					
39	2	86.67	80	–6.67	79	4	83.33	80	-3.33					
40	2	86.67	80	–6.67	80	4	63.33	70	6.67					

decisions about the skin lesions. In Table 9.2, a similar comparison is made between the Pre-test and Post-test accuracy values, with positive values indicating improved decision accuracy.

In order to conduct a pervasiveness analysis such as we have outlined above, we first need to define the effect that we are interested in detecting. In the skin cancer experiment, the aim was to detect improvement differences between the conditions. In the original analysis, the size of the improvement was not central, just whether the mean improvement observed in some groups was greater or less than the improvement observed in other groups. However, an average amount by which the accuracy of detection improved was reported. In a pervasiveness analysis it is important to define the amount of improvement we think is important enough to warrant further consideration. This is the hard bit. We could take a relaxed view and consider that any improvement in RT would be sufficient to indicate an improvement. This would likely result in many people in each group being classed as having improved, particularly since for all participants in this design it would have been at least the second time they performed the task, and it could be expected that most would improve at least a small amount for just this reason. On the other hand, we could adopt a strict attitude, and only count reductions in RT that were, for example, 50% or greater as indicating improvement. This would likely reduce the number of people in each group exhibiting such an improvement by a large amount. To illustrate how the number of people showing an effect is related to the size of the effect we are interested in, the number of people in the skin cancer experiment who exhibited improvements in RT and Acc were counted, for improvements of different size. These counts are presented in Figures 9.1 and 9.2.

The first thing to notice about both figures is the lines all decline in value as the effect sizes increase. This is to be expected, especially if the effects under observation have natural limits to their magnitude, as is the case here with RT and accuracy.

In Figure 9.1, the differences between the conditions in their effects on improvements in RT are obvious. For any particular effect size, there were more people in conditions 1 and 3 that exhibited this amount of improvement than people in the other conditions. Conditions 1 and 3 were the conditions in which participants practiced making decisions about skin lesions. Using the benchmark suggested above, we could conclude then that "most" people (i.e., 80%) in these conditions improved their response speed by at least 30%. We have included in the figure a dotted horizontal line at the 80% mark on the proportion scale, and a dotted vertical line at the 30% mark on the effect size scale to assist with determining whether most people in a condition improved by this much or more. None of the other conditions reached this benchmark for any of the effect sizes. Therefore it seems safe to conclude from this data that, insofar as the sample was representative of the population, most people would improve the speed of their decision making in this task by at least 30% by engaging in the training utilised in conditions 1 and 3, whereas few people would improve by this amount by being subject to any of the other conditions.

The differences between the conditions with respect to the accuracy of the decisions (Figure 9.2) are not as stark as for RT. Although more people in conditions 1 and 3 exhibited particular improvement amounts than people in the other conditions, as far as meeting the standard for "most" people, the greatest amount of improvement exhibited by 80% of people in conditions 1 and 3 was only 2.5%. This is substantially smaller than the amount of improvement spruiked in the original report of this experiment (12–15%). This discrepancy does not reflect some sort of arithmetic error in the original report, just a difference in perspective. The discrepancy does, however, demonstrate how reliance on means can be misleading in terms of representing

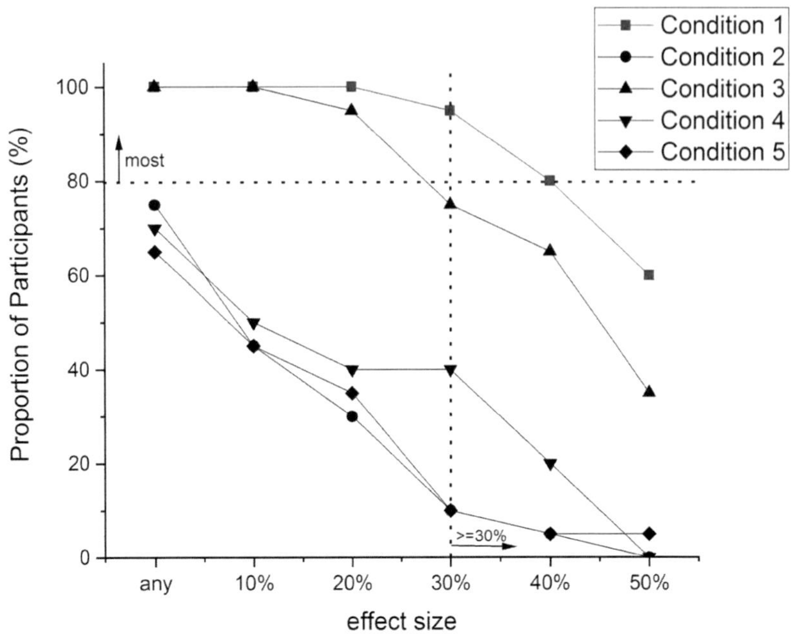

FIGURE 9.1 The proportion of people (%) in each condition of the Speelman et al. (2010) experiment that exhibited a particular "effect size" (i.e., a reduction in RT of a particular amount), or greater. Effect size was calculated as the difference between Pre-test RT and Post-test RT as a percentage of Pre-test RT (100 × (PreRT-PostRT)/PreRT). Original data values are presented in Table 9.1.

majority performance. Furthermore, this result has demonstrated how a pervasiveness analysis enables determination of whether a group effect reflects the performance of the majority of the group, or possibly the existence of a subset within the group that displayed a very large effect. Indeed, inspection of Table 9.2 indicates that there are some possible outliers in conditions 1 and 3 that would have had an inflationary effect on the means for each condition, which probably did not affect the outcome of the original analysis, but it certainly did affect the final conclusion about the amount of improvement observed. The pervasiveness analysis is not affected by such outliers to the same extent.

Advantages of a Pervasiveness Analysis

An analysis that considers the pervasiveness of an effect within a sample has several advantages over an analysis that aggregates the data of members of a sample to determine whether there has been an overall effect. We consider some of these below.

Superior Measure of Effect Size

A pervasiveness analysis can provide a more informative measure of effect size to traditional measures of effect size. In the pervasiveness method, a (minimum) effect size is stated and can

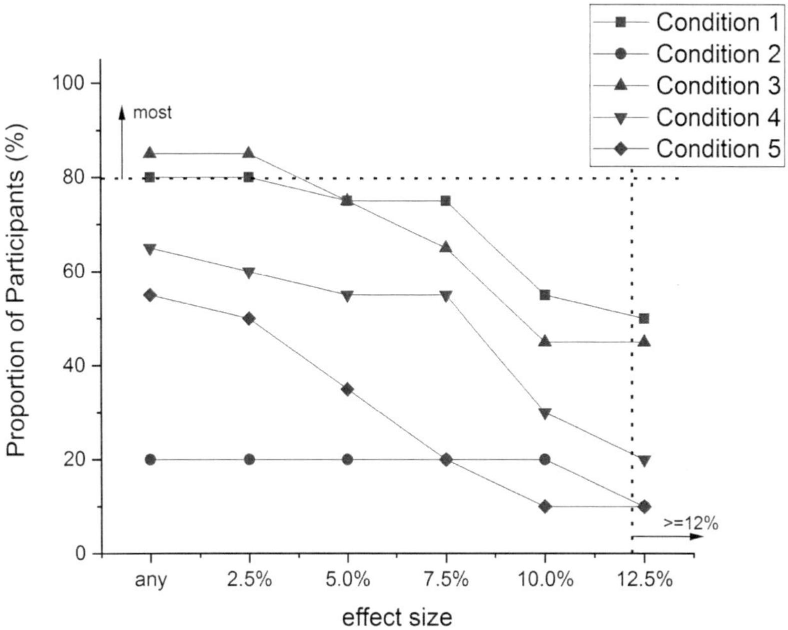

FIGURE 9.2 The proportion of people (%) in each condition of the Speelman et al. (2010) experiment that exhibited a particular "effect size" (i.e., an increase in accuracy of a particular amount), or greater. Effect size was calculated as the difference between Post-test Acc and Pre-test Acc (PostAcc-PreAcc). Original data values are presented in Table 9.2.

be plotted on a pervasiveness graph such as those in Figures 9.1 and 9.2, and the proportion of people who meet this criterion is reported. In traditional measures, the effect size reported is an average calculated from the sample. For instance, the effect size stemming from an experiment that demonstrates a performance difference between two conditions is a reflection of the size of the difference between the mean performance in one condition with the mean performance in the other condition (and often standardised by dividing by something like the standard deviation of the sample of scores, such as in Cohen's d). Just as the mean of a set of scores does not convey how most of the sample behaved, traditional effect size measures do not reveal the size of the effect revealed by most people in the sample. In contrast, a pervasiveness analysis will indicate the size of the effect demonstrated by most people in the sample.

Results Closer to What We Want to Say

Earlier we identified an issue with the way we interpret the results of experiments, where we regularly imply that our data indicates that *most* people behave in a certain way. The issue we identified was that we rarely look at our data in a way that will determine if these conclusions are a fair reflection of the behaviour of most people in the sample we have studied. Conducting a pervasiveness analysis, however, provides clear evidence that can support such statements, when warranted, and bring our science a lot closer to the types of conclusions we seem to long for but which have been justified with insufficient evidence.

Easily Combine Pervasiveness Estimates from Different Studies

The type of pervasiveness analysis outlined here results in values that are simple counts of the number of people in a sample who exhibit a particular type of performance. If other studies examine the same phenomenon with different samples, and report pervasiveness information, it would be a straightforward exercise to combine the various pervasiveness values into a new value that represents the total number of people exhibiting the target performance in the combined sample. For example, imagine five studies with similar designs, with N of 40, 65, 90, 101, and 135. Imagine further that in each of these studies, the reported number of people who exhibited a particular effect was 35, 58, 82, 96, and 120, respectively. These results could be combined, in a form of meta-analysis, to indicate that the overall pervasiveness of the effect is 391/431, or over 90%. This result is arguably more convincing that the effect is demonstrated by most people than any of the results for the individual studies.

Pervasiveness is Similar to Replicability

A pervasiveness analysis not only provides information about how pervasive an effect is, it also can be interpreted as a measure of the replicability of the effect. That is, pervasiveness explicitly represents the proportion of people in a sample that show the effect. The pervasiveness of an effect also implies the probability of observing the effect when we test one more person, or another group of people (e.g., Ince et al., 2021). The confidence we can have with claims of replicability will increase with the size of the sample we have observed. Furthermore, if the 80% rule is accepted, this could rule out small effects from being investigated further, and thus could reduce the publication of non-reproducible effects.

We (Moore et al., 2023) recently published a study in which we re-analysed data previously reported from successful replications of nine famous experiments (Zwaan et al., 2018). Rather than the null-hypothesis significance tests performed in the original study, we performed pervasiveness analyses, which examined the number of people in the original samples that demonstrated the effect each experiment is renowned for. Seven of the nine experiments met the 80% pervasiveness criteria threshold adopted in our study. That is, in each of these seven experiments, over 80% of participants demonstrated the target effect. The remaining two experiments, which utilised the shape simulation and repetition priming tasks, did not meet the threshold. This means that regardless of conditions, fewer than 80% of individuals demonstrated the effect in these two experiments. In fact, the overall pervasiveness values were only 70% and 64% for the shape simulation and repetition priming tasks, respectively. This result contrasts with those reported by Zwaan et al. (2018), who reported that all nine experiments were able to reproduce the original effects. While the Zwaan et al. (2018) work demonstrated replication of the group effects found in the original experiments, we argue that the finer grain of analysis we reported, which is very simple to undertake, provides useful further insight into what we mean by "effect" and how even successful replication can camouflage interesting and potentially important variation in outcomes of otherwise robust phenomena.

The Moore et al. (2023) study demonstrates the usefulness of pervasiveness as a greater understanding of the reproducibility of an effect. In seven of the replicated experiments analysed, the effects were observed in over 80% of the sample. This represents strong evidence that these effects are reproducible in the substantive majority of people. In contrast, in the other two replicated experiments, the effects were more varied. This then raises questions about the reproducibility of the shape simulation and repetition priming effects, and hence any claims about the universality of these effects. It suggests that there are important details yet to be understood about these phenomena, and notable questions regarding whether they can be understood as identifying phenomena common to a shared set of cognitive processes or whether there are substantially different ways of interacting with stimuli that need to be recognised and examined further. One could speculate about the validity of these effects, or possibly the selective nature of them (e.g., they may only be exhibited by people with certain psychological characteristics). At the least, these results suggest some circumspection regarding Zwaan et al.'s (2018) claim that the effects in these experiments are all "highly robust": most are, but a couple are not.

The results of the Moore et al. (2023) study suggest a means for testing the universality assumption we have identified as underlying the Aggregation Delusion. If a pervasiveness analysis indicates that the majority of a sample exhibit the same effect, then this may justify aggregating the results of that sample, or possibly the results of just the majority, in order to perform further group-based analyses. That is, identifying that a large number of people in a sample all performed in the same way may justify the assumption that they share similar cognitive processes, that they are ergodic, and so provides a rationale for aggregating their results. It is important to note, though, that if the purpose of said group-based analyses is to determine whether an effect has been detected, this fact has already been established by the pervasiveness analysis, making the group-based analyses redundant. Of course, there may be other features of the data that group-based analyses could uncover that are beyond the scope of pervasiveness analyses as described here.

Low Pervasiveness may Indicate the Existence of Homogenous Sub-groups

It is possible that, according to the 80% rule, no overall effect is observed in a sample. Closer scrutiny, however, of how individuals in the sample performed may indicate that there are sub-groups that behave in different ways. If there was some way of characterising these groups (e.g., handedness), then it might be possible to generate more refined effect descriptions (e.g., 80% of left handers performed in X way, 80% of right handers performed in Y way). Such an analysis provides similar information to that often provided by individual differences analyses using a correlational approach, particularly those exploring the existence of moderating variables. As we suggested above, identifying individuals for whom a particular intervention has an effect, and those for whom it does not, could be important information in determining whether particular interventions are useful in an applied context.

The Benefits of Observing Effects Within Subjects

Given that a pervasiveness analysis as we have outlined here requires that each person in a sample can potentially exhibit an effect, it may not be possible to apply such an analysis with all experimental paradigms or designs. For instance, some within-subject designs are well-suited to analyses of pervasiveness. In such designs a measure of a change in performance can be compared with the pre-defined change that constitutes the effect. In contrast, between-subject comparisons could be challenging, especially if there is only one observation per person. To conduct a pervasiveness analysis, as we have presented it here requires the ability to detect an effect in each individual. In a between-subjects design, the effect is examined by a comparison of the means of the various groups. In such cases, it may be necessary to reconceptualise the effect, or redesign the experiment, so that the effect can be observed within subjects. If this is not possible then an alternate method, such as OOM (Grice, 2011) or a Bayesian prevalence analysis (Ince et al., 2021), could be useful. It is worthwhile reiterating, however, that between-subjects designs suffer a logical problem with respect to inferring experimental effects. As we discussed in Chapter 3, the gold standard of research design, the Randomised Controlled Trial (RCT) is always missing half of the necessary data to fully observe an effect (Eronen, 2020). That is, such experiments possess the implicit assumption that we can infer effects that occur within people by comparing people in one condition with people in another condition. In other words, between-subject effects can be used to infer within-subject effects. But if we never observe these within-subject effects, how confident can we be that they exist? This uncertainty underlines the importance of trying to observe effects within subjects wherever possible, while recognising the potential for sequence or carryover effects (these can be alleviated to some extent by designs whereby participants undertake many trials per condition; McManus et al., 2023). The situation is made even more extreme when correlations are used to infer trend relationships between variables. In such studies, individuals contribute only one point in a trend. Indeed, "the between-person differences … simply do not exist at the level of the individual" (Lamielle, 2013, p. 70), further emphasising the need to examine trends within individuals (Lamielle, 1997; Schmiedek et al., 2020).

The pervasiveness method of analysis does not preclude concern with measurement error. In many situations, it will not be sufficient to compare two measurements of a person to determine whether or not they have exhibited an effect because each of those two measurements may not provide an accurate indication of the person's true value on the dependent variable of interest. If their performance on that variable is typically associated with a distribution of values, and reaction time is a classic example (Ratcliff, 1979), then it will be necessary to take many measurements within the two experimental conditions of interest. Such an approach may then require some form of inferential statistical test to determine whether the sample of measurements *for the individual* reflects the effect under scrutiny (Ince et al., 2021).

Effects have Clear a priori Definitions

One valuable initiative that has followed the reproducibility crisis in psychology has been the pre-registration of experiments. One advantage of pre-registering experiments prior to their onset is that many of the questionable research practices that have been identified as possible causes of poor reproducibility of psychological effects are rendered less influential (Nosek & Lakens, 2014; although see van Rooij, 2019). A similar advantage applies to pervasiveness analyses. These require a clear definition of what type of behaviour constitutes an effect prior to performing the analysis. This could be derived from previous research, theory, or some other form of reasoning about what would constitute a scientifically significant effect. For example, a researcher could argue that an experimental condition that leads to 25% or more improvement in performance speed on a particular task compared to a control condition was an effect worth testing for. Decisions about what constitutes an effect would be intimately connected with the nature of the effect, and the possible causes underlying it. In contrast, sample-based statistical analyses often use the data to define an effect (e.g., the mean performance in Condition A was faster than the mean performance in Condition B) and provide a *post hoc* characterisation of its magnitude (i.e., the effect size). Subsequent experiments on the same phenomenon are rarely concerned with finding the same-sized effect, just with whether the effect, of any size, can be found at all (Debrouwere & Rosseel, 2022). Requiring a clear *a priori* definition of an effect reduces the chances that an effect is defined by the data that is collected and so could be as much a product of the desire to obtain a statistically significant effect as a reflection of a real effect.

We have presented a relatively simple method for determining the pervasiveness of psychological effects. Although we consider the method can be straightforwardly applied to data collected in typical psychology experiments, and it provides a number of advantages over Null Hypothesis Significance Tests (NHST) techniques typically applied to those experiments, we expect great resistance to change from the majority of psychology researchers. Certainly previous attempts to change analysis behaviours have not been met with success (Speelman & McGann, 2013). We suggest two reasons for why this might be the case, one at the level of individual researchers, the other at the level of professional norms.

The first is a result of the tendencies of individual researchers. Having trained within a particular mode of defining and operationalising research questions, in accordance with the standard set of analytical tools available to us, shifting away from ergodic thinking would require a re-education which could look, on the face of it, to be rather daunting. If the rich value of such new analyses has not been fully grasped through their technical presentation, then the investment of precious time needed to get to grips with them will remain unlikely.

A second reason we believe underlies the inertia against responding to the ergodic problem is one that has been described by historians of psychological research for some time, and that is our granting of a professional imprimatur to a particular "standard" set of methods and tools which have come to define psychological research (Danziger, 1994; Flis & van Eck, 2018; Green, 2015; Stam, 2004). Indeed, the takeover and dominance of inferential statistics over psychology has been referred to as "sanctification" (Tukey, 1969) and "institutionalisation" (Gigerenzer, 1991). Over time professional practices within the science have substantially coalesced around a core set of themes and processes, into which a very diverse set of research questions and topics have been fit. Professional incentives have thus all been structured according to the principles of ergodic thinking. Even the recent, dramatic discussions around our professional incentives and methodological practices have remained focused on how to do such ergodic-thinking research well (Wallot & Kelty-Stephen, 2018), and the question, now with decades-long arguments of methodologists behind it, of whether we should be doing it at all has barely been raised. The words of a lecturer from our past, Jim Lumsden, come to mind: "If it's not worth doing, it's not worth doing well".

A common response among our peers, when presented with the pervasiveness analysis, is scepticism that the counting of cases that match a definition of an effect constitutes an appropriate approach to determining whether an effect exists. We all share years of experience at applying various statistical techniques to the question of whether the data reveals an effect, especially when a graph of a set of means suggests such an effect exists. The statistical result has always been required to provide the final imprimatur to what the difference in means suggests. And so our colleagues, and even ourselves for a time, find it difficult to believe that a mere count of cases provides sufficient and probably superior evidence of an effect. But if the question we are investigating is something like "does the majority of my sample exhibit the effect?", what could be a more convincing answer than that 80% or more of the individuals in the sample showed the effect? Once we have this result, no further information is required. And yet, we still see researchers, who have reached the same realisation as us on the informativeness of a pervasiveness analysis, then suggesting means by which the pervasiveness result can be checked with a statistical analysis (Grice, 2011; Ince et al., 2021; McManus et al., 2023). The institutionalisation of statistics runs deep.

As ever, the only reliable evidence of a "real" effect is to observe it repeatedly. The pervasiveness analysis provides one form of evidence on this point (i.e., do we observe this effect repeatedly when we test a number of individuals?). Another relevant form of evidence is to observe the same people over different occasions (i.e., does each person repeatedly show this effect?). The latter form is particularly important in circumstances where the phenomenon under investigation is controversial. For example, in an experiment investigating the existence of extra-sensory perception (ESP), a proportion of a sample may reveal ESP-like behaviour by guessing the identity of hidden cards at better than chance levels. Such performance may be unlikely according to various statistical models, but still possible (i.e., they just got lucky), and so it would be important to test people on multiple occasions to determine the reliability of this behaviour. Observing the same people exhibit the same level of ESP behaviour on multiple occasions could provide convincing evidence that these people exhibited abilities beyond mere (extraordinary) guessing (as long as other, less controversial, explanations can be ruled out).

The different kinds of reasons underlying our professional inertia about changing methodological practice warrant different kinds of responses, a two-pronged approach to tackling problems related to the non-ergodicity of human beings, which we might think of as fireproofing and firefighting. Fireproofing involves substantive institutional and structural changes to the practices of professional psychological research. Such changes will mean changes to education and training, significant revision of our research methods and procedures, as well as shifts in standards and norms around reviewing and publishing of research. These kinds of systemic changes are difficult, costly, and can only be managed through large coordinated efforts by many people – it's more like making a tide than making waves, more like building houses to be more fireproof in the first place, than trying to put out fires when they happen.

Fireproofing is long-term thinking that may not show immediate or striking benefits. There are, however, some positive actions which do offer such immediate reward, and which can be managed without the investment of effort needed for something like training in an entirely new set of statistical techniques. Firefighting the ergodic fallacy can be done in a manner that does not undermine the worth of psychological research to date, but in fact means that many of the data sets we have already available contain rich veins of un-tapped value that we can access easily, and without major investment of time or resources. In the following chapter we consider some approaches to re-considering existing data sets from different perspectives.

An immediate first step, however, is one that can be undertaken without tearing at the foundations of what we do. In this chapter we offer the straightforward consideration of the pervasiveness of effects as a firefighting measure, a means to explore our existing data in a manner that offers key insights to questions in which we are interested. (Have a within-subjects data set? Get another publication out of it!) In time, and with sufficient researcher interest, this could lead to a greater focus on observing the behaviour of individuals with a view to discovering not only how they behave in particular circumstances, but the extent to which they all behave the same way. Addressing this problem extensively requires systemic change in our professional practices, a re-fitting of our methods and analytical techniques from the ground up in the service of the kinds of questions that psychologists are actually interested in answering. Combined with individual-focused methods such as case formulation and single-case research designs, pervasiveness can facilitate forms of research that close the feedback loop between laboratory work and applied practice. Systematic examination of questions of prevalence and generalisation at the level of individual persons provides more solid, reliable foundations on which to build our understanding and theories of experience and behaviour. Such fireproofing of future research work is not a small task, though the various movements for improved theorising and research that are already extant in the discipline at present suggests that such an overhaul is at least possible, if we can learn to re-balance the levels of status and respect afforded different forms of evidence. As individual researchers we might begin to explore such new methods and consider revising our approach. What is more, in the following chapter, we will explore how some of this may even be possible by drawing new use from existing data.

10

LEARNING FROM A MIXED HISTORY

The discussion about reform of psychological research practices that has occurred in recent years has largely concerned how we can fix the research and theory that we already have – do what we are doing, asking the questions we are asking, but better (Wallot & Kelty-Stephen, 2018). The Great Psychology Delusion also requires us to think rather starkly about what can and cannot be salvaged from the existing literature. The issue is not simply about how much we can improve our answering of the questions in which we have been interested, but whether we have been asking the right questions at all.

In this chapter we explore the principles by which we can interrogate the enormous body of existing literature – what value it offers, and what hard realisations we will have to make about it. While various kinds of methodological and institutional reforms will be an important part of the process, and some of these reforms are already underway, it is vital to ask not just "How do we ensure future research is more secure?" but also whether the past research has placed us so far afield that we need dramatic or revolutionary changes not just in our methods but our very understanding of what psychology is and how it should be conducted. While the emphasis throughout the book is of course on the challenges that psychological science faces, this chapter has a significant role in contextualising the huge amount of good and valuable knowledge that exists. For instance, even where the conclusions of some existing work cannot be relied upon due to its dependence on assumptions discussed in Part I, as records of patterns of behaviour in various contexts the research remains valid, and in fact where data are available for review, may yet have more to offer the scientific community on the basis of analyses at the finer, individual participant level.

This chapter has two parts. The first considers whether we can overcome the issues identified earlier in the book by just re-analysing existing data sets with different tools. The second part then considers other strategies that are designed to respond to the specific delusions we have described. In the following chapter, we argue that avoiding these delusions when undertaking new research may require yet another set of strategies.

DOI: 10.4324/9781003503873-12

Can we Just use More Sophisticated Statistics?

A common response we have received from people who have listened to us present the ideas in this book takes the form of suggestions about statistical techniques that will address the concerns we have described as the various delusions. A popular response is to invoke the long tradition of "individual differences" research and assert that "sure, people are different, but that is taken care of by finding individual differences variables that account for that variance." Of course, such individual differences approaches most often rely on correlations between the variable of interest, and some other individual differences variable, and so this approach falls foul of the Correlation Delusion. Ultimately this approach assumes that all the people examined in this way share the same relationship between those variables. Without a check that this assumption is valid, the analytical technique should not get started (see also Yarkoni, 2022).

Another common statistical solution proposed by audiences relies on some form of multi-level modelling, preferably involving Bayesian estimation techniques. The proposers of such solutions often suggest that these techniques can provide some idea of the degree to which individuals are different. This is true, but the type of difference indicated by these techniques can be limited. What these techniques do is similar to a traditional analysis of variance, where the total variance in the data set is divided between a number of factors. Multilevel modelling techniques just enable a division of variance amongst a wider variety of factors. Depending on the design of the data set, some of the factors can relate to data from different individuals, and so it is possible to determine the amount of variance in the data that can be attributed to having different individuals in the set. To some extent such information could be useful in addressing the issue of whether individuals in the sample share a common psychological makeup with respect to the constructs being measured. However, in between-groups designs at least, because the variance attributed to individuals is variance on a measured variable, the statistical information only reflects quantitative variance, and so cannot reveal anything about qualitative differences in psychological processes.

If a multi-level modelling analysis indicates that there are significant individual differences in the data, what does that mean? One interpretation is that this result could be useful for addressing one of the central issues we have highlighted in this book. That is, such a result could help determine whether the individuals in a sample are sufficiently similar that aggregated group results can be analysed as if they are all estimates of the same parameter. Thus, when multi-level modelling is used to assess questions of individual differences, they are asking a different question to the ones typically addressed in statistical analyses, and so could be considered a useful way forward through the issues we have identified with traditional forms of analysis.

The fundamental stumbling block in such analyses is that they begin with the assumption that the individuals are sampled from the same population (Hamaker, 2012, p. 24; Veenman et al., 2024). This is especially so in Bayesian techniques where this assumption begins the process of setting prior probabilities (priors). This assumption implies that individuals will vary within this population, but this variation is within a specific variable. Thus, even though these techniques allow for different "effects" between individuals, in practical terms, these effects are just differences along some continuous variable, and so are quantitative. The differences are not qualitative, or at least, the analysis techniques cannot detect such differences.[1]

It is important to consider the information that is being provided by multi-level modelling with respect to individual differences. If all we get on this front from multi-level modelling is that people in the sample have significantly different mean values (or slope values, or intercept values, or some other value being predicted by the model), the value of this information is not clear. Although the people might differ on a particular dependent variable, it is just a difference within a particular variable. This is unlikely to tell us much about whether people differ in some qualitative sense with respect to some fundamental psychological mechanism. The problem is that a difference between people in terms of values on a scale provides only a limited amount of information about those people. This is a serious problem in psychology. We work so hard to refine our measurement scales, and indeed the situations in which we take measurements, that we refine much of the psychological richness out of the situation. So much so that two people who have fundamentally different psyches can have the same score on a particular scale, and we will have learned nothing about the differences between them.

For example, take any psychological measurement scale where a total score is derived by some procedure whereby the scores on each item are summed together. It is possible for two individuals to be given the same total score while scoring high on completely different items. It is certainly questionable whether the two people are experiencing the same psychological state, or have the same psychological trait or ability, and yet the way psychologists analyse and interpret such data would encourage exactly that conclusion. A psychological concept, such as intelligence, is complex, by which we mean multi-dimensional. Representing how smart someone is by an IQ score glosses over the range of abilities a person has, some of which they excel in, and others are more or less than average talents. A typical intelligence test that produces IQ scores will assess people on a range of intellectual tasks (e.g., vocabulary, matrix reasoning, number memory, encoding), with performance on each task combined to determine the IQ score. As a result, two people with the same IQ score may have quite different talent profiles (see *The Jaggedness Principle*, as described by Rose, 2016, chapter 4). A similar observation has been made with respect to personality assessment (Shoda et al., 1994). Thus, relying on differences in group averages on a single behavioural dimension is an extremely low-fidelity strategy for uncovering the nature of mechanisms underlying behaviour.

This is a general quandary faced by psychology. By constraining behaviour in our research settings, we often force responses to vary only along a rigid continuum (e.g., the speed of a response – reaction time (RT) – can only vary in extent). This prevents the detection of different psychological mechanisms – differences in response extent (i.e., typical variance in a variable) may be caused by different psychological mechanisms, but it is not possible to reverse engineer the variance to detect this. As we have said before, it is not possible to unscramble the omelette of aggregated data to explain individual performance. Any statistical technique that professes to do this is not actually doing the statistical job of analysing aggregated data. Statistical techniques can do just about anything, but they can't do everything, not all at once at least.

There is a more telling problem with the suggestion of ever more sophisticated statistical techniques for addressing the concerns raised in this book, and that is the apparent view that better statistical techniques are the solution to addressing methodological issues in psychology. This view reflects the attitude touched on in earlier chapters, and highlighted by Danziger and others, that psychology as a discipline fell heavily for the seduction of statistics as a pathway to a valid science of the psyche. Our forebears were entranced by a tool that analysed data from groups of people in a cold and dispassionate manner and enabled decisions about whether an intervention had an effect on people. Unfortunately, the statistical siren has led psychology along a path that heads in the opposite direction from a valid science. Any researcher who responds to the various delusions we have outlined in this book with a statistical solution must ask themselves what it is they hope to gain by aggregating the data from many individuals. If it is to see a clearer signal by averaging over the noise in individuals' data sets, then we will point out that this aim assumes that each individual's data is an estimate of the same thing.

This is the fundamental assumption of sampling statistics – an aggregate value derived from the data of several individuals (e.g., a sample mean) is considered an estimate of the corresponding population parameter (i.e., a population mean). But if we do not know if an individual's data estimates the same thing as the data from another individual in the same sample, there is no justification for aggregating the data from these individuals. It is this point in the research process that requires resolution long before a researcher should consider what statistical technique is appropriate to answer their research questions. Indeed, at this point, it is possible that no statistical technique is appropriate, especially if there is no evidence that individuals in a sample have the same relevant psychological makeup. Therefore, in our view, the first step in any analysis of group data should be to determine whether the individuals in a sample are common enough with respect to some psychological issue that aggregating their data makes sense. A technique such as a pervasiveness analysis can be useful here.

When we have presented the idea of a pervasiveness analysis to people, a common response is that measurement techniques in psychology are not precise enough for us to believe that the results obtained from individuals can be relied on to indicate whether the individuals have exhibited an effect or not. For this reason, aggregating data from many individuals is used to reduce the noise from unreliable measurements and allow an effect to be observed. Our response is that it is hardly a valid argument to rely on the outcome (a group effect is observed) to justify the means (aggregating data across individuals). Especially, when this approach has resulted in typically small effects that are difficult to replicate (Davis-Stober et al., 2024; Gelman, 2018; Gernigon et al., 2023).

A better approach is to reduce noise in individual measurements by increasing the power of estimates at that level. That is, we should measure individuals many times, possibly using statistical tools such as Null Hypothesis Significance Tests (NHSTs) to determine whether each person demonstrates the effect (Ince et al., 2021; McManus et al., 2023). If we are confident about the validity of the measurement of individual behaviour, and of the determination of the existence of an effect in each person, we are then safe to determine the prevalence of the effect in the sample (how many people show it), and whether it is pervasive (e.g., prevalence > 80%). When an experiment's design allows for such clear observations of whether individuals have exhibited an effect, this then allows for the use of some promising new statistical techniques for interrogating the proportion of people showing the effect. For instance, Rouder and Haaf (2021) described a form of Bayesian hierarchical analysis that specifically tests for whether variance between individuals reflects only quantitative differences or may indicate qualitative differences. Musfeld et al. (2023) used a similar technique to determine the nature of individual learning curves in a particular task, finding a clear distinction in curve shape between those who learned the task, and those who did not. Alternatively, Ingendahl et al. (2024) showed how quantile regression can be used to specifically test the hypothesis that group effects are due to large effects in a small number of people.

Strategies for Evaluating Existing research

We have just considered whether the problems we have identified in previous research can be addressed by using more sophisticated statistical techniques. Our conclusion is that such a strategy may be fruitful, but it depends on specific features of the research, particularly the design. Where statistics may not be helpful, other non-statistical strategies might be useful. In this section we outline a number of such strategies. Each strategy is designed to avoid the problems associated with particular delusions. Some stem from avoiding the theoretical assumptions underlying a delusion, others relate to alternate methods for addressing the same question, and another set involves asking different questions.

The Aggregation Delusion and the Delusion of Experimental Control

A fundamental question that underlies these delusions is the quest for knowledge of universal principles underlying behaviour. Unless we have good evidence that such things exist, we may have to abandon this as a driving force behind scientific psychology. Given how much psychological research shares this goal, the worst-case scenario is that the data that has been collected to pursue this goal is barely useful for addressing less lofty goals. Still, let's not throw the baby out with the bathwater just yet. At the least, a great deal of this data could be useful for detecting whether general principles do exist. In particular, if such principles exist, this means the psychological mechanisms underlying behaviour are similar. We would therefore expect behaviours to also be similar. Defining "similar" will be a challenge, but once this is achieved in a convincing manner (i.e., convincing to the sceptical editors, reviewers, and readers of psychology journal papers), the following strategies may be useful as a starting point for establishing whether people respond similarly when exposed to the same conditions and therefore could be the same with respect to some underlying psychological mechanism.

Count the Number of People Who Show an Effect

If the data collected in a study is such that it is possible to test whether individuals exhibited an effect of interest, it is worthwhile counting the number of people in a group who exhibited this effect. It is then possible to make statements about the pervasiveness of an effect. If there is a sizeable majority in the group that showed the effect this enables statements such as "people do X". In the previous chapter, we suggested that 80% is a good-sized majority, by which we mean that few would argue against this being a majority. It is a percentage value that deserves the descriptor "most", and is a proportion we all might consider initial evidence for something that might ultimately be identified as a universal behaviour. This strategy could be applied to re-visiting classic effects in a particular field. In one example of this (Moore et al., 2023), we had access to complete data sets from replications of some classic effects in cognitive psychology, made openly available by Zwaan et al. (2018). We found that several such effects were exhibited by most people in the study's sample, supporting the conclusions based on traditional statistical analyses of aggregated group results. Importantly, these same group-based statistical analyses indicated that a couple of other such effects were replicated in the new study, according to the results of traditional group-based NHST statistical techniques, but a pervasiveness analysis indicated these effects were not exhibited by an 80% majority of the people in the sample. Pervasiveness analyses can therefore provide us with confidence in earlier conclusions derived from analyses of aggregated data, as well as an indication of when such conclusions should be re-evaluated. In particular, it would be valuable to know whether the original conclusions about an effect were likely the result of aggregating results from many people where only a subset exhibited the effect, but to a large extent.

Plot Individual Data

If a study produced data where the original observation of an effect was deduced by a comparison of group performance, a pervasiveness analysis as described above is not possible. Nonetheless, it still might be possible to develop a sense of the pervasiveness of a particular behaviour. There are many graphical techniques for displaying data so that individual performance is represented. That is, no aggregation is performed. Displaying such data for the various conditions in a study can provide, at a glance, an estimate of the degree of overlap in the behaviours of the individuals between the conditions (e.g., West et al., 2022).

Consider Figure 10.1. Panel A represents a bar graph of data from three groups, with 95% confidence intervals indicated. These confidence intervals (and ANOVAs with alpha set to 0.05) indicate statistically significant differences between each pairing of the three groups because none of the intervals overlap. A traditional treatment of such a result would conclude that whatever variable has been manipulated to create the three groups has had an effect on the average performance of the three groups. That is, Group B's performance was superior to Group C's performance, which in turn was superior to Group A's performance. And yet, when the performances of the individuals in this experiment are included in the figure, as in Panel B, very few people would be convinced by an effect that was only indicated by a significant difference between the means. When there is considerable overlap in the data of the groups, such as between Groups A and C, and Groups B and C, the significant difference between the means of these groups probably only reflects the effects of extremely high and low scorers. In contrast, the complete lack of overlap in scores in Groups A and B justifies a conclusion that the performances of these two groups were different, and indeed that all people in Group A were lower performers than all people in Group B.

Counting the number of people who show an effect and plotting individual data cannot provide information directly about whether people share common psychological mechanisms. At best these strategies will provide information as to whether people responded similarly to the same research context. As we have discussed above and in earlier chapters, it is still possible

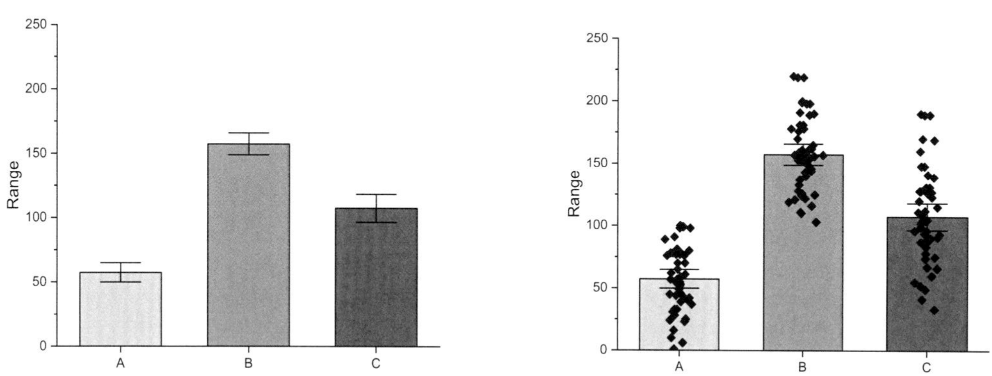

FIGURE 10.1 A fictional data set, presented without (A) and with (B) individual data points. Error bars are 95% confidence intervals.

for the same behaviours to result from different psychological mechanisms. It is also possible for the same psychological mechanisms to produce different behaviours. This speaks to the limited nature of behavioural measurement, which constrains our ability to observe different mechanisms, an issue we pick up below.

The Delusion of Group Comparison

As presented in Chapter 3, the logic underlying group comparison, particularly in an experimental context, is fundamentally flawed. Not only does it rest on the assumptions underlying the Aggregation and Experimental Control delusions, but it also assumes that people in one condition would perform in an equivalent manner to the people in another condition if they had been exposed to that condition. If an existing data set comes from a study where groups have been subject to different conditions, and their behaviours have been compared, then there is probably little that can be retrieved from such a design, at least in relation to the questions that were originally addressed by the design. There are other potential uses for the data, however.

Establish Standards for Common Tasks

A large number of experimental paradigms have been developed in the last century and a half and have been adopted and utilised by many independent researchers. Although many studies will have between-subjects designs where we argue the group comparison aspect is questionable (unless, perhaps, they show results as clear as the comparison between Groups A and B in Figure 10.1), many will have similar elements in their designs to those using similar paradigms. It may be possible that there are sufficient similarities between studies performed by different groups of researchers that they can pool their data to establish standards – values such as means, medians, modes, standard deviations, and ranges – for the particular tasks and conditions they have examined. Such pooled data establish the natural history that psychology lacked in the genesis of the discipline (Flake et al., 2022; Heft, 2001, 2018; Morris, 2009).

The Delusions of Pervasiveness, Generalisation, and Specificity

The Delusions of Pervasiveness, Generalisation, and Specificity essentially reflect the propensity of researchers to overstate the extent to which people in their studies exhibited the effects implied by their analyses. That is, there might be some statistical difference between the means of some conditions in an experiment, and researchers characterise their results as "people" exhibiting the effect, without checking on the pervasiveness of the effect amongst the people in the study. Such an effect is then over-extended to being a property of a wider population and subsequently applied to individuals from that population. We have already outlined in Chapter 9 some methods for establishing the sort of evidence that would support such claims. Counting the number of people who show an effect and plotting individual data could also be useful in re-examining pre-existing data along these lines. But there is an alternate way of looking at data that might be equally valuable, if not more so.

Examine the Variety of Behaviour

Similar to establishing standards for common tasks, it is important that we understand the variety of behaviours that are possible and likely in any given situation. As we have mentioned, the aim of the typical paradigm in psychology research is to discover the universal in behaviour. Unfortunately, this approach has not been all that successful, for the reasons we have outlined, but mainly because there may be precious little universality in the factors underlying human behaviour. With this in mind, a more fruitful approach could be to focus on documenting the range of behaviours that occur under prescribed circumstances. Previous research, both published and unpublished, possess a treasure trove of information documenting the nature, extremes, and variety of human behaviour recorded in myriad situations. The published versions of this data will primarily have been reported in aggregated form. Providing access to all versions of this data, including data from each individual observed, will help to establish where, if anywhere, universal principles lie. Furthermore, in the case of cognitive psychology, there will be areas where the same task is used by many researchers, or at least similar versions of the task have been used, but invariably different stimuli are used by each research team. Including this information in the combined data sets will enrich the knowledge base underpinning the behaviours examined.

Nonetheless, when it comes to re-assessing past research, particularly if we decide to re-analyse data in a way that avoids aggregation, we will still need to consider the narrow ways in which the phenomena of interest have been examined (e.g., the specific task used, the experimental context) (Yarkoni, 2022). We do not underestimate the vastness of the task we have outlined. It is, to some extent, the price to be paid for psychology skipping its butterfly collection stage. The effort should be worthwhile though as it will produce information on the range of behaviours humans engage in, and the nuance associated with each form of behaviour. This information is rarely made available by research that seeks to aggregate information about behaviour across many individuals.

The Correlation Delusion

There are several ways in which correlational techniques are used to examine psychological data. One is to establish associations between two or more variables, which are typically interpreted in some sort of causal manner. This causal interpretation ranges from the absolutely explicit to the implicit and unadmitted and can encompass simple two-variable relationships all the way to complicated structural equation models with mediating and moderating variables. A specific case of the latter is in individual differences analyses, where one or more variables are seen to moderate the relationship between some other grouping of variables (e.g., the effect of expertise on the performance of a task is influenced by the working memory capacity of the individuals).

The second way correlations are used is to collect large sets of associations between variables to examine whether there are a smaller number of factors (or similar things) underlying the responses to the measured variables (e.g., factor analysis). This approach underlies the development of most psychometric tests, such as intelligence tests, personality tests, and tests for diagnosing clinical disorders.

In Chapter 3 we discussed several issues with the use of correlation as an indicator of causal relationships. The fact that such correlations are derived from so little data collected from each individual means that no information about the operations of variables within individuals is ever examined. As a result, nothing informative about the causal relationship between variables can really be gleaned from the data collected in such studies. But is the data of no use at all? Well, given that so little data is collected from each individual, such data is probably less useful than the data considered applicable to the strategies already described. Nonetheless, the data could still be useful for establishing databases that record the range of behaviours under specific circumstances, as would be appropriate in examining the variety of behaviour.

If data from more than two variables has been recorded for each individual, the data could also be useful for examining whether sub-groups exist within a dataset. For instance, people who report they do not listen to music while reading may show a correlation between the level of distraction they experience when music is playing and the complexity of the music. In contrast, people who listen to music while reading may show no association between distraction and music complexity. There are many analytical techniques for addressing such situations, none of which will address a question regarding causal relationships. However, grouping information might be useful in indicating potential future research into what makes some individuals similar and therefore different to others. Although this strategy points away from universal principles of behaviour, it might lead the way to general principles that apply to prescribed groups of people and/or situations.

Data that has been collected for psychometric purposes may be similarly useful for the establishment of databases. Quite often when someone is classified as having a particular personality type, or potentially suffering from a specific psychological disorder, the temptation is to draw conclusions about the likelihood of them exhibiting particular behaviours, or experiencing certain states or emotions. The word "likelihood" implies some form of probability estimate. Researchers are keen to make statements such as "high scorers on X are likely to be high scorers on Y" or "low scorers on Z are more likely to do A" and yet the magnitude of this likelihood is rarely specified and is not readily available from a correlation coefficient or its many derivatives. Indeed the correlation between personality test scores and behaviours is typically quite low (i.e., less than 0.3) (Rose, 2016, p. 102).

To establish the probability of a specific outcome, we need information about how often that outcome occurs given certain conditions. For example, the probability of a certain card hand being dealt in a game of blackjack can be estimated by observing thousands of games of blackjack and noting the hands dealt in each game.[2] Similarly, the data collected to establish the psychometric properties of a test could be used instead to establish the number of people who have a particular profile of scores on a range of tests out of some large sample of people who have completed these tests. Since data has primarily been collected to serve enquiries regarding the associations between variables, we really do not know the prevalence of specific behavioural and emotional profiles in the population to the degree that we can confidently make statements such as "if someone scores above a particular value on the personality scale Y of personality test X, there is a 70% chance they will fall victim to a cyber security phishing scam." We are not suggesting these sorts of statements will necessarily be supported by existing data. Nonetheless, researchers appear to want to say such things but are not justified in doing so by the types of analyses they currently use. Such a strategy for looking at existing data may go some way towards enabling psychology to provide such predictions in a valid manner.

The Simplicity Delusion

The Simplicity Delusion reflects a general mode of operation in psychological research that cuts across theorising and the development of research questions, study design, data collection, data analysis, and interpretation. To overcome this delusion requires more than just a new strategy for re-assessing existing data. Instead, we propose something like a meta-strategy that is more a state of mind for undertaking psychology research. This strategy is one we propose be adopted if one attempts to mine existing research for previously undiscovered gems, but we also advocate that it be the driving force behind any new research in psychology.

Have an Open Mind and Expect Complex Explanations

As we have noted throughout the book, psychology skipped the natural history phase of its science. Perhaps because we (both early and current psychology researchers) belong to the set from which the subject of our research is selected (i.e., human beings), we believed we have a good idea of the sorts of behaviours that are out there, and so there was no need to document them in the way a biologist would study the behaviours of insect specimens in a particular location. When it became apparent that a scientific enterprise looking at psychological phenomena was possible, researchers quickly jumped to testing theories about the nature of common behaviours such as memory, learning, perception, communication, and social interaction. So keen have researchers been to end a journal paper with a theoretical account of the reported results, it has often been suggested that each new psychology study engenders a new theory (Eronen & Bringmann, 2021; Meehl, 1978). This approach quickly became the norm, and then the expectation of editors, reviewers, and university hiring committees alike. Given the poor state of current theories, theorising, and relevant data, it seems prudent to now call a halt to proceedings, and suggest a new way forward. Furthermore, this could involve a new way of looking backward at what has been done, in order to move forward.

The strategy we propose here involves adopting a mindset that is the complete opposite of the current modal perspective underlying research in psychology, which is to approach a data set as if it is only capable of addressing one research question, and as such the measurements reflect one view of a psychological construct, and can be analysed and interpreted in a specific manner. Instead, we suggest approaching the data as if it is a gift you were not involved in selecting, and for which the purpose is unclear. When confronted with such a gift, adopt a curious and careful attitude, and explore the data as if it is a newly discovered island about which no one knows anything. In such a circumstance, note the things you observe and the ones you find interesting, and importantly why you find them interesting. The observations will help you to note things that happen together and things that never occur with other things (Debrouwere & Rosseel, 2022, pp. 856–857, p. 860). Your musings about why you find some things interesting, or not, may suggest early hypotheses, but will also help you to understand your biases.

At the least, this cataloguing of behaviour measurements will feed into knowledge of what is possible with respect to human behaviour, what is common, what is rare, and ultimately, who does what, when. A dataset that represents the pooling of a multitude of similar data collection efforts is likely to generate evidence about not only varieties of behaviour but also the relative prevalence of each. This will be far more valuable and realistic than a generalisation about "all" people who are commonly encountered as the summary of a study that is based on a relatively small sample (Speelman et al., 2024).

Conclusion

We have devoted considerable attention in this book to critiquing the efforts psychology researchers have made to uncover mechanisms underlying behaviour. As we outlined in Chapter 7, psychology is replete with situations where data and interpretations of that data exist at different scales, and so are not necessarily connected in any valid manner. This is akin to the substitution error described by Kahneman (2011) – when people make decisions, they often try to solve one problem by solving a different, often easier, one, and so make erroneous decisions. Psychology research is full of such examples: the things we really want to know about peoples' mental functioning are difficult to uncover, so we tend to focus on something else that we hope will give us clues about the main question of interest (Hamaker, 2012). Unfortunately, as we have discussed, this hope is a forlorn one and indeed is delusional. As a result, the history of psychology is overflowing with data sets that may not be of any value for answering the questions that originally sparked their collection. Nonetheless, there may be other questions for which this database, at the very least, provides rich background information and context, if not answers. In the following chapter, we consider means by which future research in psychology can avoid the various delusions that make up the Great Psychology Delusion. We suggest that by ensuring data and their interpretations are kept to the same scale, we can avoid substitution errors and address the questions we really want answered. We also suggest, though, that there may be some questions currently occupying psychology research that cannot be addressed in any valid manner.

Notes

1 This applies to between-groups comparisons. It is a different story with within-subject comparisons, as we discuss further on.

2 Of course in blackjack this can be established more definitively knowing the constraints of the game (Krumme, 2023), but we do not have a similar luxury with respect to psychological phenomena.

11

FROM DELUSION TO DREAM

We do not underestimate the difficulty we face as a community of professionals to shake ourselves loose from the Great Psychology Delusion. The challenges of moving towards ever more valid and reliable practices for the psychological sciences are not just methodological and analytic, but also political, professional, and even personal.

The incentives that have acted as maintaining factors in the various delusions we have explored in these pages remain very common across the academic sector. As psychologists we have learned, practised, and advanced in our careers based on our capacity to meet those incentives. Being a *good psychologist* has meant implementing, upholding, and defending those structures (Nosek et al., 2012, 2022). The discomfort and uncertainty that come with a critical reflection on those values are real, as is the difficulty in knowing how to move forward more positively and how to honestly and accurately assess the value of our existing bodies of work.

We are optimistic for the future of psychology. The open, frank, and difficult conversations that are now more common (if not quite pervasive) in the research literature are a new standard of practice. These discussions provide a forum for critical consideration that, while niche in its way, is still much wider in its participation than previous such debates. What is more, an array of methodologies has now been developed and effectively deployed across the spectrum of research domains that are not just improved versions of aggregationist statistics but are genuinely alternative means of framing questions and producing evidence to address them. The hammer of the null-hypothesis significance test remains in our toolbox, but it is far from the only tool.

In this final chapter, then, we consider this broad scale of the scientific community of psychological science and the prospect of a richer, more productive, and more effective set of practices in which the community of psychologists can engage. We begin by addressing one last delusion – one that is not particular to psychology, but shared across a wide range of scientific communities – the delusion of neutrality, of a value-free science. We look at how understanding this final delusion involves understanding the relationship between the scientific community and the broader civil society in which science is undertaken. And finally, we look at some of the

DOI: 10.4324/9781003503873-13

steps that we can take in order to overcome this delusion by expanding and strengthening the communication between different groups of people with a stake in scientific practice.

One Last Delusion, and the Biggest Feedback Loop

We have repeatedly observed in these pages that aggregationist thinking abstracts prematurely from the specifics of particular psychological phenomena. In treating individual variability as error (the Aggregation Delusion), both individuality and the contexts of particular measurements are considered noise and suppressed. Indeed, it removes the possibility of examining the particular relationship between any two sets of measurements (the Correlation Delusion). This destroys the relationship between the phenomenon being measured and its context and implicitly endorses an abstract, general, and interchangeable notion of human beings and their psyches. To commit the ergodic fallacy is to attempt to provide a description of experience or behaviour that transcends contextual or personal specificity – that is abstracted from the messy details of particulars to the encompassing perspective of what is sometimes called the View from Nowhere (Nagel, 1986). Over the past several decades, research undertaken by historians and philosophers of science across a spectrum of scientific fields – from physics and biology to chemistry, ecology, and evolution – have made it clear that the conception of a value-free science and the View from Nowhere it implies are simply untenable (Brown, 2024; Douglas, 2009; Longino, 1990). Study of scientific practice by those working in Science and Technology Studies and the History and Philosophy of Science has made it clear that scientific practice is always embedded in social norms and values.

Thus we find ourselves having to be wary of a final delusion, that of a value-free or neutral scientific practice. We will call this the Neutrality Delusion.

***The Neutrality Delusion*:** Inferences and decision making in scientific practice are governed by logic and data alone, and the only values which play a role in this process are those that promote an unbiased search after objective truth.

Researchers working within the fields of the History and Philosophy of Science, Science and Technology Studies, and related domains have long pointed out the extent to which actual scientific practice invariably, inevitably, involves much more than just the data and the sets of logic that are used to discern sustainable conclusions on the basis of those data. A host of cultural, social, and professional values are typically implicit within decisions about what research questions are worthwhile, what methods properly represent effective truth-seeking, and what kinds of evidence are considered valid. This was perhaps most famously described by Kuhn (1970) but has been explored in immense depth by many researchers since (some well-known examples include Barad, 2007; Douglas, 2009; Longino, 1990; Shapin & Schaffer, 2011, among many others). This interweaving of the technical and the social in the professional practice of science is unavoidable. It is not something that can be overcome or set aside even with extensive practice. It therefore needs to be recognised, acknowledged, and incorporated into our understanding of how we produce new knowledge (Brown, 2024; Douglas, 2023; Longino, 1990).

That all practice is valued, shaped, and driven by social norms may seem to some as counter to the very virtues of science. The authority of science within society does at least in part depend on the notion of science as being *objective*, unaligned, and impersonal. To argue against the possibility of neutrality would seem to undermine that authority, a vandalism of science's worth and reputation.

Perhaps ironically, such a pessimistic view depends on a certain scale blindness regarding science and the development of new facts and knowledge. While objectivity is considered impossible for an individual scientist, it *can* be approached by a *community* (Jadreškić, 2021; Levitt et al., 2022; Longino, 1990). The great virtue of science is its corrigibility – the always tentative, always accountable, always improvable way the work is done.

To see objectivity as something that holds not in the individual scientist, but at the scale of the community, is not an abdication of responsibility for individual researchers. The full and accurate description of actions taken in the course of a series of observations, measurements, experiments, or studies remains essential. Discipline in the conduct of research and careful following of principles of good practice and research integrity is similarly vital. That individual sets of observations are necessarily incomplete and questionable is not a counsel for nihilism. It is just a recognition that understanding advances through multiple studies, which can be sensibly and effectively placed in the right kinds of relationships to each other, over time, by a community of critical professionals. It is this recognition of incompleteness and the need for coordination and collaboration between different perspectives to provide a better overall picture that underlies our suggestions regarding a federation of psychological sciences in Chapter 7. Such a multifarious view of the scientific process sees significant acknowledgement and explication in the History and Philosophy of Science literature. For example, Longino (1990) describes four interlocking aspects to the process of objectivity in a scientific community. The first is clear fora for critical discourse, such as peer review, post-publication criticism and evaluation, discussion at conferences and other professional channels of communication. The second is a set of standards – values and stable routines agreed by the community by which differing viewpoints can be compared. These tend to vary substantially between different specialisms. Third is the responsiveness of the community, to wit, community members' willingness to be corrected, and to adapt their thinking and approaches in response to that critical discussion such that the group as a whole continually revise their consensus. And finally, the sharing of intellectual authority amongst appropriately qualified practitioners means that power and reputation alone cannot long distort or suppress revision and development of understanding over time.

Thus, while a single View from Nowhere would seem unachievable, a more dynamic viewpoint that allows us to move between multiple perspectives, each providing particular insights, understandings, and opportunities for action, offers the possibility of a comprehensive grasp that is less ideal but more concrete.

By its very nature, accountability is something negotiated. It is a relationship of responsibility that holds between people and between groups that must be actively managed and enacted. In one of the classic works of science scholarship, Shapin and Shaffer (2011) examined how this task was vociferously debated in the early years of modern science. Their work focused on the unfolding of an argument between one of the founders of the Royal Society, Robert Boyle, and the political philosopher Thomas Hobbes. They analyse how important not just technical, but social innovation was in building authority for science within society, and in the organisation of a scientific community around the effective formation of new knowledge.

Douglas and Branch (2024) describe how a more explicit discussion of the relationship between social norms and values was negotiated following the Second World War (particularly, though not exclusively, in the United States). They argue that the defence of the value-free ideal in science was crucial to the upholding of a particular social contract between researchers and civil society. A division between "basic" and "applied" research allowed a division of funding sources between governments and industry. Governments would fund pure or basic research that had no clear application, undertaken without any concern for potential implications because of its value-free character. The initial investment would then later pay off for society when applications for the outcomes of basic research were conceived and the development of them funded by industry.

In an environment in which the value-laden character of science has become increasingly clear, it has become necessary to re-negotiate this social contract (Douglas & Branch, 2024). It remains to be seen how this negotiation might be managed, but Douglas and Branch argue persuasively that it be so, and our own considerations in these pages support the general thrust of their conclusion. Divisions between pure and applied research are less tenable, more problematic, than previously thought, and it behoves scientists of all stripes to be able to articulate, justify, and if necessary revise, the values driving their work.

This is neither a negative nor pessimistic view of science. It is one which is decidedly optimistic. It is one which sees scientific activity as never perfect, but always subject to improvement, though only if it is undertaken in a way that is reflective and therefore deliberate and accountable. This will mean a noticeable change of practice for psychologists.

Pluralism Implies Greater Inter-Disciplinarity

As different forms of behaviourism came to hold prominence within the psychological research literature during the early twentieth century, so the kinds of things that psychologists did in the conduct of that research changed. Laboratory work involving trained introspectors waned (though has never quite disappeared), while work with animals waxed (though had already been happening for decades). Similarly, as different forms of cognitive psychology arose and came to dominate research work across a range of fields later in the century, so animal work waned (though has never disappeared) (Danziger, 1994).

If we are recommending a new calibration of methods and analyses, what changes in the behaviour and experiences of psychologists are we likely to see? If the principles that we have argued for in this book have real value, then what would this more successful psychological science look like?

We have argued for a pluralistic, contextualised practice that is sensitive to both scale and individual cases. We have pointed out (and are far from the first to do so) the limitations of professional silos, and so a more successful psychology will involve a greater degree of inter-disciplinary awareness.

McGann et al. (2024) identify four bodies of literature that provide insight into the ecosystems of experience and behaviour. These include behavioural ecology (as it has been developed and deployed with non-human animals), ecological psychology (as derived from the work of James and Eleanor Gibson and their colleagues), and also, crucially, anthropology. Within the inter-disciplinary field of cognitive science, anthropology has been lamented as the "lost" discipline (Boden, 2006). Originally included in statements of member domains of cognitive science, its influence has never been great. Though there have been important impacts from anthropological work, they have been relatively few, and certainly the interaction between anthropology and other cognitive sciences has been unsystematic and unreliable (Bender et al., 2010). Influence and impact in more mainstream areas of the psychological sciences have been fewer again.

A psychological science that is aware of the importance of phenomena at a variety of scales will involve, and indeed incorporate, anthropological work. Though anthropology as a discipline has challenges of its own to face and overcome (Bender et al., 2010; Ingold, 2016), it is certainly the case that psychological scientists that are scale-aware and who include contexts and settings in their typical and routine practice will be familiar with and sensitive to the nature of ethnographies and other outputs of anthropological work.

The fourth body of literature noted by McGann et al. (2024) is that of behaviour settings theory, about which we have written in earlier chapters. Barker (1978) argued that the existence of behaviour settings implied a new discipline – one of "eco-behavioural science" – that operated explicitly at the scale of the setting. He was not at all suggesting the building of a new silo, however. It was the recognition of the need for different methods and analyses than those characteristic of mainstream laboratory psychology for which he was advocating. The result is another argument for the necessary, unavoidable, inter-disciplinary character of psychological work and the need for psychological researchers to be able to converse with and collaborate with those working at other scales of behavioural and experiential phenomena.

We do not propose that a successful psychology will have only *this* theoretical framework or *that* set of methods. But we do strongly believe that a successful psychology involves professionals who are aware of the nested character of our phenomena, inter-connected across scales, and capable of theorising and collaborating across those scales in inter-disciplinary teams.

Better Inter-Disciplinary Practice

Cultivating a wider range of more appropriate scientific practice will involve changes and interventions across the scales at which behaviour is organised. That means considering the ecosystem of the behaviour in question, as well as the individual cases and instances of particular researchers.

That we need to revise the structure of professional incentives in psychological science is not only something that has been previously examined, but progress has been made in some quarters. Given the value of a scientific pluralism, and the need to more effectively engage with other disciplines due to the wide range of scales at which psychologically relevant phenomena occur, it behoves us to explore how we might foster a value of inter-disciplinarity. Recognising that range of scales in the professional ecosystem, we might begin at the broadest level and work our way to finer grains of intervention.

Community leaders and policy makers within academic work represent what they value and shape the work undertaken within the field through the creation of policies and provision of awards of various kinds. We should recognise that many of the people involved in these decisions are not practising psychological researchers. A crucial step to fostering changes of practice with regard to policies and awards will involve an honest and direct communication beyond any perceived boundaries of professional psychology.

The ways in which policies and awards constrain and facilitate the practice of research are varied. Most direct of course is the awarding of funding. There already exist examples of funding allocation that is earmarked for research of particular kinds, with the explicit aim of encouraging work of a more innovative or exploratory kind. These models could be extended with care to support inter-disciplinary work. This could be done with an explicit intention to investigate the differences between scales of activity as well as the interaction of the dynamics between those scales.

Funding is not the only kind of award that matters, however. Professional awards of different kinds operate as currency in applications for jobs, for tenure, and for promotion. While professional bodies may have few direct means of shaping practice within universities and other institutions who support and facilitate research, through such professional recognition they represent and cultivate the values of the profession and support the transformation of the makeup of the community over the longer timescales of such changes.

Looking beyond the setting of policies and different forms of awards to researchers, however, there is one key way in which professional bodies can have a direct influence on the practices within universities, and that is through the criteria for accreditation of qualifications. It is quite possible for professional societies to explicitly require engagement with fields of endeavour from cognate but distinct areas of work beyond psychology.

While some guidelines for this incorporation of greater inter-disciplinarity can and should be developed, it is not the case that there will be a single best approach in this regard. Indeed, the point is not to find the one best other perspective by which to amplify particular aspects of an undergraduate or postgraduate curriculum. Rather, the point is to take steps to ensure that students are exposed to alternative perspectives and told explicitly that being able to engage with such perspectives and use them as reflective tools on their own practice through their careers is the reason for such exposure. This is one means by which young researchers can be supported to develop intellectual humility and foundations for skills of reflective and critical practice, all of which should be central to formation as a scientist.

In outlining such a suggestion, of course, we can already hear the horrified cries of programme developers whose timetables are already overstuffed, curricula packed to bursting with the need to cover every angle and all of the various core aspects of psychological science.

We are sorry to say that we have no simple panacea to such concerns. Unfortunately, given the strong consensus on the delusory character of the neutrality claim among the specialists in the field, our options are few. Increasing the capacity of the community for critical reflection from multiple perspectives seems a most valuable and concrete step to achieving the kind of accountability and explicit justification that underpin the practice of social objectivity. This is an important skill that cannot be expected to be developed by accident within members of the community. Our options are to embed such potential for reflection throughout the community through an inclusion of it as a crucial part of professional formation or the empowerment of specialists to shape policies, procedures, and standards for the community. Most likely, some balance of these approaches will be involved. Given the strength of evidence on the issue at this point, to ignore it is tantamount to the kind of denialism that causes many of us such concern when we encounter it in wider public discourse.

Holden Thorp, editor of *Science*, has recently argued for the embedding of History and Philosophy of Science within core curricula (Thorp, 2024). This is a very useful and clear first step towards such revising of our programmes of professional formation, and the cultivation of a more reflective discipline that better manages both its own practices of objectivity and its relationship with the norms and values of the societies in which it is embedded.

Certainly it is the case that every undergraduate and postgraduate programme makes compromises in this regard. Every decision is a prioritisation of one aspect of the wide, diverse field of psychological science over others. If we can come to recognise that decisions to maintain a low priority for inter-disciplinarity, a comparative belittling of the importance of different scales and scientific pluralism, then we can at least be honest and more explicit in that assessment. The status quo is a decision made too, and if the arguments presented in these pages, and in the works on which we have built our points of view count for anything, then decisions that maintain the status quo are ones which support a problematically narrow form of scientific practice that is likely to be a maintaining factor for the troubles of our science.

Big Psychological Science

Vlaeyen et al. (2020) consider some of the potential future developments of single-case research designs. They raise the prospect of open databases of such studies – each with data relevant to individual cases, but building up over time to provide sound bases for generalisations, or the understanding of distributions of patterns of behaviour, characteristics, or responses to interventions. It is easy to imagine infrastructure such as the Open Science Framework (Center for Open Science, 2024), facilitating such repositories, where standardised sets of recording and data storage are developed across professional communities.

The crucial point is that big, ambitious science does not necessarily require a small number of very large studies. Where research aims to address questions of specific behaviour and examination of systematic generalisation of findings, then big science can and should be composed of a very large number of small studies. For instance, academic researchers could offer a service to practitioners by volunteering to take their clinical data (maybe after providing advice on what form this should take) and provide analyses of individual cases that can both assist the clinician in their work with each client and provide them with a picture of how their client base responds to various therapeutic strategies. Further, the researcher could integrate data from many practitioners to provide a corpus of individual data and analyses and highlight clusters of similarities as well as pervasiveness of symptoms and responses to treatments. In this way, psychological practice can move closer to the science it professes to be.

The Psychological Science Accelerator (Moshontz et al., 2018) is a large international collaboration of dozens of psychological laboratories which aims to coordinate and implement large psychological studies. Its organisation seems just as easily suited to the coordination of these large numbers of small studies, however. With the adoption of standards of analysis that can resolve phenomena at the scale of the individual case (a person), then the deployment of simple pervasiveness analyses or more complex forms of case studies are entirely possible.

Such large international collaborations are not only suited to person-scale work.

As our theories and understanding of the psychological ecosystem improve, a similar possibility emerges for natural historical work – be it ethnographic (or similar disciplinary practice by anthropologists) or eco-behavioural (supported by behaviour settings researchers). Such databases would provide a means to understand not just the distributions of particular kinds of settings, but the key relationships between elements of settings that should be maintained or reproduced in the laboratory in order for experimental work to have sound external validity.

The work of the Midwest team (Barker, 1968, 1978) provides the basis of a taxonomy of settings, which can help guide systematic planning for surveys of diversity and consistency of settings across the range of human experience (see, in particular, their accounts of the behaviour settings survey of Midwest detailed in Barker, 1968). Their close examination of the single case of Midwest is rich but of course limited by its singularity, leaving open the need for a programme of coordinated generalisation research and replication. That work will be challenging, but very fruitful.

Of course, while it is essential that we deliberately seek a transformation of our disciplines at the scale of institutions and community practices, and better understand how science operates at scale, we are also individual working professionals, and changes in practice will be visible at this more personal scale too.

Small Psychological Science – Or, What Does this Mean for Me?

For those of us who don't have direct access to the levers of policy development for institutions and professional organisations, our first responsibility must be to appreciate better the importance of being engaged with those social aspects of our profession. Even so, there are actions that we can take solely within our own practice as researchers that will make a significant difference to the validity and robustness of psychological scientific work. What suggestions we make here, of course, are only guidelines as we reiterate our resistance to any One True Psychology.

To begin, we might carefully frame our research without regard to methodology, but rather in terms of real-world experiences and activities. Being very explicit about the scale of the phenomenon we are interested in is surprisingly powerful here. Doing so will both help us resist the lure of our aggregationist habits and help us think clearly about what kinds of evidence would be directly informative about the question we really want answered, helping us reflect on "what do psychologists want to know?" and what kinds of evidence would be genuinely relevant (Lakens, 2021). Make decisions not on the basis of whether you are ideologically a qualitative or quantitative psychologist, nor on the basis of what statistical methods are currently in vogue, but on the basis of what evidence is most directly relevant to the research question.

In thinking about phenomena, we might start by focusing on experiences and behaviours that are "obvious" in the real world. While there is a known "lure" to the surprising and the counterintuitive psychological research finding (Krueger & Funder, 2004), it is perhaps also true that if our theories don't first robustly describe and explain the obvious, then we might have started in the wrong place. If it takes hundreds of people, comparisons between several groups, aggregation of data analysed with inferential statistics, for an effect to be detected, ask yourself if the effect relates to anything like real behaviour. Can anything you've learned from your experiment be realistically generalised to any behaviour that impacts daily life? Probably not (Diener et al., 2022). Instead, start with a question that concerns some obvious observation. For example, why does cutlery go missing in a communal kitchen? When you start with something that no one will argue over its existence, you can then get on with the business of trying to establish the underlying principles that govern its functioning. In the cutlery example, it doesn't matter if the underlying principles do not apply to everyone (i.e., not everyone brings the cutlery back to their office and forgets to return it). Indeed "sometimes this happens" observations can still be valuable (Baumeister et al., 2023). Ultimately, the concern is to minimise the loss of cutlery from the kitchen, so the discovery of any factor that effectively reduces this loss is inherently important.

Further, as a useful exercise, be particularly critical and resistant to the use of inferential statistics until their logic and value for a specific proposed study (with its consideration of scale and context) are made explicit. Alzahawi and Monin (2022) suggest the whole edifice of psychology will be torn down if we adopt this strategy. They don't argue for this to happen. Instead they propose doing inferential statistics better (i.e., don't use it as a rote decision machine), but also encourage more active judgement at every stage of the research. We don't see a problem with the first point. Inferential statistics have been used by psychology researchers as a crutch, however, and have ultimately engendered bad scientific behaviour. The mathematics behind the statistics is not the problem (although there are plenty of people who take issue with many aspects of the Null Hypothesis Significance Tests (NHSTs). See, for example, Trafimow et al., in press). The problem is how the statistics have been used (Lakens, 2021). If we cast aside statistics completely, even temporarily, as a salutary exercise, we would alleviate many of the problems with psychology research we have identified here and have been identified by others (e.g., Gigerenzer, 1998b; Meehl, 1978; Tukey, 1969). We certainly agree on Alzahwai and Monin's argument for active judgement at every stage of research (a statistical parallel to that of Guest & Martin, 2021, on theory and models). Researchers need to carefully consider their assumptions at every stage of the research. Importantly, if there can be no justification for the aggregation assumption early in the conception of a research project, then there will be no valid reason for analysing aggregated data with inferential statistics.

A final habit to bring to bear on local scientific practice concerns the specificity of conclusions. Don't assume there are universal principles underlying behaviour waiting to be discovered. The incentives may currently be high to be the discoverer of such a thing, but they may not truly exist, and so pronouncing you have found one could lead to fame in the short term but egg on your face in the long term. The great advantage humans have enjoyed over other organisms in the world is the extent of our adaptability. This happens not only at the level of the species, but also down to the level of the individual. As a result, adult humans are likely to have developed through experience a variety of behavioural organisation that is distinct for each person (Beck & Jackson, 2022; Kroupin et al., 2024). There may be similarities between some peoples' psychological mechanisms, but these are likely to be highly context-specific, and when virtually equivalent, probably due to highly constrained circumstances. Such cases may be entirely predictable and so not worth discovering in the first place.

Coda

What we describe in this chapter is not as far removed from current practice as it may seem to some. Our professional silos sometimes make the extent and richness of research in other domains easy to underestimate. To a great extent, it is those silos that are the problem, both between different fields and between academic work and naturally occurring behaviour. The absence of natural historical means of connecting and contextualising cases in applied practice or laboratory activities is a challenge that does need genuinely new efforts. It does not require the *invention* of entirely new methods, however, as the immense output of the Midwest Psychological Field Station provides a wealthy foundation. Similarly, the absence of a theory of the person is a challenge, but we do not need a fully developed theory of the person to address person-level phenomena. Rather, so long as we engage the full person in immersive tasks (Kroupin et al., 2024), rather than trying to isolate or itemise behaviours (sub-personal phenomena that can only be isolated effectively with procedures derived from well-developed theories), we can still do research on persons until we do understand them (us).

These grand efforts and moonshot projects seem unreasonable. But so would a description of what any scientific community does on a grand scale. What humanity, and even the subset of scientific professional communities, can and do achieve is deeply unreasonable. Even in the face of such existence proofs of effective (if not centrally controlled) coordination, the difficulty may make our descriptions in this chapter seem naive or utopian. People will scoff.

They'll say we're delusional.

REFERENCES

Addis, M.E. (2002). Methods for disseminating research products and increasing evidence-based practice: Promises, obstacles, and future directions. *Clinical Psychology: Science and Practice*, *9*(4), 367–378. https://doi.org/10.1093/clipsy.9.4.367

Adolph, K.E., & Hoch, J.E. (2019). Motor development: Embodied, embedded, enculturated, and enabling. *Annual Review of Psychology*, *70*, 141–164. https://doi.org/10.1146/annurev-psych-010418-102836

Adolph, K.E., Karasik, L.B., & Tamis-Lemonda, C.S. (2010). Motor skill. In M.H. Bornstein (Ed.), *Handbook of cultural developmental science* (pp. 61–88). Psychology Press.

Ægisdóttir, S., White, M.J., Spengler, P.M., Maugherman, A.S., Anderson, L.A., Cook, R.S., Nichols, C.N., Lampropoulos, G.K., Walker, B.S., Cohen, G., & Rush, J.D. (2006). The meta-analysis of clinical judgment project: Fifty-six years of accumulated research on clinical versus statistical prediction. *The Counseling Psychologist*, *34*(3), 341–382. https://doi.org/10.1177/0011000005285875

Allport, G.W. (1937). *Personality: A psychological interpretation*. Holt.

Alzahawi, S., & Monin, B. (2022). There is no psychology without inferential statistics. Comment on Yarkoni T. (2022) The generalizability crisis. *Behavioral and Brain Sciences*, *45*, e1, 1–78. https://doi.org/10.1017/S0140525X2100056X, e2

Anastasi, A. (1937). *Differential psychology: Individual and group differences in behavior*. The Macmillan Company.

Anderson, J.G.T. (2017). Why ecology needs natural history. *American Scientist*, *105*(5), 290–297. https://doi.org/10.1511/2017.105.5.290

Anderson, J.R. (1982). Acquisition of cognitive skill. *Psychological Review*, *89*, 369–406. https://doi.org/10.1037/0033-295X. 89.4.369

Archer, V., Jones, O.A.H., Sands, D., Isaacson, R., Sword, H., Sanders, D.A., Majumdar, S., & Hendon, C.H. (2019, August 22). How can academics keep up with the literature? *Times Higher Education (THE)*. www.timeshighereducation.com/features/how-can-academics-keep-literature

Arnett, J.J. (2008). The neglected 95%: Why American psychology needs to become less American. *American Psychologist*, *63*(7), 602–614.

Arnulf, J.K., Olsson, U.H., & Nimon, K. (2024). Measuring the menu, not the food: "Psychometric" data may instead measure "lingometrics" (and miss its greatest potential). *Frontiers in Psychology, 15*. https://doi.org/10.3389/fpsyg.2024.1308098

Aspers, P., & Corte, U. (2019). What is qualitative in qualitative research? *Qualitative Sociology*, *42*(2), 139–160. https://doi.org/10.1007/s11133-019-9413-7

Avram, C.M., Jones, A.E., Lucas, M.L., & Barrett, L. (2024). Reclaiming behaviour settings: Reviewing empirical applications of Barker's behaviour settings theory. *Philosophical Transactions of the Royal Society B: Biological Sciences*, *379*(1910), 20230283. https://doi.org/10.1098/rstb.2023.0283

Aydin, O. (2024). Rise of single-case experimental designs: A historical overview of the necessity of single-case methodology. *Neuropsychological Rehabilitation*, *34*(3), 301–334. https://doi.org/10.1080/09602011.2023.2181191

Ayoub, C.C., & Fischer, K.W. (2006). Developmental pathways and intersections among domains of development. In *Handbook of early child development*. Blackwell.

Baggs, E., & Sanches de Oliveira, G. (2024). Rewilding psychology. *Philosophical Transactions of the Royal Society B: Biological Sciences*, *379*(1910), 20230287. https://doi.org/10.1098/rstb.2023.0287

Balashov, Y., & Janssen, M. (2003). Presentism and relativity. *British Journal for the Philosophy of Science*, *54*(2), 327–346. https://doi.org/10.1093/bjps/54.2.327

Balota, D.A., & Yap, M.J. (2011). Moving beyond the mean in studies of mental chronometry the power of response time distributional analyses. *Current Directions in Psychological Science*, *20*, 160–166. https://doi.org/10.1177/0963721411408885

Barad, K. (2007). *Meeting the universe halfway: Quantum physics and the entanglement of matter and meaning*. Duke University Press.

Bargh, J.A., Chen, M., & Burrows, L. (1996). Automaticity of social behavior: Direct effects of trait construct and stereotype activation on action. *Journal of Personality and Social Psychology*, *71*(2), 230–244.

Barker, R.G. (1968). *Ecological psychology: Concepts and methods for studying the environment of human behavior*. Stanford University Press.

Barker, R.G. (1978). The need for an eco-behavioral science. In R.G. Barker & Associates (Eds.), *Habitats, environments, and human behavior* (pp. 36–48). Jossey-Bass Publishers.

Barker, R.G. (1979). Settings of a professional lifetime. *Journal of Personality and Social Psychology*, *37*(12), 2137–2157. https://doi.org/10.1037/0022-3514.37.12.2137

Barker, R.G., & Associates (1978). *Habitats, environments, and human behavior*. Jossey-Bass Incorporated Pub.

Barlow, D.H., Nock, M., & Hersen, M. (2008). *Single case research designs: Strategies for studying behavior change*. Allyn and Bacon.

Barrett, L. (2009). A guide to practical babooning: Historical, social, and cognitive contingency. *Evolutionary Anthropology*, *18*, 91–109. https://doi.org/10.1002/evan.20210

Barrett, L., & Stulp, G. (2013). Four more reasons why ethology matters: Tinbergen and the human sciences. *Human Ethology Bulletin*, *28*(4), 39–49.

Barrows, C.W., Murphy-Mariscal, M.L., & Hernandez, R.R. (2016). At a crossroads: The nature of natural history in the twenty-first century. *BioScience*, *66*(7), 592–599.

Bartholomew, G.A. (1986). The role of natural history in contemporary biology. *BioScience*, *36*(5), 324–329. https://doi.org/10.2307/1310237

Bates, M. (2014). *The nature of natural history* (Vol. 1138). Princeton University Press.

Baumeister, R.F., Tice, D.M., & Bushman, B.J. (2022). A review of multisite replication projects in social psychology: Is it viable to sustain any confidence in social psychology's knowledge base? *Perspectives on Psychological Science*, *18*(4), 912–935. https://doi.org/10.1177/17456916221121815

Beck, E.D., & Jackson, J.J. (2022). Personalized prediction of behaviors and experiences: An idiographic person-situation test. *Psychological Science*, *33*(10), 1767–1782. https://doi.org/10.1177/09567976221093307

Belar, C.D. (2000). Scientist-practitioner ≠ science + practice: Boulder is bolder. *American Psychologist*, *55*(2), 249–250. https://doi.org/10.1037/0003-066X.55.2.248

Bender, A., Hutchins, E., & Medin, D. (2010). Anthropology in cognitive science. *Topics in Cognitive Science*, *2*(3), 374–385.

Bennett, C.M., & Miller, M.B. (2010). How reliable are the results from functional magnetic resonance imaging? *Annals of the New York Academy of Sciences*, *1191*(1), 133–155.

Bennett, C.M., & Miller, M.B. (2013). fMRI reliability: Influences of task and experimental design. *Cognitive, Affective, & Behavioral Neuroscience*, *13*, 690–702. https://doi.org/10.3758/s13415-013-0195-1

Beutler, L.E., Moleiro, C., & Talebi, H. (2002). How practitioners can systematically use empirical evidence in treatment selection. *Journal of Clinical Psychology*, *58*(10), 1199. https://doi.org/10.1002/jclp.10106

Birkhoff, G.D. (1931). Proof of the ergodic theory. *Proceedings of the National Academy of Science (USA)*, *17*, 656–660.

Bishop, D. (2023, November 19). BishopBlog: Defence against the dark arts: A proposal for a new MSc course. *BishopBlog*. https://deevybee.blogspot.com/2023/11/defence-against-dark-arts-proposal-for.html

Boden, M.A. (2006). *Mind as machine: A history of cognitive science*. Oxford University Press.

Boring, E.G. (1920). The logic of the normal law of error in mental measurement. *American Journal of Psychology*, *31*, 1–33. https://doi.org/10.2307/1413989

Borsboom, D. (2013, November 20). Theoretical amnesia. *Open Science Collaboration*. http://osc.centerforopenscience.org/2013/11/20/theoretical-amnesia/

Borsboom, D., Kievit, R.A., Cervone, D., & Hood, S.B. (2009). The two disciplines of scientific psychology, or: The disunity of psychology as a working hypothesis. In J. Valsiner, P.C.M. Molenaar, M.C.D.P. Lyra, & N. Chaudhary (Eds.), *Dynamic process methodology in the social and developmental sciences* (pp. 67–97). Springer.

Boutron, I. (2020). Spin in scientific publications: A frequent detrimental research practice. *Annals of Emergency Medicine*, *75*(3), 432–434. https://doi.org/10.1016/j.annemergmed.2019.11.002

Brisson, J., & Markovits, H. (2020). Reasoning strategies and semantic memory effects in deductive reasoning. *Memory & Cognition*, *48*(6), 920–930. https://doi.org/10.3758/s13421-020-01027-3

Broekkamp, H., & van Hout-Wolters, B. (2007). The gap between educational research and practice: A literature review, symposium, and questionnaire. *Educational Research and Evaluation*, *13*(3), 203–220. https://doi.org/10.1080/13803610701626127

Brown, M.J. (2024). For values in science: Assessing recent arguments for the ideal of value-free science. *Synthese*, *204*(4), 112. https://doi.org/10.1007/s11229-024-04762-1

Bruch, M. (2015). The development of case formulation approaches. In M. Bruch (Ed.), *Beyond diagnosis* (pp. 1–23). John Wiley & Sons, Ltd. https://doi.org/10.1002/9781394259557.ch

Brunswik, E. (1947). Systematic and representative design of psychological experiments. In J. Neyman (Ed.), *Proceedings of the Berkeley symposium on mathematical statistics and probability* (pp. 143–202). University of California Press.

Brunswik, E. (1955). Representative design and probabilistic theory in a functional psychology. *Psychological Review*, *62*(3), 193–217.

Bucciarelli, M., & Johnson-Laird, P.N. (1999). Strategies in syllogistic reasoning. *Cognitive Science*, *23*(3), 247–303. https://doi.org/10.1207/s15516709cog2303_1

Bugatti, M., Owen, J., Reese, R.J., Richardson, Z., Rasmussen, W., & Newton, D.A. (2023). The effectiveness of psychotherapy for depression in private practice: Benchmarking and trajectories of change. *Professional Psychology: Research and Practice*, *54*(5), 327–335. https://doi.org/10.1037/pro0000518

Buzbas, E.O., & Devezer, B. (2023). Tension between theory and practice of replication. *Journal of Trial & Error*. https://doi.org/10.36850/mr9

Callaghan, C.T., Martin, J.M., Kingsford, R.T., & Brooks, D.M. (2018). Unnatural history: Is a paradigm shift of natural history in 21st century ornithology needed? *Ibis*, *160*(2), 475–480.

Cantor, P., Osher, D., Berg, J., Steyer, L., & Rose, T. (2019). Malleability, plasticity, and individuality: How children learn and develop in context. *Applied Developmental Science*, *23*(4), 307–337.

Carlisi, C.O., Reed, K., Helmink, F.G.L., Lachlan, R., Cosker, D.P., Viding, E., & Mareschal, I. (2021). Using genetic algorithms to uncover individual differences in how humans represent facial emotion. *Royal Society Open Science*, *8*(10), 202251. https://doi.org/10.1098/rsos.202251

Carter, J.A. (2002). Integrating science and practice: Reclaiming the science in practice. *Journal of Clinical Psychology*, *58*(10), 1285–1290. https://doi.org/10.1002/jclp.10112

Cattell, J.M. (1890). Mental tests and measurements. *Mind*, *os-XV*(59), 373–381. https://doi.org/10.1093/mind/os-XV.59.373

Cattell, J.M. (1896). Address of the president before the American Psychological Association, 1895. *Psychological Review, 3*(2), 134–148. https://doi.org/10.1037/h0071520

Catts, S.V., O'Toole, B.I., Carr, V.J., Lewin, T., Neil, A., Harris, M.G., Frost, A.D.J., Crissman, B.R., Eadie, K., & Evans, R.W. (2010). Appraising evidence for intervention effectiveness in early psychosis: Conceptual framework and review of evaluation approaches. *Australian and New Zealand Journal of Psychiatry, 44*(3), 195–219. https://doi.org/10.3109/00048670903487167

Center for Open Science. (2024). OSF. Open Science Framework. https://osf.io/

Chambers, C. (2017). *The seven deadly sins of psychology: A manifesto for reforming the culture of scientific practice*. Princeton University Press.

Chang, H. (2004). *Inventing temperature: Measurement and scientific progress*. Oxford University Press.

Chang, H. (2012). *Is water H2O?: Evidence, realism and pluralism* (Vol. 293). Springer. https://doi.org/10.1007/978-94-007-3932-1

Chang, H. (2017). Epistemic iteration and natural kinds: Realism and pluralism in taxonomy. In *Philosophical issues in psychiatry IV: Classification of psychiatric illness* (pp. 229–245). Oxford University Press.

Chang, H. (2022). *Realism for realistic people*. Cambridge University Press.

Chemero, A. (2023). Abduction and deduction in dynamical cognitive science. *Topics in Cognitive Science*, 1–13. https://doi.org/10.1111/tops.12692

Christodoulou, D. (2014). *Seven myths about education*. Routledge.

Cialdini, R.B. (2009). We have to break up. *Perspectives on Psychological Science, 4*(1), 5–6. https://doi.org/10.1111/j.1745-6924.2009.01091.x

Coetzee, J.P., & Monti, M.M. (2018). At the core of reasoning: Dissociating deductive and non-deductive load. *Human Brain Mapping, 39*(4), 1850–1861. https://doi.org/10.1002/hbm.23979

Cohen, J. (1977). *Statistical power analysis for the behavioural sciences*. Academic Press.

Cohen, J. (1994). The earth is round ($p < .05$). *American Psychologist, 49*(12), 997–1003. https://doi.org/10.1037/0003-066X.49.12.997

Cowan, R.S. (1972). Francis Galton's statistical ideas: The influence of eugenics. *Isis, 63*(4), 509–528. https://doi.org/10.1086/351000

Craig, D.P.A., & Abramson, C.I. (2018). Ordinal pattern analysis in comparative psychology: A flexible alternative to null hypothesis significance testing using an observation oriented modeling paradigm. *International Journal of Comparative Psychology, 31*, 1–21.

Cronbach, L.J. (1957). The two disciplines of scientific psychology. *American Psychologist, 12*(11), 671–684. https://doi.org/10.1037/h0043943

Cronbach, L.J. (1975). Beyond the two disciplines of scientific psychology. *American Psychologist, 30*(2), 116–127. https://doi.org/10.1037/h0076829

Crossman, E.R. (1959). A theory of the acquisition of speed-skill. *Ergonomics, 2*, 153–166. https://doi.org/10.1080/00140135908930419

Cumming, G. (2008). Replication and p intervals: p Values predict the future only vaguely, but confidence intervals do much better. *Perspectives on Psychological Science, 3*, 286–300. https://doi.org/10.1111/j.1745-6924.2008.00079.x

Cumming, G. (2012). *Understanding the new statistics: Effect sizes, confidence intervals, and meta-analysis*. Routledge.

Cumming, G., & Finch, S. (2005). Inference by eye: Confidence intervals and how to read pictures of data. *American Psychologist, 60*, 170–180. https://doi.org/10.1037/0003-066X.60.2.170

Cummins, F. (2018). *The ground from which we speak*. Cambridge Scholars.

D'Amato, M.R. (1979). *Experimental psychology: Methodology, psychophysics and learning.* Tata McGraw-Hill.

Dana, J., & Thomas, R. (2006). In defense of clinical judgment … and mechanical prediction. *Journal of Behavioral Decision Making, 19*(5), 413–428. https://doi.org/10.1002/bdm.537

Dancey, C.P., & Reidy, J. (2008). *Statistics without maths for psychology: Using SPSS for windows.* Pearson Education.

Danziger, K. (1994). *Constructing the subject: Historical origins of psychological research*. Cambridge University Press.

Dar, R. (1987). Another look at Meehl, Lakatos, and the scientific practices of psychologists. *American Psychologist*, *42*(2), 145–151.

Davis-Stober, C.P., Dana, J., Kellen, D., McMullin, S.D. & Bonifay, W. (2024). Better accuracy for better science ... through random conclusions. *Perspectives on Psychological Science*, *19*(1), 223–243. https://doi.org/10.1177/17456916231182097

Dawes, R.M. (2005). The ethical implications of Paul Meehl's work on comparing clinical versus actuarial prediction methods. *Journal of Clinical Psychology*, *61*(10), 1245–1255. https://doi.org/10.1002/jclp.20180

Debrouwere, S., & Rosseel, Y. (2022). The conceptual, cunning, and conclusive experiment in psychology. *Perspectives on Psychological Science*, *17*(3), 852–862. https://doi.org/10.1177/17456916211026947

De Leeuw, J.R., Motz, B.A., Fyfe, E.R., Carvalho, P.F., & Goldstone, R.L. (2022). Generalizability, transferability, and the practice-to-practice gap. Comment on Yarkoni T. (2022) The generalizability crisis. *Behavioral and Brain Sciences, 45*, e1, 1–78. https://doi.org/ 10.1017/S0140525X21000406, e11

DeJesus, J.M., Callanan, M.A., Solis, G., & Gelman, S.A. (2019). Generic language in scientific communication. *Proceedings of the National Academy of Sciences*, *116*(37), 18370–18377.

Devezer, B., Nardin, L.G., Baumgaertner, B., & Buzbas, E.O. (2019). Scientific discovery in a model-centric framework: Reproducibility, innovation, and epistemic diversity. *PLOS One*, *14*(5), e0216125. https://doi.org/10.1371/journal.pone.0216125

Devlieger, P., Rusch, F., & Pfeiffer, D. (2003). Rethinking disability as same and different! Towards a cultural model of disability. In P. Devlieger, F. Rusch, & D. Pfeiffer (Eds.), *Rethinking disability: The emergence of new definitions, concepts and communities* (pp. 9–16). Garant.

Dewsbury, D.A. (2009). Is psychology losing its foundations? *Review of General Psychology*, *13*(4), 281–289. https://doi.org/10.1037/a0017760

DiCaglio, J. (2021). *Scale theory: A nondisciplinary inquiry*. University of Minnesota Press

De Haan, S. (2020). *Enactive psychiatry.* Cambridge University Press.

Diener, E., Northcott, R., Zyphur, M.J., & West, S.G. (2022). Beyond experiments. *Perspectives on Psychological Science*, *17*(4), 1101–1119. https://doi.org/10.1177/17456916211037670

Doherty, M.E., Shemberg, K.M., Anderson, R.B., & Tweney, R.D. (2013). Exploring unexplained variation. *Theory & Psychology*, *23*, 81. https://doi.org/10.1177/0959354312445653

Donald, M. (2001). *A mind so rare*. Norton.

Douglas, H. (2023). The importance of values for science. *Interdisciplinary Science Reviews*, *48*(2), 251–263. https://doi.org/10.1080/03080188.2023.2191559

Douglas, H., & Branch, T.Y. (2024). The social contract for science and the value-free ideal. *Synthese*, *203*(2), 40. https://doi.org/10.1007/s11229-023-04477-9

Douglas, H.E. (2009). *Science, policy, and the value-free ideal*. University of Pittsburgh Press.

Doyen, S., Klein, O., Pichon, C.-L. & Cleeremans, A. (2012). Behavioral priming: It's all in the mind, but whose mind? *PLOS One*, *7*(1), e29081. https://doi.org/10.1371/journal.pone.0029081

Dupré, J. (1993). *The disorder of things: Metaphysical foundations of the disunity of science*. Harvard University Press.

Dykiert, D., Der, G., Starr, J.M., & Deary, I.J. (2012). Age differences in intra-individual variability in simple and choice reaction time: Systematic review and meta-analysis. *PLOS One*, *7*(10), e45750. https://doi.org/10.1371/journal.pone.0045759

Ebbinghaus, H. (1885). *Memory*. Columbia University/Dover.

Ebersole, C.R., Atherton, O.E., Belanger, A.L., Skulborstad, H.M., Allen, J.M., Banks, J.B., Baranski, E., Bernstein, M.J., Bonfiglio, D.B., & Boucher, L. (2016). Many Labs 3: Evaluating participant pool quality across the academic semester via replication. *Journal of Experimental Social Psychology*, *67*, 68–82.

Ebersole, C.R., Mathur, M.B., Baranski, E., Bart-Plange, D.-J., Buttrick, N.R., Chartier, C.R., Corker, K.S., Corley, M., Hartshorne, J.K., & IJzerman, H. (2020). Many Labs 5: Testing pre-data-collection peer review as an intervention to increase replicability. *Advances in Methods and Practices in Psychological Science*, *3*(3), 309–331.

Eells, T.D. (2015). *Psychotherapy case formulation.* American Psychological Association. https://psycnet.apa.org/record/2015-00669-000

Einstein, A. (1919, November 28). Time, space, and gravitation. *London Times*, 13–14.

Elmes, D.G., Kantowitz, B.H. & Roediger, H.L. III (1995). *Research methods in psychology* (5th Ed.). West.

Ericsson, K.A., & Chase, W.G. (1982). Exceptional memory: Extraordinary feats of memory can be matched or surpassed by people with average memories that have been improved by training. *American Scientist*, *70*(6), 607–615.

Eronen, M.I. (2020). Causal discovery and the problem of psychological interventions. *New Ideas in Psychology*, *59*, 100785. https://doi.org/10.1016/j.newideapsych.2020.100785

Eronen, M.I. (2024). Causal complexity and psychological measurement. *Philosophical Psychology*, *0*(0), 1–16. https://doi.org/10.1080/09515089.2023.2300693

Eronen, M.I., & Bringmann, L.F. (2021). The theory crisis in psychology: How to move forward. *Perspectives on Psychological Science*, *16*(4), 779–788. https://doi.org/10.1177/1745691620970586

Espino, O., & Byrne, R.M.J. (2020). The suppression of inferences from counterfactual conditionals. *Cognitive Science*, *44*(4), e12827. https://doi.org/10.1111/cogs.12827

Estes, W.K. (1960). Learning theory and the new "mental chemistry". *Psychological Review*, *67*, 207–223. https://doi.org/10.1037/h0041624

Favela, L.H. (2020). Dynamical systems theory in cognitive science and neuroscience. *Philosophy Compass*, *15*(8), e12695. https://doi.org/10.1111/phc3.12695

Feldman Barrett, L., Mesquita, B., & Smith, E.R. (2010). The context principle. In B. Mesquita, L. Feldman Barrett, & E.R. Smith (Eds.), *The mind in context* (1st ed., pp. 1–22). Guilford Press.

Felline, L. (2011). Scientific explanation between principle and constructive theories. *Philosophy of Science*, *78*(5), 989–1000. https://doi.org/10.1086/662270

Ferguson, C.J. (2015). "Everybody knows psychology is not a real science": Public perceptions of psychology and how we can improve our relationship with policymakers, the scientific community, and the general public. *American Psychologist*, *70*(6), 527–542. https://doi.org/10.1037/a0039405

Ferguson, C.J., & Heene, M. (2012). A vast graveyard of undead theories: Publication bias and psychological science's aversion to the null. *Perspectives on Psychological Science*, *7*(6), 555–561.

Fernández-Álvarez, J., Prado-Abril, J., Sanchez-Reales, S., Molinari, G., Gómez Penedo, J. M., & Youn, S. J. (2020). The gap between research and practice: Towards the integration of psychotherapy. *Papeles Del Psicologo*, *41*, 81–90.

Fischer, K.W., & Bidell, T.R. (2006). Dynamic development of action and thought. In W. Damon & R.M. Lerner (Eds.), *Handbook of child psychology: Theoretical models of human development* (Vol. 1, pp. 467–561). Wiley.

Fisher, A.J., Medaglia, J.D., & Jeronimus, B.F. (2018). Lack of group-to-individual generalizability is a threat to human subjects research. *Proceedings of the National Academy of Sciences (USA)*, *115*, E6106–E6115. https://doi.org/10.1073/pnas.1711978115

Fisher, R.A. (1925). *Statistical methods for research workers.* Oliver & Boyd.

Fishman, D.B. (2000). Transcending the efficacy versus effectiveness research debate: Proposal for a new, electronic "Journal of Pragmatic Case Studies." *Prevention and Treatment*, *3*, Article 8, 1-25.

Flake, J.K., Luong, R., & Shaw, M. (2022). Addressing a crisis of generalizability with large-scale construct validation. Commentary on Yarkoni, T. (2022). The generalizability crisis. *Behavioral & Brain Sciences*, *45*, e1, 1–78. https://doi.org/ 10.1017/S0140525X21000376, e14

Fleischner, T.L. (2011). The mindfulness of natural history. In T.L. Fleischner (Ed.), *The way of natural history* (pp. 3–15). Trinity University Press.

Flis, I., & van Eck, N.J. (2018). Framing psychology as a discipline (1950–1999): A large-scale term co-occurrence analysis of scientific literature in psychology. *History of Psychology*, *21*(4), 334–362.

Flores, F. (1999). Einstein's theory of theories and types of theoretical explanation. *International Studies in the Philosophy of Science*, *13*(2), 123–134. https://doi.org/10.1080/02698599908573613

Flynn, J.R. (2007). *What is intelligence?* Cambridge University Press.

Flyvbjerg, B. (2006). Five misunderstandings about case-study research. *Qualitative Inquiry*, *12*(2), 219–245. https://doi.org/10.1177/1077800405284363

Franklin, R., Allison, D.B., & Gorman, B.S. (Eds.). (1996). *Design and analysis of single-case research*. Psychology Press.

Freedman, D.A. (1985). Statistics and the scientific method. In W.M. Mason & S.E. Fienberg (Eds.), *Cohort analysis in social research: Beyond the identification problem* (pp. 343–366). Springer. https://doi.org/10.1007/978-1-4613-8536-3_11

Freeman, W.J. (1975). *Mass action in the nervous system: Examination of the neurophysiological basis of adaptive behavior through the eeg*. Academic Press.

Freeman, W.J. (1995). *Societies of brains: A study in the neuroscience of love and hate* (1st ed.). Psychology Press.

Fuchs, E., & Flügge, G. (2014). Adult neuroplasticity: More than 40 years of research. *Neural Plasticity*, *2014*, e541870. https://doi.org/10.1155/2014/541870

Gallo, K.P., & Barlow, D.H. (2012). Factors involved in clinician adoption and nonadoption of evidence-based interventions in mental health. *Clinical Psychology: Science and Practice*, *19*(1), 93–106.

Garb, H.N., & Wood, J.M. (2019). Methodological advances in statistical prediction. *Psychological Assessment*, *31*(12), 1456–1466. https://doi.org/10.1037/pas0000673

Garfinkel, H. (1967). *Studies in ethnomethodology*. Prentice-Hall.

Gastelum-Vargas, M., Chemero, A., & Raja, V. (2024). Places for reasoning. *Philosophical Transactions of the Royal Society B: Biological Sciences*, *379*(1910), 20230294. https://doi.org/10.1098/rstb.2023.0294

Gelman, A. (2018). The failure of null hypothesis significance testing when studying incremental changes, and what to do about it. *Personality and Social Psychology Bulletin*, *44*(1), 16–23. https://doi.org/10.1177/0146167217729162

Georgiou, D., Diery, A., Mok, S.Y., Fischer, F., & Seidel, T. (2023). Turning research evidence into teaching action: Teacher educators' attitudes toward evidence-based teaching. *International Journal of Educational Research Open*, *4*, 100240. https://doi.org/10.1016/j.ijedro.2023.100240

Gernigon, C., Den Hartigh, R.J.R., Vallacher, R.R., & van Geert, P.L.C. (2023). How the complexity of psychological processes reframes the issue of reproducibility in psychological science. *Perspectives on Psychological Science*, *19*(6), 952–977. https://doi.org/10.1177/17456916231187324

Ghaderi, A. (2011). Does case formulation make a difference to treatment outcome? In *Forensic case formulation* (pp. 61–79). John Wiley & Sons, Ltd. https://doi.org/10.1002/9781119977018.ch3

Gigerenzer, G. (1991). From tools to theories: A heuristic of discovery in cognitive psychology. *Psychological Review*, *98*(2), 254.

Gigerenzer, G. (1998a). Surrogates for theories. *Theory and Psychology*, *8*, 195–204.

Gigerenzer, G. (1998b). We need statistical thinking, not statistical rituals. *Behavioral and Brain Sciences*, *21*(2), 199–200.

Gigerenzer, G. (2004). Mindless statistics. *Journal of Socio-Economics*, *33*(5), 587–606. https://doi.org/10.1016/j.socec.2004.09.033

Gigerenzer, G. (2024). Can psychology learn from the natural sciences? *Theory & Psychology*, *34*(3), 295–310. https://doi.org/10.1177/09593543231209342

Goldberg, L.R. (1970). Man versus model of man: A rationale, plus some evidence, for a method of improving on clinical inferences. *Psychological Bulletin*, *73*(6), 422.

Goldberger, A.L., Amaral, L.A.N., Hausdorff, J.M., Ivanov, P.Ch., Peng, C.-K., & Stanley, H.E. (2002). Fractal dynamics in physiology: Alterations with disease and aging. *Proceedings of the National Academy of Sciences*, *99*(suppl_1), 2466–2472. https://doi.org/10.1073/pnas.01257949

Gottman, J.M., & Notarius, C.I. (2000). Decade review: Observing marital interaction. *Journal of Marriage and Family*, *62*(4), 927–947. https://doi.org/10.1111/j.1741-3737.2000.00927.x

Gray, K. (2017). How to map theory: Reliable methods are fruitless without rigorous theory. *Perspectives on Psychological Science*, *12*(5), 731–741.

Green, C.D. (2015). Why psychology isn't unified, and probably never will be. *Review of General Psychology*, *19*(3), 207–214. https://doi.org/10.1037/gpr0000051

Green, L.W. (2008). Making research relevant: If it is an evidence-based practice, where's the practice-based evidence? *Family Practice*, *25*(suppl_1), i20–i24. https://doi.org/10.1093/fampra/cmn055

Grenier, M.-L. (2021). Patient case formulations and oppressive disability discourses in occupational therapy education. *Canadian Journal of Occupational Therapy*, *88*(3), 266–272. https://doi.org/10.1177/00084174211005882

Grice, J.W. (2011). *Observation Oriented Modeling: Analysis of cause in the behavioral sciences.* Academic Press.

Grice, J.W. (2015). From means and variances to persons and patterns. *Frontiers in Psychology*, *6*, 1007. https://doi.org/10.3389/fpsyg.2015.01007

Grice, J.W., Barrett, P., Cota, L., Felix, C., Taylor, Z., Garner, S., et al. (2017). Four bad habits of modern psychologists. *Behavioural Sciences*, *7*(3), 53. https://doi.org/10.3390/bs7030053

Grice, J.W., Craig, D.P.A., & Abramson, C.I. (2015). A simple and transparent alternative to repeated measures ANOVA. *SAGE Open*, July-September, 1–13. https://doi.org/10.1177/2158244015604192

Grice, J.W., Jackson, B.J., & McDaniel, B.L. (2006). Bridging the idiographic-nomothetic divide: a follow-up study. *Journal of Personality*, *74*, 1191–1218. https://doi.org/10.1111/j. 1467- 6494.2006.00407.x

Griffiths, S., Rhodes, G., Jeffrey, L., Palermo, R., & Neumann, M.F. (2018). The average facial expression of a crowd influences impressions of individual expressions. *Journal of Experimental Psychology: Human Perception and Performance*, *44*(2), 311–319. http://dx.doi.org/10.1037/xhp0000446

Grove, W. M., & Vrieze, S. I. (2013). The clinical versus mechanical prediction controversy. In K. F. Geisinger, B. A. Bracken, J. F. Carlson, J.-I. C. Hansen, N. R. Kuncel, S. P. Reise, & M. C. Rodriguez (Eds.), *APA handbook of testing and assessment in psychology, Vol. 2. Testing and assessment in clinical and counseling psychology* (pp. 51–62). American Psychological Association. https://doi.org/10.1037/14048-004

Grove, W.M., Zald, D.H., Lebow, B.S., Snitz, B.E., & Nelson, C. (2000). Clinical versus mechanical prediction: A meta-analysis. *Psychological Assessment*, *12*(1), 19–30. https://doi.org/10.1037/1040-3590.12.1.19

Grubbs, J.B. (2022). The cost of crisis in clinical psychological science. Comment on Yarkoni T. (2022) The generalizability crisis. *Behavioral and Brain Sciences*, *45*, e1, 1–78. https://doi.org/ 10.1017/S0140525X21000388, e18

Guest, O. (2024). What makes a good theory, and how do we make a theory good? *Computational Brain & Behavior*. https://doi.org/10.1007/s42113-023-00193-2

Guest, O., & Martin, A.E. (2021). How computational modeling can force theory building in psychological science. *Perspectives on Psychological Science*, *16*(4), 789–802. https://doi.org/10.1177/1745691620970585

Haaf, J.M., & Rouder, J.N. (2019). Some do and some don't? Accounting for variability of individual difference structures. *Psychonomic Bulletin and Review*, *26*, 772–789. https://doi.org/10.3758/s13423-018-1522-x

Haefell, G.J. (2022). Psychology needs to get tired of winning. *Royal Society Open Science*, *9*, 1–8. https://doi.org/10.1098/rsos.220099

Hale, J., Hastings, J., West, R., Lefevre, C.E., Direito, A., Bohlen, L.C., Godinho, C., Anderson, N., Zink, S., Groarke, H., & Michie, S. (2020). An ontology-based modelling system (OBMS) for representing behaviour change theories applied to 76 theories. *Wellcome Open Research*, *5*, 177. https://doi.org/10.12688/wellcomeopenres.16121.1

Halford, W.K. & Frost, A.D.J. (2021). Depression anxiety stress scale-10: A brief measure for routine psychotherapy outcome and progress assessment. *Behaviour Change*, *38*, 221–234. https://doi.org/10.1017/bec.2021.12

Hamaker, E.L. (2012). Why researchers should think "within-person": A paradigmatic rationale. In M.R. Mehl & T.S. Conner (Eds.), *Handbook of research methods for studying daily life* (pp. 43–61). Guildford Press.

Hamaker, E.L., Nesselroade, J.R., & Molenaar, P.C. (2007). The integrated trait–state model. *Journal of Research in Personality*, *41*(2), 295–315.

Hardwick, R.M., Forrence, A.D., Costello, M.G., Zackowski, K., & Haith, A.M. (2022). Age-related increases in reaction time result from slower preparation, not delayed initiation. *Journal of Neurophysiology*, *128*, 582–592. https://doi.org/10.1152/jn.00072.2022

Hargreaves, D.H. (1997). In defence of research for evidence-based teaching: A rejoinder to Martyn Hammersley. *British Educational Research Journal*, *23*(4), 405–419. https://doi.org/10.1080/0141192970230402

Haslam, S.A., & McGarty, C. (2003). *Research methods and statistics in psychology*. Sage Foundations of Psychology Series (2nd ed.). SAGE.

Heathcote, A.S., Brown, S., & Mewhort, D.J.K. (2000). The power law repealed: The case for an exponential law of practice. *Psychological Bulletin and Review*, *7*, 185–207. https://doi.org/10.3758/BF03212979

Heft, H. (1979). Background and focal environmental conditions of the home and attention in young children. *Journal of Applied Social Psychology*, *9*(1), 47–69. https://doi.org/10.1111/j.1559-1816.1979.tb00794.x

Heft, H. (1988). Affordances of children's environments: A functional approach to environmental description. *Children's Environments Quarterly*, 29–37. https://doi-org/10.1111/j.1559-1816.1979.tb00794.x

Heft, H. (2001). *Ecological psychology in context: James Gibson, Roger Barker, and the legacy of William James's radical empiricism* (1st ed.). Lawrence Erlbaum Associates.

Heft, H. (2014). What makes an ecological psychology ecological? *Man-Environment Research Journal (人間・環境学会誌)*, *16*(2), 11–16. https://doi.org/10.20786/mera.16.2_11

Heft, H. (2018). Places: Widening the scope of an ecological approach to perception – Action with an emphasis on child development. *Ecological Psychology*, *30*(1), 99–123. https://doi.org/10.1080/10407413.2018.1410045

Heft, H. (2024). Behaviour settings, situated action and complexity theory. *Philosophical Transactions of the Royal Society B: Biological Sciences*, *379*(1910), 20230284. https://doi.org/10.1098/rstb.2023.0284

Henrich, J., Heine, S.J., & Norenzayan, A. (2010). Beyond WEIRD: Towards a broad-based behavioral science. *Behavioral and Brain Sciences*, *33*(2–3), 111–135.

Hersen, M. (2002). Rationale for clinical case studies: An editorial. *Clinical Case Studies*, *1*(1), 3–5.

Hoffmann, S., Deutsch, L., Klein, J.T., & O'Rourke, M. (2022). Integrate the integrators! A call for establishing academic careers for integration experts. *Humanities and Social Sciences Communications*, *9*(1), Article 1. https://doi.org/10.1057/s41599-022-01138-z

Holton, G. (1979, Summer). Constructing a theory: Einstein's model. *The American Scholar*, *48*(3), 309–340. www.jstor.org/stable/41210527

Horton, Z. (2021). *The cosmic zoom: Scale, knowledge, and mediation* (1st ed.). University of Chicago Press.

Howell, D.C. (2002). *Statistical Methods for Psychology* (5th ed.). Duxbury.

Howitt, D., & Cramer, D. (2011). *An Introduction to Statistics in Psychology* (5th ed.). Prentice Hall.

Hughes, B. (2018). *Psychology in crisis* (1st ed.). Red Globe Press.

Hunter, M.D., Fisher, Z.F., & Geier, C.F. (2024). What ergodicity means for you. *Developmental Cognitive Neuroscience*, *68*, 101406. https://doi.org/10.1016/j.dcn.2024.101406

Hutchins, E. (1995). *Cognition in the wild*. MIT Press.

IJzerman, H., Lewis, N.A.Jr., Weinstein, N., DeBruine, L., Ritchie, S.J., Vazire, S., Forscher, P.S., Morey, R.D., Ivory, J.D., Anvari, F., & Przybylski, A.K. (2020). Psychological Science is not yet a crisis-ready discipline. *PsyArxiv* April 23.

Ince, R.A.A., Paton, A.T., Kay, J.W., & Schyns, P.G. (2021). Bayesian inference of population prevalence. *eLife*, *10*(e62461), 1–22. https://doi.org/10. 7554/ eLife. 6246

Ingendahl, M., Woitzel, J., & Alves, H. (2024). *Who* shows the unlikelihood effect – And *why? Psychonomic Bulletin & Review*, *31*, 1768–1781. https://doi.org/10.3758/s13423-024-02453-z

Ingold, T. (2016). From science to art and back again: The pendulum of an anthropologist. *Anuac*, *5*(1), 5–23. https://doi.org/10.7340/anuac2239-625X-2237

Ioannidis, J.P., Munafo, M.R., Fusar-Poli, P., Nosek, B.A., & David, S.P. (2014). Publication and other reporting biases in cognitive sciences: Detection, prevalence, and prevention. *Trends in Cognitive Sciences*, *18*(5), 235–241.

Jadreškić, D. (2021). Diversity as an epistemic value – From individual to social objectivity. In R. Natarajan (ed.), *Sprache – Bildung – Geschlecht: Interdisziplinäre Ansätze in Flucht- und Migrationskontexten* [Internet]. Springer Fachmedien; 2021 [cited 2024 Dec 17], 241–258. Available from: https://doi.org/10.1007/978-3-658-28341-4_11

James, W. (1890). *The principles of psychology*. Macmillan.

James, W. (1892). *Psychology: A briefer course*. Henry Holt and Company.

Jarke, H., Anand-Vembar, S., Alzahawi, S., Andersen, T.L., Bojanić, L., Carstensen, A., Feldman, G., Garcia-Garzon, E., Kapoor, H., Lewis, S., Todsen, A.L., Većkalov, B., Zickfeld, J.H., & Geiger, S.J. (2022). A roadmap to large-scale multi-country replications in psychology. *Collabra: Psychology*, *8*(1), 57538. https://doi.org/10.1525/collabra.57538

Jayaraman, S., Fausey, C.M., & Smith, L.B. (2015). The faces in infant-perspective scenes change over the first year of life. *PLOS One*, *10*(5), e0123780. https://doi.org/10.1371/journal.pone.0123780

John, L.K., Loewenstein, G., & Prelec, D. (2012). Measuring the prevalence of questionable research practices with incentives for truth telling. *Psychological Science*, *23*(5), 524–532.

Jonas, E., & Kording, K.P. (2017). Could a neuroscientist understand a microprocessor? *PLOS Computational Biology*, *13*(1), e1005268. https://doi.org/10.1371/journal.pcbi.1005268

Kagan, J. (2012). *Psychology's ghosts: The crisis in the profession and the way back*. Yale University Press.

Kahneman, D. (2011). *Thinking, fast and slow*. Farrar, Strauss and Giroux.

Karasik, L.B., Tamis-LeMonda, C.S., & Adolph, K.E. (2011). Transition from crawling to walking and infants' actions with objects and people. *Child Development*, *82*(4), 1199–1209. https://doi.org/10.1111/j.1467-8624.2011.01595.x

Karasik, L.B., Tamis-LeMonda, C.S., Adolph, K.E., & Bornstein, M.H. (2015). Places and postures: A cross-cultural comparison of sitting in 5-month-olds. *Journal of Cross-Cultural Psychology*, *46*(8), 1023–1038. https://doi.org/10.1177/0022022115593803

Karmiloff-Smith, A. (2000). Why babies' brains are not Swiss army knives. In H. Rose & S. Rose (Eds.), *Alas, poor Darwin: Arguments against evolutionary psychology* (pp. 144–156). Vintage.

Kazdin, A.E. (2008). Evidence-based treatment and practice: New opportunities to bridge clinical research and practice, enhance the knowledge base, and improve patient care. *American Psychologist*, *63*(3), 146–159. https://doi.org/10.1037/0003-066X.63.3.146

Kazdin, A.E. (2016). Closing the research–practice gap: How, why, and whether. *Clinical Psychology: Science and Practice*, *23*(2), 201–206. https://doi.org/10.1111/cpsp.12155

Kazdin, A.E. (2021a). Single-case experimental designs: Characteristics, changes, and challenges. *Journal of the Experimental Analysis of Behavior*, *115*(1), 56–85. https://doi.org/10.1002/jeab.638

Kazdin, A.E. (2021b). *Single case research designs: Methods for clinical and applied settings* (3rd ed.). Oxford University Press.

Kelso, J.A.S. (1995). *Dynamic patterns*. MIT Press.

Kelty-Stephen, D.G. (2024). Scaling up: Lawfulness of affordances requires independence from any single "scale of behavior". In M. Mangalam, A. Hajnal, & D.G. Kelty-Stephen (Eds.), *The modern legacy of Gibson's affordances for the sciences of organisms* (pp.176–195). Routledge.

Kievit, R.A., Frankenhuis, W.E., Waldorp, L.J., & Borsboom, D. (2013). Simpson's paradox in psychological science: a practical guide. *Frontiers in Psychology*, *4*, 513. https://doi.org/10.3389/fpsyg.2013.00513

Kirsner, K., & Speelman, C. (1996). Skill acquisition and repetition priming: One principle, many processes. *Journal of Experimental Psychology: Learning, Memory & Cognition*, *22*, 563–575. https://doi.org/10.1037/0278-7393. 22.3.563

Klein, G.A. (1993). A recognition-primed decision model of rapid decision making. In G.A. Klein, J. Orasanu, R. Calderwood, & C.E. Zsambok (Eds.), *Decision making in action: Models and methods* (pp. 138–147). Ablex.

Klein, R.A., Cook, C.L., Ebersole, C.R., Vitiello, C., Nosek, B.A., et al. (2022). Many Labs 4: Failure to replicate mortality salience effect with and without original author involvement. *Collabra: Psychology*, *8*(1): 35271. https://doi.org/10.1525/collabra.35271

Klein, R.A., Vianello, M., Hasselman, F., Adams, B.G., Adams, R.B., Alper, S., Aveyard, M., Axt, J.R., Babalola, M.T., Bahník, Š., Batra, R., Berkics, M., Bernstein, M.J., Berry, D.R., Bialobrzeska, O., Binan, E.D., Bocian, K., Brandt, M.J., Busching, R., … Nosek, B.A. (2018). Many Labs 2: Investigating variation in replicability across samples and settings. *Advances in Methods and Practices in Psychological Science*, *1*(4), 443–490. https://doi.org/10.1177/2515245918810225

Knight, C.C., & Fischer, K.W. (1992). Learning to read words: Individual differences in developmental sequences. *Journal of Applied Developmental Psychology*, *13*(3), 377–404. https://doi.org/10.1016/0193-3973(92)90037-I

Kolers, P.A. (1976). Reading a year later. *Journal of Experimental Psychology: Human Learning and Memory*, *2*, 554–565. https://doi.org/10.1037/ 0278-7393.2.5.554

Kratochwill, T.R., & Levin, J.R. (Eds.). (1992). *Single-case research design and analysis: New directions for psychology and education*. Erlbaum.

Krause, M., & Behn, A. (2022). Case formulation as a bridge between theory, clinical practice, and research: A commentary. *Journal of Clinical Psychology*, *78*(3), 454–461. https://doi.org/10.1002/jclp.23328

Kroupin, I., Davis, H.E., & Henrich, J. (2024). Beyond Newton: Why assumptions of universality are critical to cognitive science, and how to finally move past them. *Psychological Review*. Advance online publication. https://dx.doi.org/10.1037/rev0000480

Krueger, J.I., & Funder, D.C. (2004). Towards a balanced social psychology: Causes, consequences, and cures for the problem-seeking approach to social behavior and cognition. *Behavioral and Brain Sciences*, *27*(3), 313–327.

Krumme, C. (2023). *Optimal illusions: The false promise of optimization*. Riverhead.

Kuhn, T.S. (1970). *The structure of scientific revolutions*. University of Chicago Press.

Lakens, D. (2021). The practical alternative to the p-value is the correctly used p-value. *Perspectives on Psychological Science*, *16*(3), 639–648. https://doi.org/10.1177/1745691620958012

Lamiell, J.T. (1997). Individuals and the differences between them. In R. Hogan, J. Johnson, & S. Briggs (Eds.), *Handbook of personality psychology* (pp. 117–141). Academic Press.

Lamiell, J.T. (2013). Statisticism in personality psychologists' use of trait constructs: What is it? How was it contracted? Is there a cure? *New Ideas in Psychology*, *31*, 65–71. https://doi.org/10.1016/j.newideapsych.2011.02.0 09

Lamiell, J.T. (2019). *Psychology's misuse of statistics and persistent dismissal of its critics*. Palgrave.

Lampropoulos, G.K., & Spengler, P.M. (2002). Introduction: Reprioritizing the role of science in a realistic version of the scientist-practitioner model. *Journal of Clinical Psychology*, *58*(10), 1195. https://doi.org/10.1002/jclp.10105

Lange, M. (2014). Did Einstein really believe that principle theories are explanatorily powerless? *Perspectives on Science*, *22*(4), 449–463. https://doi.org/10.1162/POSC_a_00145

Leiper. (2013). Psychodynamic formulation. In L. Johnstone & R. Dallos (Eds.), *Formulation in psychology and psychotherapy* (pp. 45–66). Routledge.

Levitt, H.M., Surace, F.I., Wu, M.B., Chapin, B., Hargrove, J.G., Herbitter, C., Lu, E.C., Maroney, M.R., & Hochman, A.L. (2022). The meaning of scientific objectivity and subjectivity: From the perspective of methodologists. *Psychological Methods*, *27*(4), 589–605. https://doi.org/10.1037/met0000363

Lewin, K. (1951). *Field theory in social science*. Harper Torchbooks.

Lilienfeld, S.O. (2007). Psychological treatments that cause harm. *Perspectives on Psychological Science*, *2*(1), 53–70. https://doi.org/10.1111/j.1745-6916.2007.00029.x

Lilienfeld, S.O., Fowler, K.A., Lohr, J.M., & Lynn, S.J. (2013). Pseudoscience, nonscience, and nonsense in clinical psychology: Dangers and remedies. In *Destructive trends in mental health* (pp. 187–218). Routledge.

Lilienfeld, S.O., Ritschel, L.A., Lynn, S.J., & Latzman, R.D. (2019). The insufficiently appreciated raison d'être of evidence-based practice. In S. Dimidjian (Ed.), *Evidence-based practice in action: Bridging clinical science and intervention* (pp. 43–63). The Guilford Press.

Logan, G.D. (1988). Toward an instance theory of automatization. *Psychological Review*, *95*, 492–527. https://doi.org/10.1037/0033- 295X.95.4.492

Logie, R. (2018). Human cognition: Common principles and individual variation. *Journal of Applied Research in Memory and Cognition*, *7* (4), 471–486 https://doi.org/10.1016/j.jarmac.2018.08.001

Longino, H.E. (1990). *Science as social knowledge: Values and objectivity in scientific inquiry*. Princeton University Press.

Lovibond, P.F., & Lovibond, S.H. (1995). The structure of negative emotional states: Comparison of the Depression Anxiety Stress Scales (DASS) with the Beck Depression and Anxiety Inventories. *Behaviour Research and Therapy*, *33*, 335–343.

Lyall, C. (2019). *Being an interdisciplinary academic: How institutions shape university careers*. Springer International Publishing. https://doi.org/10.1007/978-3-030-18659-3

Lykken, D.T. (1991). What's wrong with psychology anyway. In D. Cicchetti & W.M. Grove (Eds.), *Thinking clearly about psychology* (Vol. 1, pp. 3–39). University of Minnesota Press.

McBeath, A., Bager-Charleson, S., & Abarbanel, A. (2019). Therapists and academic writing: "Once upon a time psychotherapy practitioners and researchers were the same people." *European Journal for Qualitative Research in Psychotherapy*, *9*, 103–116.

McClelland, L. (2013). Reformulating the impact of social inequalities. In L. Johnstone & R. Dallos (Eds.), *Formulation in psychology and psychotherapy* (pp. 121–144). Routledge.

McGann, M., Lucas, M., McHugh, C., & Barrett, L. (2024). People, places, things and communities: Expanding behaviour settings theory in the twenty-first century. *Philosophical Transactions of the Royal Society B: Biological Sciences*, *379*(1910), 20230282. https://doi.org/10.1098/rstb.2023.0282

McGann, M., & Speelman, C.P. (2020). Two kinds of theory: What psychology can learn from Einstein. *Theory & Psychology*, *30*(5), 674–689. https://doi.org/10.1177/0959354320937804

Mac Giolla, E., Karlsson, S., Neequaye, D.A., & Bergquist, M. (2022, July 8). *Evaluating the replicability of social priming studies*. https://doi.org/10.31234/osf.io/dwg9v

MacKenzie, D.A. (1981). *Statistics in Britain, 1865–1930: The social construction of scientific knowledge*. Edinburgh University Press.

Maguire, E.A., Gadian, D.G., Johnsrude, I.S., Good, C.D., Ashburner, J., Frackowiak, R.S.J., & Frith, C.D. (2000). Navigation-related structural change in the hippocampi of taxi drivers. *Proceedings of the National Academy of Sciences*, *97*(8), 4398–4403. https://doi.org/10.1073/pnas.070039597

Mandelbrot, B. (1967). How long is the coast of Britain? Statistical self-similarity and fractional dimension. *Science*, *156*(3775), 636–638. https://doi.org/10.1126/science.156.3775.636

Marmolejo-Ramos, F., & Matsunaga, M. (2009). Getting the most from your curves: exploring and reporting data using informative graphical techniques. *Tutorials in Quantitative Methods for Psychology*, *5*, 40–50.

Maxwell, S.E., & Delaney, H.D. (1990). *Designing experiments and analyzing data*. Brooks/Cole.

McManus, R.M., Young, L., & Sweetman, J. (2023). Psychology is a property of persons, not averages or distributions: Confronting the group-to-person generalizability problem in experimental psychology. *Advances in Methods and Practices in Psychological Science*, *6*(3), 1–23. https://doi.org/10.1177/2515459231186615

Medaglia, J.D., & Fernandez, K.A. (2022). The "'Crisis' Crisis" in psychology. *Behavioral and Brain Sciences*, *45*, e28. https://doi.org/10.1017/S0140525X21000364

Meehl, P.E. (1954). *Clinical versus statistical prediction: A theoretical analysis and review of the evidence*. University of Minnesota Press.

Meehl, P.E. (1967). Theory-testing in psychology and physics: A methodological paradox. *Philosophy of Science*, *34*(2), 103–115.

Meehl, P.E. (1978). Theoretical risks and tabular asterisks: Sir Karl, Sir Ronald, and the slow progress of soft psychology. *Journal of Consulting and Clinical Psychology*, *46*(4), 806–834. https://doi.org/10.1037/0022-006X. 46.4.806

Mehoudar, E., Arizpe, J., Baker, C.I., & Yovel, G. (2014). Faces in the eye of the beholder: Unique and stable eye scanning patterns of individual observers. *Journal of Vision*, *14*(7), 1–11.

Meyer, V., & Turkat, I.D. (1979). Behavioral analysis of clinical cases. *Journal of Behavioral Assessment*, *1*, 259–270.

Micceri, T. (1989). The unicorn, the normal curve, and other improbable creatures. *Psychological Bulletin*, *105*, 156–166. https://doi.org/10.1037/0033-2909.105. 1.156

Miller, J., & Schwarz, W. (2018). Implications of individual differences in on-average null effects. *Journal of Experimental Psychology: General*, *147*(3), 377–397. https://doi.org/10.1037/xge0000367

Milne, D., & Paxton, R. (1998). A psychological re-analysis of the scientist–practitioner model. *Clinical Psychology & Psychotherapy*, *5*(4), 216–230. https://doi.org/10.1002/(SICI)1099-0879(199812)5:4<216::AID-CPP165>3.0.CO;2-P

Mlodinow, L. (2009). *The Drunkard's walk: How randomness rules our lives*. Vintage Books.

Molenaar, P.C. (2004). A manifesto on psychology as idiographic science: Bringing the person back into scientific psychology, this time forever. *Measurement*, *2*(4), 201–218.

Molenaar, P.C. (2008a). On the implications of the classical ergodic theorems: Analysis of developmental processes has to focus on intra-individual variation. *Developmental Psychobiology*, *50*(1), 60–69. https://doi.org/10.1002/dev.20262

Molenaar, P.C. (2008b). Consequences of the ergodic theorems for classical test theory, factor analysis, and the analysis of developmental processes. In S.M. Hofer & D.F. Alwin (Eds.), *Handbook of cognitive aging* (pp. 90–104). Sage.

Molenaar, P.C., & Campbell, C.G. (2009). The new person-specific paradigm in psychology. *Current Directions in Psychological Science*, *18*(2), 112–117. https://doi.org/10.1111/j.1467-8721.2009.01619.x

Monteiro, S., Sherbino, J., Sibbald, M., & Norman, G. (2020). Critical thinking, biases and dual processing: The enduring myth of generalisable skills. *Medical Education*, *54*(1), 66–73. https://doi.org/10.1111/medu.13872

Moore, S., Speelman, C.P., & McGann, M. (2023). Pervasiveness of effects in sample-based experimental psychology: A re-examination of replication data from nine famous psychology experiments. *New Ideas in Psychology*, *68*, 100978. https://doi.org/10.1016/j.newideapsych.2022.100978

Morris, E.K. (2009). Behavior analysis and ecological psychology: Past, present, and future. A review of Harry Heft's Ecological Psychology in Context. *Journal of the Experimental Analysis of Behavior*, *92*(2), 275–304. https://doi.org/10.1901/jeab.2009.92-275

Moshontz, H., Campbell, L., Ebersole, C.R., IJzerman, H., Urry, H.L., Forscher, P.S., Grahe, J., McCarthy, R.J., Musser, E.D., Protzko, F.J.K., Forero, D.A., Janssen, S.M.J., Keene, J., Aczel, B., Ansari, D., Antfolk, J., Baskin, E., Batres, C., … Chartier, C.R. (2018). The psychological science accelerator: Advancing psychology through a distributed collaborative network. *PsyArXiv*. https://doi.org/10.31234/osf.io/785qu

Munafò, M.R., Nosek, B.A., Bishop, D.V., Button, K.S., Chambers, C.D., Du Sert, N.P., Simonsohn, U., Wagenmakers, E.-J., Ware, J.J., & Ioannidis, J.P. (2017). A manifesto for reproducible science. *Nature Human Behaviour*, *1*(1), 0021.

Munsterberg, H. (1899). Psychology and history. *Psychological Review*, *6*(1), 1–31. https://doi.org/10.1037/h0071306

Musfeld, P., Souza, A.S., & Oberauer, K. (2023). Repetition learning is neither a continuous nor an implicit process. *PNAS*, *120*(16), e2218042120. https://doi.org/10.1073/pnas.2218042120

Muthukrishna, M., & Henrich, J. (2019). A problem in theory. *Nature Human Behaviour*, *3*(3), 221–229. https://doi.org/10.1038/s41562-018-0522-1

Nagel, T. (1986). *The view from nowhere*. Oxford University Press.

Nathoo, F.S., & Masson, M.E.J. (2016). Bayesian alternatives to null-hypothesis significance testing for repeated-measures designs. *Journal of Mathematical Psychology*, *72*, 144– 157. https://doi.org/10.1016/j.jmp.2015.03.003

National Institutes of Health. (2024, July 19). *NIH Director's Pioneer Award | NIH Common Fund*. https://commonfund.nih.gov/pioneer

Neumann, M., Niessen, A.S.M., Hurks, P.P.M., & Meijer, R.R. (2023). Holistic and mechanical combination in psychological assessment: Why algorithms are underutilized and what is needed to increase their use. *International Journal of Selection and Assessment*, *31*(2), 267–285. https://doi.org/10.1111/ijsa.12416

Newell, A. (1973). You can't play 20 questions with nature and win: Projective comments on the papers of this symposium. In W.G. Chase (Ed.), *Visual information processing*. Academic Press.

Newell, A. (1990). *Unified theories of cognition*. Harvard University Press.

Newell, A., & Rosenbloom, P.S. (1981). Mechanisms of skills acquisition and the law of practice. In J.R. Anderson (Ed.), *Cognitive skills and their acquisition* (pp. 1-55). Erlbaum.

Nisbett, R.E., Peng, K., Choi, I., & Norenzayan, A. (2001). Culture and systems of thought: Holistic versus analytic cognition. *Psychological Review*, *108*(2), 291–310. https://doi.org/10.1037/0033-295X.108.2.291

Normand, M.P. (2016). Less is more: Psychologists can learn more by studying fewer people. *Quantitative Psychology and Measurement*, 934. https://doi.org/10.3389/fpsyg.2016.00934

Nosek, BA., Hardwicke, T. E., Moshontz, H., Allard, A., Corker, K.S., Dreber, A., Fidler, F., Hilgard, J., Kline Struhl, M., Nuijten, M.B., Rohrer, J.M., Romero, F., Scheel, A.M., Scherer, L.D., Schönbrodt, F.D., & Vazire, S. (2022). Replicability, robustness, and reproducibility in psychological science. *Annual Review of Psychology*, *73*(1), 719–748. https://doi.org/10.1146/annurev-psych-020821-114157

Nosek, B.A., & Lakens, D. (2014). Registered reports. *Social Psychology*, *45*, 137–141.

Nosek, B.A., Spies, J.R., & Motyl, M. (2012). Scientific utopia: II. Restructuring incentives and practices to promote truth over publishability. *Perspectives on Psychological Science*, *7*(6), 615–631.

Noss, R.F. (1996). The naturalists are dying off. *Conversation Biology*, *10*(1), 1–3.

Novick, M.R. (1966). The axioms and principal results of classical test theory. *Journal of Mathematical Psychology*, *3*, 1–18. https://doi.org/10.1016/0022-2496(66) 90002-2

Nuijten, M.B., Hartgerink, C.H.J., Assen, M.A.L.M. van, Epskamp, S., & Wicherts, J.M. (2015). The prevalence of statistical reporting errors in psychology (1985–2013). *Behavior Research Methods*, 1–22. https://doi.org/10.3758/s13428-015-0664-2

Oberauer, K., & Lewandowsky, S. (2019). Addressing the theory crisis in psychology. *Psychonomic Bulletin & Review*. https://doi.org/10.3758/s13423-019-01645-2

O'Donnell, J.M. (with Internet Archive). (1985). *The origins of behaviorism: American psychology, 1870–1920*. New York University Press.

Olson, A., Kämmer, J.E., Taher, A., Johnston, R., Yang, Q., Mondoux, S., & Monteiro, S. (2024). The inseparability of context and clinical reasoning. *Journal of Evaluation in Clinical Practice*, *30*(4), 533–538. https://doi.org/10.1111/jep.13969

Open Science Collaboration. (2012). An open, large-scale, collaborative effort to estimate the reproducibility of psychological science. *Perspectives on Psychological Science*, *7*(6), 657–660. https://doi.org/10.1177/1745691612462588

Open Science Collaboration. (2015). Estimating the reproducibility of psychological science. *Science*, *349*(6251), Article aac4716. https://doi.org/10.1126/science.aac4716

Pashler, H., & Harris, C.R. (2012). Is the replicability crisis overblown? Three arguments examined. *Perspectives on Psychological Science*, *7*(6), 531–536. https://doi.org/10.1177/1745691612463401

Pastore, N. (1949). *The nature-nurture controversy*. King's Crown Press.

Patel, R., Spreng, R.N., & Turner, G.R. (2013). Functional brain changes following cognitive and motor skills training: a quantitative meta-analysis. *Neurorehabilitation and Neural Repair*, *27*, 187–199. https://doi.org/10.1177/ 1545968312461718

Peterson, D.R. (1991). Connection and disconnection of research and practice in the education of professional psychologists. *American Psychologist*, *46*(4), 422–429. https://doi.org/10.1037/0003-066X.46.4.422

Pinker, S. (1997). *How the mind works*. Allen Lane.

Plutynski, A. (2024). How is a therapist like a modeler? *Philosophy, Psychiatry, & Psychology*, *31*(2), 151–161.

Popov, V. (2023). If God handed us the ground-truth theory of memory, how would we recognize it? *Social and Behavioral Sciences; Cognitive Psychology; Memory, ay5cm*. www.zora.uzh.ch/id/eprint/233473/

Raimy, V.C. (Ed.). (1950). *Training in clinical psychology*. Prentice-Hall.

Ratcliff, R. (1979). Group reaction time distributions and an analysis of distribution statistics. *Psychological Bulletin*, *86*(3), 446–461. http://dx.doi.org/10.1037/0033-2909.86.3.446
Ray, W.J. (2000). *Methods toward a science of behavior and experience* (6th ed.). Wadsworth.
Reicher, G.M. (1969). Perceptual recognition as a function of meaningfulness of stimulus material. *Journal of Experimental Psychology*, *81*, 275–280. https://doi.org/10.1037/ h0027768
Reynolds-Vaughn, V., Riddle, J., Brown, J., Schiesel, M., Wayant, C., & Vassar, M. (2020). Evaluation of spin in the abstracts of emergency medicine randomized controlled trials. *Annals of Emergency Medicine*, *75*(3), 423–431. https://doi.org/10.1016/j.annemergmed.2019.03.011
Richards, G. (2010). *Putting psychology in its place: Critical historical perspectives* (3rd ed.). Routledge.
Richardson, A.W. (2006). The many unities of science: Politics, semantics, ontology. In S.H. Kellert, H.E. Longino & C.K. Waters (Eds.), *Scientific pluralism* (pp. 1–25). University of Minnesota Press.
Richardson, M., Dale, R., & Marsh, K. (2014). Complex dynamical systems in social and personality psychology: Theory, modeling and analysis. In *Handbook of research methods in social and personality psychology* (pp. 251–280). Cambridge University Press.
Richardson, T.H. (2009). Challenges for the scientist-practitioner model in contemporary clinical psychology. *Psych-Talk*, *62*, 20–26.
Richters, J.E. (2021) Incredible utility: The lost causes and causal debris of psychological science. *Basic and Applied Social Psychology*, *43*(6), 366–405. https://doi.org/10.1080/01973533.2021.1979003
Riley, M.A., Richardson, M.J., Shockley, K., & Ramenzoni, V.C. (2011). Interpersonal synergies. *Frontiers in Psychology*, *2*. https://doi.org/10.3389/fpsyg.2011.00038
Roald, T., Køppe, S., Bechmann Jensen, T., Moeskjær Hansen, J., & Levin, K. (2021). Why do we always generalize in qualitative research? *Qualitative Psychology*, *8*(1), 69–81. https://doi.org/10.1037/qup 0000138
Robinson, P.W. (1981). *Fundamentals of experimental psychology* (2nd ed.). Prentice Hall.
Roe, A.W., Pallas, S.L., Hahm, J.-O., & Sur, M. (1990). A map of visual space induced in primary auditory cortex. *Science*, *250*(4982), 818–820. https://doi.org/10.1126/science.2237432
Romero, F. (2018). Who should do replication labor? *Advances in Methods and Practices in Psychological Science*, *1*(4), 516–537. https://doi.org/10.1177/2515245918803619
Rose, T. (2016). *The end of average: How to succeed in a world that values sameness*. Harper Collins.
Rossmanith, N., Costall, A., Reichelt, A.F., López, B., & Reddy, V. (2014). Jointly structuring triadic spaces of meaning and action: Book sharing from 3 months on. *Frontiers in Psychology*, *5*. https://doi.org/10.3389/fpsyg.2014.01390
Rouder, J.N., & Haaf, J.M. (2021). Are there reliable qualitative individual differences in cognition? *Journal of Cognition*, *4*(1), 46, 1–16. https://doi.org/10.5334/joc.131
Ryan, P. (2020). *Enhancing clinical case formulation*. Routledge.
Ryan, P., & Kilroe, A. (2020). Enhancing formulation. In P. Ryan (Ed.), *Enhancing clinical case formulation* (pp. 1–10). Routledge.
Sacks, H. (1992). *Lectures on conversation*. Blackwell.
Sauer, S. (2018). Observation oriented modeling revised from a statistical point of view. *Behavior Research Methods*, *50*, 1749–1761. https://doi.org/10.3758/s13428-017-0949-8
Scheel, A.M., Tiokhin, L., Isager, P.M., & Lakens, D. (2020). Why hypothesis testers should spend less time testing hypotheses. *Perspectives on Psychological Science*, *16*(4), 744–755. https://doi.org/10.1177/1745691620966795
Schilpp, P.A. (Ed.). (1949). *Albert Einstein: Philosopher-scientist.* The Library of Living Philosophers.
Schmiedek, F., Lövdén, M., von Oertzen, T., & Lindenberger, U. (2020). Within-person structures of daily cognitive performance differ from between-person structures of cognitive abilities. *PeerJ*, *8*, e9290. https://doi.org/10.7717/peerj.9290
Schoggen, P. (1989). *Behavior settings: A revision and extension of Roger G. Barker's "Ecological Psychology."* Stanford University Press.
Schwaber, M.K., Garraghty, P.E., & Kaas, J.H. (1993). Neuroplasticity of the adult primate auditory cortex following cochlear hearing loss. *Otology & Neurotology*, *14*(3), 252.

Scott, M.M. (2005). A powerful theory and a paradox: Ecological psychologists after Barker. *Environment and Behavior*, *37*(3), 295–329. https://doi.org/10.1177/0013916504270696
Sechrest, L., & Sidani, S. (1995). Quantitative and qualitative methods: Is there an alternative? *Evaluation and Program Planning*, *18*(1), 77–87.
Segall, M.H., Campbell, D.T., & Herskovits, M.J. (1963). Cultural differences in the perception of geometric illusions. *Science*, *139*(3556), 769–771. https://doi.org/10.1126/science.139.3556.769
Shapin, S., & Schaffer, S. (2011). *Leviathan and the air-pump*. Princeton University Press.
Shapiro, M.B. (1966). The single case in clinical-psychological research. *Journal of General Psychology*, *74*, 3–23.
Shenoy, K.V., Sahani, M., & Churchland, M.M. (2013). Cortical control of arm movements: A dynamical systems perspective. *Annual Review of Neuroscience*, *36*, 337–359. https://doi.org/10.1146/annurev-neuro-062111-150509
Shepard, R.N., & Metzler, J. (1971). Mental rotation of three-dimensional objects. *Science*, *171*, 701–703.
Shoda, Y., Mischel, W., & Wright, J.C. (1994). Intraindividual stability in the organization and patterning of behavior: Incorporating psychological situations into the idiographic analysis of personality. *Journal of Personality and Social Psychology*, *67*(4), 674–687. https://doi.org/10.1037/0022-3514.67.4.674
Shotter, J. (1998). Resurrecting people in academic psychology: A celebration of the ordinary. In W. E. Smythe (Ed.), *Toward a psychology of persons* (pp. 245–271). Lawrence Erlbaum Associates.
Sievers, B., & DeFilippis, E. (2022). Causal complexity demands community coordination. Comment on Yarkoni T. (2022) The generalizability crisis. *Behavioral and Brain Sciences*, *45*, e1, 1–78. https://doi.org/10.1017/S0140525X20001685
Silva, P.R., Farias, T., Cascio, F., Santos, L. dos, Peixoto, V., Crespo, E., Ayres, C., Ayres, M., Marinho, V., Bastos, V.H., Ribeiro, P., Velasques, B., Orsini, M., Fiorelli, R., de Freitas, M.R.G., & Teixeira, S. (2018). Neuroplasticity in visual impairments. *Neurology International*, *10*(4). https://doi.org/ 10.1017/S0140525X21000418, e31
Simmons, J.P., Nelson, L.D., & Simonsohn, U. (2011). False-positive psychology: Undisclosed flexibility in data collection and analysis allows presenting anything as significant. *Psychological Science*, *22*(11), 1359–1366.
Simon, H.A. (1973). The organization of complex systems. In H.H. Pattee (Ed.), *Hierarchy theory: The challenge of complex systems* (pp. 1–27). George Braziller.
Simpson, E.H. (1951). The interpretation of interaction in contingency tables. *Journal of the Royal Statistics Society, Series B*, *13*, 238–241.
Simpson, R.H. (1944). The specific meanings of certain terms indicating different degrees of frequency. *Quarterly Journal of Speech*, *30*, 328–330.
Sinclair, U. (1934, December 11). I, candidate for governor and how I got licked. *Oakland Tribune*, *19*.
Smaldino, P.E., & McElreath, R. (2016). The natural selection of bad science. *Royal Society Open Science*, *3*(9), 160384. https://doi.org/10.1098/rsos.160384
Smedslund, J. (2016). Why psychology cannot be an empirical science. *Integrative Psychological and Behavioral Science*, *50*, 185–195. https://doi.org/10.1007/s12124-015-9339-x
Smith, P.L., & Little, D.R. (2018). Small is beautiful: In defense of the small-N design. *Psychonomic Bulletin and Review*, *85*, 2083–2101. https://doi.org/10.3758/s13423-018-1451-8
Speelman, C.P., & Kirsner, K. (2005). *Beyond the learning curve: The construction of mind.* Oxford University Press.
Speelman, C.P., & McGann, M. (2013). How mean is the mean? *Frontiers in Psychology*, *4*, 451. https://doi.org/10.3389/fpsyg.2013. 00451
Speelman, C., Martin, K., Flower, S., & Simpson, T. (2010). Skill acquisition in skin cancer detection. *Perceptual & Motor Skills*, *110*(1), 277–297.
Speelman, C.P., & McGann, M. (2020). Statements about the pervasiveness of behaviour require data about the pervasiveness of behaviour. *Frontiers in Psychology*, 11, 594675. https://doi.org/10.3389/fpsyg.2020.594675

Speelman, C.P., Parker, L., Rapley, B.J., & McGann, M. (2024). Most psychological researchers assume their samples are ergodic: Evidence from a year of articles in three major journals. *Collabra: Psychology*, *10*(1), 1–8. https://doi.org/10.1525/collabra.92888

Spivey, M. (2008). *The continuity of mind*. Oxford University Press.

Stam, H.J. (2000). Theoretical psychology. In K. Pawlik & M.R. Rosenzweig (Eds.), *International handbook of psychology* (pp. 551–569). Sage.

Stam, H.J. (2004). Unifying psychology: Epistemological act or disciplinary maneuver? *Journal of Clinical Psychology*, *60*(12), 1259–1262. https://doi-org/10.1002/jclp.20069

Stanovich, K.E. (2013). *How to think straight about psychology* (10th ed.). Pearson.

Stephen, D.G., Dixon, J.A., & Isenhower, R.W. (2009). Dynamics of representational change: Entropy, action, and cognition. *Journal of Experimental Psychology: Human Perception and Performance*, *35*(6), 1811–1832. https://doi.org/10.1037/a0014510

Stephen, D.G., & Van Orden, G. (2012). Searching for general principles in cognitive performance: Reply to commentators. *Topics in Cognitive Science*, *4*, 94–102. https://doi.org/10.1111/j.1756-8765.2011.01171.x

Stewart, R.E., Stirman, S.W., & Chambless, D.L. (2012). A qualitative investigation of practicing psychologists' attitudes toward research-informed practice: Implications for dissemination strategies. *Professional Psychology: Research and Practice*, *43*(2), 100–109. https://doi.org/10.1037/a0025694

Stone, G.O., & Van Orden, G.C. (1993). Strategic control of processing in word recognition. *Journal of Experimental Psychology: Human Perception and Performance*, *19*(4), 744.

Strack, F., Martin, L.L., & Schwarz, N. (1988). Priming and communication: Social determinants of information use in judgments of life satisfaction. *European Journal of Social Psychology*, *18*, 429–442.

Stricker, G. (2002). What is a scientist-practitioner anyway? *Journal of Clinical Psychology*, *58*(10), 1277–1283. https://doi.org/10.1002/jclp.10111

Stricker, G., & Cummings, N.A. (1992). The professional school movement. In D.K. Freedheim, H.J. Freudenberger, J.W. Kessler, S.B. Messer, D.R. Peterson, H.H. Strupp, & P.L. Wachtel (Eds.), *History of psychotherapy: A century of change* (pp. 801–828). American Psychological Association. https://doi.org/10.1037/10110-024

Stricker, G., & Trierweiler, S.J. (1995). The local clinical scientist: A bridge between science and practice. *American Psychologist*, *50*(12), 995–1002.

Sunderland, M.E., Klitz, K., & Yoshihara, K. (2012). Doing natural history. *BioScience*, *62*(9), 824–829. https://doi.org/10.1525/bio.2012.62.9.8

Syed, M., & McLean, K.C. (2022). Disentangling paradigm and method can help bring qualitative research to post-positivist psychology and address the generalizability crisis. Commentary on Yarkoni, T. (2022). The generalizability crisis. *Behavioral & Brain Sciences*, *45*(e1), 1–78. https://doi.org/10.1017/S0140525X21000431, e32

Szollosi, A., & Donkin, C. (2019). Neglected sources of flexibility in psychological theories: From replicability to good explanations. *Computational Brain & Behavior*. https://doi.org/10.1007/s42113-019-00045-y

Szollosi, A., & Donkin, C. (2021). Arrested theory development: The misguided distinction between exploratory and confirmatory research. *Perspectives on Psychological Science*, *16*(4), 717–724. https://doi.org/10.1177/1745691620966796

Tang, R., & Braver, T.S. (2020). Towards an individual differences perspective in mindfulness training research: Theoretical and empirical considerations. *Frontiers in Psychology*, *11*, 818. https://doi.org/10.3389/fpsyg.2020.00818

Tavris, C. (2003). Mind games: Psychological warfare between therapists and scientists. *Chronicle of Higher Education*, *49*(25), B7.

Teachman, B.A., Drabick, D.A.G., Hershenberg, R., Vivian, D., Wolfe, B.E., & Goldfried, M.R. (2012). Bridging the gap between clinical research and clinical practice: Introduction to the special section. *Psychotherapy*, *49*(2), 97–100. https://doi.org/10.1037/a0027346

Tewksbury, J.J., Anderson, J.G.T., Bakker, J.D., Billo, T.J., Dunwiddie, P.W., Groom, M.J., Hampton, S.E., Herman, S.G., Levey, D.J., Machnicki, N.J., del Rio, C.M., Power, M.E., Rowell, K., Salomon, A.K.,

Stacey, L., Trombulak, S.C., & Wheeler, T.A. (2014). Natural history's place in science and society. *BioScience, 64*(4), 300–310. https://doi.org/10.1093/biosci/biu032

Thalmayer, A.G., Toscanelli, C., & Arnett, J.J. (2021). The neglected 95% revisited: Is American psychology becoming less American? *American Psychologist, 76*(1), 116.

Thelen, E. (1995). Time-scale dynamics and the development of an embodied cognition. In T. van Gelder & R.F. Port (Eds.), *Mind as motion: Explorations in the dynamics of cognition* (pp. 69–100). MIT Press.

Thelen, E., & Smith, L. (1994). *A dynamic systems approach to the development of cognition and action.* MIT Press.

Thorngate, W., & Carroll, B. (1986). Ordinal pattern analysis: A strategy for assessing hypotheses about individuals. In J. Valsiner (Ed.), *The individual subject and scientific psychology* (pp. 201–232). Springer.

Thorp, H.H. (2024). Teach philosophy of science. *Science, 384*(6692), 141–141. https://doi.org/10.1126/science.adp7153

Tinbergen, N. (1963). On aims and methods of Ethology. *Zeitschrift Für Tierpsychologie, 20*(4), 410–433. https://doi.org/10.1111/j.1439-0310.1963.tb01161.x

Townsend, J.T., & Busemeyer, J. (1995). Dynamic representation of decision making. In T. van Gelder & R.F. Port (Eds.), *Mind as motion: Explorations in the dynamics of cognition* (pp. 101–120). Bradford Books.

Trafimow, D. (2025). Theory-refuting findings in psychology: How much should they matter? *Journal for the Theory of Social Behaviour, 55*(1), e70000. https://doi.org/10.1111/jtsb.70000

Trafimow, D., & Osman, M. (2022). Barriers to converting applied social psychology to bettering the human condition. *Basic and Applied Social Psychology, 44*(1), 1–11. https://doi.org/10.1080/01973533.2022.2051327

Trafimow, D., Tang, T., Wang, T., Choy, S.T.B., Hu, L., Chen, X., Wang, C. & Wang, Z. (in press). Improving inferential analyses pre-data and post-data. *Psychological Methods.*

Tukey, J.W. (1969). Analyzing data: Sanctification or detective work? *American Psychologist, 24*(2), 83–91. https://doi.org/10.1037/h0027108

Tukey, J.W. (1977). *Exploratory data analysis*. Addison-Wesley.

Turkat, I.D. (2014). An historical perspective on the impact of case formulation. *Behavior Therapist, 37*(7), 180–188.

Uher, J. (2022a). Functions of units, scales and quantitative data: Fundamental differences in numerical traceability between sciences. *Quality & Quantity, 56*, 2519–2548. https://doi.org/10.1007/s11135-021-01215-6

Uher, J. (2022b) Rating scales institutionalise a network of logical errors and conceptual problems in research practices: A rigorous analysis showing ways to tackle psychology's crises. *Frontiers in Psychology, 13*, 1009893. https://doi.org/10.3389/fpsyg.2022.1009893

Uher, J. (2023). What's wrong with rating scales? Psychology's replication and confidence crisis cannot be solved without transparency in data generation. *Social and Personality Psychology Compass, 17*(5), e12740. https://doi.org/10.1111/spc3.12740

UK Research and Innovation (UKRI). (2021, August 17). *Introduction to transformative research.* www.ukri.org/councils/epsrc/guidance-for-applicants/types-of-funding-we-offer/transformative-research/introduction-to-transformative-research/

UNESCO. (2018). *Open science training handbook*. Open Science Training Handbook. www.unesco.org/en/open-science/open-science-training-handbook

Valsiner, J. (1986). Between groups and individuals: Psychologists' and laypersons' interpretations of correlational findings. In J. Valsiner (Ed.), *The individual subject and scientific psychology* (pp. 113–152). Plenum.

Valsiner, J. (2019). Generalization in science: Abstracting from unique events. In C. HØjholt & E. Schraube (Eds.), *Subjectivity and knowledge: Generalization in the psychological study of everyday life* (pp. 79–97). Springer, Ch.5.

van Geert, P., & de Ruiter, N. (2022). *Toward a process approach in psychology*. Cambridge University Press.

van Gelder, T. (1995). What might cognition be if not computation. *Journal of Philosophy, 92*(7), 345–381.

van Gelder, T., & Port, R.F. (1995). It's about time: An overview of the dynamical approach to cognition. In T. van Gelder & R. Port (Eds.), *Mind as motion: Explorations in the dynamics of cognition* (Vol. 1, p. 43). MIT Press.

Van Orden, G.C., Holden, J.G., Podgornik, M.N., & Aitchison, C.S. (1999). What swimming says about reading: Coordination, context, and homophone errors. *Ecological Psychology, 11*(1), 45–79. https://doi.org/10.1207/s15326969eco1101

Van Orden, G.C., Holden, J.G., & Turvey, M.T. (2003). Self-organization of cognitive performance. *Journal of Experimental Psychology: General, 132*(3), 331–350. https://doi.org/10.1037/0096-3445.132.3.331

Van Orden, G.C., Holden, J.G., & Turvey, M.T. (2005). Human cognition and 1/f scaling. *Journal of Experimental Psychology: General, 134*(1), 117–123. https://doi.org/10.1037/0096-3445.134.1.117

Van Orden, G. & Stephen, D.G. (2012). Is cognitive science usefully cast as complexity science? *Topics in Cognitive Science, 4*, 3–6. https://doi.org/10.1111/j.1756-8765.2011.01165.x

van Rooij, I. (2019, January 18). *Psychological science needs theory development before preregistration.* Retrieved January 19, 2019, from Psychonomic Society Featured Content website: https://featuredcontent.psychonomic.org/psychological-science-needs-theory-development-before-preregistration/

van Rooij, I., & Baggio, G. (2020). Theory development requires an epistemological sea change. *Psychological Inquiry, 31*(4), 321–325. https://doi.org/10.1080/1047840X.2020.1853477

van Rooij, I., & Baggio, G. (2021). Theory before the test: How to build high-verisimilitude explanatory theories in psychological science. *Perspectives on Psychological Science, 16*(4), 682–697. https://doi.org/10.1177/1745691620970604

van Rooij, I., Guest, O., Adolfi, F.G., Haan, R. de, Kolokolova, A., & Rich, P. (2024). *Reclaiming AI as a theoretical tool for cognitive science.* https://doi.org/10.31234/osf.io/4cbuv

Veenman, M., Stefan, A.M. & Haaf, J.M. (2024). Bayesian hierarchical modelling: an introduction and reassessment. *Behavior Research Methods*, *56*, 4600–4631. https://doi.org/10.3758/s13428-023-02204-3

Vlaeyen, J.W., Wicksell, R.K., Simons, L.E., Gentili, C., De, T.K., Tate, R.L., Vohra, S., Punja, S., Linton, S.J., & Sniehotta, F.F. (2020). From Boulder to Stockholm in 70 years: Single case experimental designs in clinical research. *The Psychological Record*, *70*, 659–670.

Voss, P., Thomas, M.E., Cisneros-Franco, J.M., & de Villers-Sidani, É. (2017). Dynamic brains and the changing rules of neuroplasticity: Implications for learning and recovery. *Frontiers in Psychology*, *8*. https://doi.org/10.3389/fpsyg.2017.01657

Wallot, S., & Kelty-Stephen, D.G. (2018). Interaction-dominant causation in mind and brain, and its implication for questions of generalization and replication. *Minds & Machines*, *28*, 353–374. https://doi.org/10.1007/s11023-017-9455-0

Ward, L.M., & Greenwood, P.E. (2007). 1/f noise. *Scholarpedia*, *2*(12), 1537. https://doi.org/10.4249/scholarpedia.1537

Wasserstein, R.L., Schirm, A.L. & Lazar, N.A. (2019). Moving to a world beyond "p < 0.05." *The American Statistician*, *73*, 1–19.

Watkins, M.J. (1984). Models as toothbrushes. *Behavioral and Brain Sciences*, *7*(1), 86–86. https://doi.org/10.1017/S0140525X00026303

West, K.L., Soska, K.C., Cole, W.G., Han, D., Hoch, J.E., Hospodar, C.M., & Kaplan, B.E. (2022). From description to generalization, or there and back again. Commentary on Yarkoni, T. (2022). The generalizability crisis. *Behavioral & Brain Sciences*, *45*, e1, 1–78. https://doi.org/10.1017/S0140525X21000522, e37

Westerlund, A., Nilsen, P., & Sundberg, L. (2019). Implementation of implementation science knowledge: The research-practice gap paradox. *Worldviews on Evidence-Based Nursing*, *16*(5), 332–334. https://doi.org/10.1111/wvn.12403

Wheeler, D.D. (1970). Processes in word recognition. *Cognitive Psychology*, *1*, 59–85. https://doi.org/10.1016/0010-0285(70) 90005-8

Wohlleben, P. (2016). *The hidden life of trees: What they feel, how they communicate* (J. Billinghurst, Trans.; First English Language Edition, 8th Printing). Greystone Books.

Wicker, A.W. (1978). The importance of church size for new members. In R.G. Barker & Associates (Eds.), *Habitats, environments, and human behavior* (pp. 257–264). Jossey-Bass.

Wilcove, D.S., & Eisner, T. (2000). The impending extinction of natural history. *The Chronicle of Higher Education; Washington*, *47*(3), B24.

Williams, D.R., Mulder, J., Rouder, J.N., & Rast, P. (2020). Beneath the surface: Unearthing within-person variability and mean relations with Bayesian mixed models. *Psychological Methods*, *26*(1), 74–89. https://doi.org/10.1037/met0000270

Willig, C. (2019). What can qualitative psychology contribute to psychological knowledge? *Psychological Methods*, *24*(6), 796–804. https://doi.org/10.1037/met0000218

Wilson, A. (2011). Theory, and why it's time psychology got one. Notes from two scientific psychologists. http://psychsciencenotes.blogspot.com/2011/11/theory-and-why-its-time-psychology-got.html

Wohlleben, P. (2016). *The hidden life of trees: What they feel, how they communicate* (J. Billinghurst, Trans.; First English Language Edition, 8th Printing). Greystone Books.

Woods, D.L., Wyma, J.M., Yund, E.W., Herron, T.J., & Reed, B. (2015). Age-related slowing of response selection and production in a visual choice reaction time task. *Frontiers in Human Neuroscience*, *9*, 193. https://doi.org/10.3389/fnhum.2015.00193

Wulf, A. (2015). *The invention of nature: Alexander von Humboldt's new world*. Knopf.

Yarkoni, T. (2020, May 6). *Induction is not optional (if you're using inferential statistics): Reply to Lakens [Tumblr]*. Retrieved November 12, 2024, from https://talyarkoni.org/blog/2020/05/06/induction-is-not-optional-if-youre-using-inferential-statistics-reply-to-lakens/

Yarkoni, T. (2022). The generalizability crisis. *Behavioral & Brain Sciences*, *45*(e1), 1–78. https://doi.org/10.1017/S0140525X20001685

Zhao, K. (2021). Sample representation in the social sciences. *Synthese*, *198*(10), 9097–9115. https://doi.org/10.1007/s11229-020-02621-3

Zilles, K., & Amunts, K. (2013). Individual variability is not noise. *Trends in Cognitive Sciences*, *17*(4), 153–155.

Zwaan, R.A., Pecher, D., Paolacci, G., Bouwmeester, S., Verkoeijen, P., Dijkstra, K., & Zeelenberg, R. (2018). Participant nonnaiveté and the reproducibility of cognitive psychology. *Psychonomic Bulletin & Review*, *25*(5), 1968–1972. https://doi.org/10.3758/s13423-017-1348-y

INDEX

Note: Endnotes are indicated by the page number followed by 'n' and the endnote number e.g., 20n1 refers to endnote 1 on page 20.

Kolibri 360 GmbH
Ferdinand-Jühlke-Straße 7
99095 Erfurt, Deutschland
produktsicherheit@kolibri360.de